THE LAST
CUCKOO

THE LAST CUCKOO

The very best letters to

THE TIMES

since 1900

Chosen and introduced
by
KENNETH GREGORY

UNWIN HYMAN
London   Sydney

First published in Great Britain by Unwin Hyman, an
imprint of Unwin Hyman Limited, 1987

This edition and selection
© Unwin Hyman and Times Newspapers Ltd 1987

UNWIN HYMAN LIMITED
Denmark House,
37-39 Queen Elizabeth Street,
London SE1 2QB
and
40 Museum Street, London WC1A 1LU

Allen & Unwin Australia Pty Ltd
8 Napier Street, North Sydney, NSW 2060, Australia

Allen & Unwin New Zealand Ltd with the Port Nicholson Press
60 Cambridge Terrace, Wellington, New Zealand

British Library Cataloguing in Publication Data

The Last cuckoo : the very best letters to
The Times since 1900.
1. English letters
I. Gregory, Kenneth   ii. The Times
826'.912'08   PR1347

ISBN 0–04–808063–2

Set in 10 on 11 point Times by Grove Graphics, Tring, and
printed and bound in Great Britain by
Billings & Sons Ltd, London and Worcester

CONTENTS

Ackowledgements   *page*   vi

Foreword by Bernard Levin   vii

Introduction by Kenneth Gregory   1

THE PERFECT LETTER   13
THE CUCKOO   23
YESTERDAY   33
THE MENU   69
FINDING WASPS' NESTS   79
INFORMATION 1   83
NAMES   105
IN TIME OF PEACE 1   113
FLIGHT   134
IN TIME OF WAR   143
SARTORIAL   159
EDUCATION   165
THIS SPORTING LIFE   175
THE ENGLISH LANGUAGE   187
FROM THE HORSE'S MOUTH   202
INFORMATION 2   207
THE ARTS   239
SHARING THE CUP   279
IN TIME OF PEACE 2   285
AMERICANA   297
THE FAMOUS   303
THIS ENGLAND   315
TILL THE COWS COME HOME   331

Index of Subjects   336

Index of Correspondents   340

ACKNOWLEDGEMENTS

The editor and publishers wish to thank all those who have so readily given permission for inclusion of the letters which appear in this volume. The many writers, literary agents and executors to whom thanks are owed are too numerous to be named individually here but their friendly help and many interesting comments and postscripts have been invaluable. The letters on pp. 6, 13–15, and 189–91 are reproduced by permission of the Society of Authors on behalf of the Bernard Shaw Estate.

Every effort has been made to trace the writers of the letters or their heirs and executors. Inevitably, we have not always met with success in tracking down the writers of letters in some cases published as many as eighty years ago. To those whom it has proved impossible to trace we would offer our sincerest apologies and express the earnest hope that they will find pleasure in the reproduction of their letters in these pages.

Kenneth Gregory would also personally like to thank all those who have helped him in his researches, especially the Master of Trinity College, Cambridge, the Archivist of *The Times*, and the staff of the Bath Public Reference Library.

FOREWORD

To The Editor of The Times

Sir,

Many years ago − I think it was about 1893, or possibly a little earlier, or later, though I have a feeling that the Zulu War was going on at the time, which would settle the matter (or at any rate would settle it if I could remember the dates of the Zulu War) − I wrote a letter to *The Times*, suggesting that the then newly-invented hollow bicycle-tyre might be used by enemy agents who, disguised as, say, clergymen of the Church of England, could pedal about this country with impunity, carrying treasonable messages and even weapons (albeit, of course, small ones) inside the apparently harmless covering for the wheels of the innocent velocipide.

To my astonishment and alarm, *the letter was not published.* I made discreet enquiries in certain influential circles (I flatter myself that my name and reputation are not wholly unknown to those who handle the levers of power), and was assured that the letter had been studied carefully, but was not printed because it was thought that it came from a 'nutter' − a term unfamiliar to me, but which I took to mean (in the absence of any other possible explanation) one whose information is of such crucial importance that its publication would endanger the security of the realm; I assumed that its contents must have been communicated to those who would be bound to act upon them, and was well content, since it could hardly be supposed that I wrote for purposes of what I am reliably informed (by one of my grand-nephews) is called 'publicity'.

Imagine my astonishment when, a few weeks later, I read in your correspondence columns a letter which suggested that at times of international tension, elderly men and women with walking-sticks should be watched carefully, since nothing could be easier than for enemy agents, thus disguised, to carry seditious and similar messages within the said sticks, hollowed out for the purpose.

I need hardly say that from that moment until the present day, I have refused to put pen to paper in the form of correspondence to your newspaper, convinced as I am that you are either in the pay of Foreign Powers, or at the very least have a seriously defective sense of priorities.

Why then, do I now break my silence, which has lasted (give or take a Zulu War or two) for nigh on a century? I do so, Sir, in a spirit of magnanimity. I understand that a final volume of selected letters from The Times is shortly to be published, following the great success of the three earlier volumes (which success, were I not seized of the spirit of magnanimity aforesaid, I would characterize as entirely unjustified). It may surprise you to learn that I have read all three of the volumes in question, and done so with much pleasure, no little amusement, and even some instruction. It seems that the British public has not lost, and gives every assurance of never losing, its curiosity, its sense of humour, its ability to put great thoughts into brief garments, above all its refusal to be flustered, let alone frightened, when terrible things are happening elsewhere in the world. If it were not already common knowledge that the British were a nation unlike other nations, these volumes would make it clear, and I have no doubt that the fourth compendium will carry on the tradition set by the first three, and indeed by the British people themselves throughout the years.

It goes without saying that I shall expect my own letter about the bicycle-tyres to be printed, in the forthcoming collection, very prominently. True, it was written a very long time ago, but its message seems to be to be as urgent as ever it was, and possibly more so.

I remain, Sir,

your humble and obedient servant,
BERNARD LEVIN

INTRODUCTION

by Kenneth Gregory

Mr Charles John Cornish lay, looked and listened, then rose in triumph to write a letter to *The Times*. Once a soccer blue at Oxford, Mr Cornish had graduated to birdwatching in Chiswick where a cuckoo had recently taken up residence in an osier bed from which it refused to budge. The other birds were clearly put out because the cuckoo screeched – here the recumbent Cornish put aside a spy-glass and consulted his watch – one hundred times a minute. The birds of Chiswick deliberated, then detailed two sedge warblers to feed the cuckoo. Again applying his spy-glass, Mr Cornish noted that the sedge warblers seemed 'unhappy', the cuckoo finding their efforts inadequate. Sundry sparrows next lined up to lend a beak, a policy of appeasement which worked. Then one morning, as Mr Cornish lay, looked and listened, he heard only the song of happy birds. He investigated. The screeching cuckoo had left Chiswick. Research reveals that while many have written to *The Times* claiming to have heard the first cuckoo, only Mr Cornish – on 30 July 1900 – reported hearing the last cuckoo. As this book now has a title, Mr Cornish is retired with thanks, the case of the departed cuckoo helping us to decide when the twentieth century began.

The precise date was one of two mighty controversies exercising the minds of *Times* readers during the weeks before and after 1 January 1900: when would the twentieth century begin, and what exactly was going on in South Africa? Fellows of the Royal Society debated the former, retired colonels the latter. The so-called 'Black Week' of December 1899 jarred on military sensibilities: Gatacre surprised at Stormberg on the 10th, Methuen defeated at Magersfontein on the 11th, Buller repulsed at Colenso on the 15th. Only one conclusion could be drawn: the Boers had fought when the British weren't ready. A retired colonel, shown by the *Army List* to have been in the Crimea almost half a century earlier, asked the pertinent question – 'What would Frederick the Great have done?' The answer came in the form of another question – 'Why doesn't every soldier of the Queen carry a shield?' *The Times* man

1

besieged in Ladysmith hinted at the enemy's lack of good manners; every time the British started to play cricket, the Boers fired shells at the pitch. In short, Gatacre, Methuen, Buller and the cricketers were not pitted against gentlemen. For proof of this, *The Times* related an unpleasant incident. From time to time it was customary for a British officer to wander over to the enemy lines to have a chat. One new to the job spoke slowly: 'You – understand – English?' The reply was typical of men who would shell a cricket pitch: 'Of course I understand English. I just refuse to speak the . . . language.'

The precise moment at which the twentieth century would begin was a matter for philosophical discussion. Certainly the First of January was the day, but was 1900 or 1901 the year? Correspondents in favour of the latter called upon Tacitus, Shakespeare and Goethe to bear witness; they would later receive support from an ailing Oscar Wilde in Paris. 'I shall not outlive the century,' he murmured in October 1900 – and died a month later. A brave counter-attack by the pro-1900 men floundered when their adversaries dragged in Dionysius the Little who, though dead since AD 650, was highly esteemed by certain members of the Athenaeum. Suddenly Mr Hastings C. Dent intervened: the twentieth century would begin at 180°E, midnight 31 December 1900 – or at midday 31 December at Greenwich. 'Nonsense!' roared an army type who had apparently wandered in from the what-exactly-is going-on-in-South Africa argument on another page, now in its shields-should-be-made-of-stainless steel stage. 'The twentieth century began when I wrote 19.. at the top of this letter.' No less firmly did General Sir Redvers Buller announce his intention of advancing once he had found means of transport.

The Last Cuckoo here declares an interest: himself. If he chooses 1900 as the first year of the century, it is not merely because he wishes to include Conan Doyle's letter on the stupidity of the War Office. Nor is it for the pleasure of drawing the reader's attention to a particular Honours List. *The Times* of today needs more than one page to print the names of those rewarded by a gracious Sovereign on the advice of her prime minister; not so on 1 January 1900 when the names numbered only 65 – two peers, four privy councillors, 24 knights and 35 companions. One-quarter of all awards were for services to the Indian Empire; captains of industry and entrepreneurs there may have been in plenty but they were not recognised by an aristocratic Conservative prime minister, Lord Salisbury. The Cuckoo insists on recognising himself. *The Times* of 5 April 1899 informed readers of the bird's arrival, that of 30 July 1900

2

of his departure; 1901 passed without a cuckoo letter. The twentieth century therefore began in 1900.

The first letter in this book is separated from the last by almost four decades, two world wars, revolutions in four continents and the appearance of cricketers wearing pyjamas in Australia, the dissolution of empires and the toppling of monarchies, the formation by some women of a third sex, and changes in the ownership of *The Times*. Nine editors have guided the destinies of the paper since George Buckle at the turn of the century when stark slabs of reading matter defied the keenest eye. In 1900, each page of *The Times* held twice as many words as in 1987; however, the increase in the cost of the paper since 1900 has been less than half that of the postage letter rate, which may prove something. The relationship between the old Printing House Square and correspondents was an odd one, many of the latter modestly identifying themselvs as Viator, Senex, Public School Man, Disgusted, or XYZ. The editor's response was to use letters − from however eminent the senders − as fillers. On Monday 1 January 1900, letters surfaced on nine different pages. Then *The Times* was very upper class in its attitude to life:

> O! when degree is shak'd,
> Which is the ladder to all high designs,
> The enterprise is sick.

In other words, the weekend's soccer results were crammed into one-sixth of a column, though this may have been due to the teams in the League Championship − five from the Birmingham area, thirteen from the North of England, and none from the South. The world was expected to know its place. After Lord Roberts had left to take charge in South Africa, he was replaced as Commander-in-Chief, Ireland by Queen Victoria's youngest son, the Duke of Connaught. His Royal Highness would certainly be a popular choice decided *The Times*, 'for even among the anti-British masses, birth and breeding count for much'.

The world has changed since January 1900. Then Blackfriars station opposite *The Times* building invited travellers to St Petersburg or Constantinople. Bishops of the Church of England, baptised James, did not sign their letters 'Jim'; sixty years would elapse before the Authorised Version's 'Neither cast ye your pearls before swine' gave way to the New English Bible's 'Do not feed your pearls to pigs'. In January 1900, Dan Leno starred in pantomime at Drury Lane, Beerbohm Tree was about

3

to launch *A Midsummer Night's Dream* with a female Oberon, an uncut Mendelssohn score, and a carpet of wild flowers in the wood scene. If this was the occasion when Tree added rabbits to the cast, *The Times* critic ignored their presence as well as their performance. At the Albert Hall *Messiah* was projected by 1,000 instrumentalists and singers, the abundant contralto of Clara Butt telling glad tidings to Zion and probably − had the windows been open − to all points as far west as Hammersmith. The best hotels in London charged 12s 6d (63p) for a bed and four meals, the *Court Circular* informed the Empire that the Queen had gone for her afternoon drive. 'Feel very low and anxious about the war,' the old lady had written in her *Journal* a few weeks earlier. Now she swung into action, denouncing red-tape, urging the Government to be firm and courageous, comprehending the present − 'No doubt the War Office is greatly at fault, but it is the whole system which must be changed' − and peering intuitively into the future. Queen Victoria wrote to the Colonial Secretary on 14 February 1900: "Please let me know what steps you intend to take to protect the Zulus from being attacked by the Boers. Feel certain you agree with me that we are bound in honour to stand by my native subjects.'

Two things 1900 did have in common with the present: reverence for a masterwork and awareness of a social problem. On 19 June 1899, Hans Richter had conducted the first performance of Elgar's *Variations on an Original Theme, 'Enigma',* destined to become the most popular orchestral piece by an English composer and championed by non-English-born talents such as Toscanini, Monteux, Solti, Haitink and Bernstein. The social problem was discussed in a *Times* leading article on 30 October 1900: 'What are we to do with the "Hooligan"? Who or what is responsible for his growth? Every week some incident shows that certain parts of London are more perilous for the peaceable wayfarer than remote districts of Calabria, Sicily, or Greece, once the classic haunts of brigands.' This leading article was realistic in tone: when hooligan attacked hooligan, there was little to regret. But when thugs hustled and waylaid old gentlemen with gold watches . . . 'Too often the "Hooligan" is, physically as well as morally, a *dégénéré*. Sometimes, however, there is the making of a good football player in him.' Perhaps, given the chance, he would have made a good football supporter. In 1900, neither football player nor football supporter could travel to Calabria, Sicily, or Greece, there to express himself. Now he may indulge his tastes for frivolity home or away. On 9 February 1987, a purge of right-wing hooligans was called for by the Chairman of the Young Conservatives, proving that the British are socially mobile.

The *Last Cuckoo* is a history of England – with American *obligati* – in the twentieth century as told in letters to *The Times*. It is a collection of letters which the anthologist would have written had he been of the appropriate period, and capable of the wit, wisdom, eccentricity, and moral passion contained therein. These qualities cannot be acquired to order. In 1975, writing an Introduction to *The First Cuckoo*, the anthologist remembered the three-decker heading formerly given to the day's top letter in Stanley Morison's newly designed *Times* – aesthetically the noblest of all papers – which first appeared on 3 October 1932. 'In spacious pre-war days, when the theme of the top letter was introduced first by the orchestra, and then in turn by brass and wind . . .' Rarely can any anthologist have known such self-satisfaction. He preened. Convinced that Morison's type was meant for this occasion, and for this occasion alone, he knocked off a brief letter. He read it aloud in what were felt to be the tones used by the Alec Guinness cleric in *Kind Hearts and Coronets*. That evening the anthologist thought he deserved a second glass of port, and would indeed

5

have had one if the bottle had not been empty before pouring the first glass. The reaction to this letter was unusual.

Five reviewers – two British, two American and one French – read the letter as a genuine article. One congratulated the Archbishop of Canterbury on his brevity; another, accustomed to nothing more exotic in front of Cantuar than the first given name of Cosmo Gordon Lang, paused to reproach parents for saddling their children with impossible names; yet another suggested that Cantuar was a misprint for Carter or Cantor. Doubtless in some Middle Western theological seminary a professor is indexing meaningful sermons of the century:

Family Life, Responsibility in – Cuckoo interrupts . . . Cantuar, O. and seeking the manuscript. The anthologist looks forward to his royalty.

The response of readers to *The First Cuckoo* and his younger brothers showed a virtual unanimity in placing the winning letters, included in these pages, together with many new classics long hidden in bound volumes of *The Times*. Far ahead of the field was Bernard Shaw's rebuke to a female opera-goer when he was trying to concentrate on *Don Giovanni* (Caruso sang Ottavio: did he in 1905 wear the fierce moustache of later years? If so, was the Commendatore sporting a walrus?). Shaw was an indefatigible writer to *The Times*; his first letter appeared in 1898 when he was 42, his last shortly before his death in 1950. Probably not since Swift had anyone rivalled Shaw for lucidity in argument. At least, a Canadian high school teacher was so moved by Shaw at the opera that she resolved to make her senior pupils emulate his prose style. She eventually confessed to failure. Runners-up in the letters stakes were in reaction to Shaw's trail of devastation, indicating men and women of sentiment. Numerous hearts bled for Mr Lydekker who heard the cuckoo which wasn't, sighs were Neville Chamberlain's reward for discovering a grey wagtail in St James's Park (one French reviewer lauded a finance minister who could turn his mind to more civilised matters). A. P. Herbert caused many to wish they had heard him in the House of Commons, while Lord Fisher's turn of phrase captivated: it was dazzling, bewildering, or downright impossible. An American lady fell in love with Mr Branson whose menu qualified him as 'the cutest Englishman since General Burgoyne. My husband, who plays golf, would like to know if people eat like Mr Branson at St Andrews.' The Cuckoo, putting in a plug for the British Tourist Board, replied: 'Why don't you both come over and see?' Silence followed: perhaps they did come, ate in the Branson manner, and perished.

6

'*The Times* correspondence page is the last resort of the piquant, the idiosyncratic, the nutty, the dotty and the potty.' This reviewer in the *Jerusalem Post* might have added 'and the first resort of the grand denunciation, esoteric information casually passed on for the benefit of mankind, and flashes of inspiration'. How best to present letters reflecting such different moods? Past *Cuckoos* have adopted a more or less chronological order, thus subjecting the anthologist to unpleasing comment. He thought hard but was unable to counter the logic of

Sir,
 I have just bought the First Cuckoo.
There is no letter for March 3, 1906, the day on which I was born. WHY?
 I joined my regiment, of which I later became adjutant, on June 5, 1928. There is no letter for this date either. WHY! To be more exact, WHY NOT!
 I am giving my copy of your book to the vicar's wife who is collecting jumble.

Yours, in disgust . . .

To avoid giving pain to vicars' wives who take *The Daily Telegraph* and collect jumble, *The Last Cuckoo* is planned more artfully; the reader will consult the Contents page, choose a theme, then browse accordingly. Not until he has finished the book will he know if the date of his birth coincided with a selected letter to *The Times*.

Esoteric information shall now be passed on for the enlightenment of readers. A regular feature in *The Times* for more than half a century was the 'Fourth Leader', the peg on which many of the letters here were wittily hung. The Fourth Leader did not grow but shot up overnight in response to a telegram from the paper's proprietor, Lord Northcliffe, in Paris on 25 January 1914.

HUMBLY BEG FOR LIGHT LEADING ARTICLE DAILY
TILL I RETURN – CHIEF.

The next day 'Anticipation and Memory' appeared (beta minus?); then, on 28 January, a vintage alpha plus 'Blue Hair and Gilded Faces' – not a hint of punkery to come, but noting the influence of the Russian Ballet. In due course, *The Times* would publish in book form the best of the year's Fourth Leaders, aware they would be reviewed in the right spirit. 'These happy little essays,'Harold Nicolson wrote of one collection: 'They entertain, they comfort, and they assuage.... We lay the little book down with the impression that it is indeed a privilege to belong to so tolerant, so gifted and so humane a race.' Fourth Leaders would toss off literary quotations and assume that Latin tags were stored away in rusty compartments of *The Times*' universal mind. Oxbridge dons scanned the day's Fourth Leader before descending to tutorials. The Fourth Leader was unashamedly élitist. It was put to death after the issue of 13 January 1967, returning furtively not so long ago on Saturdays. No whimsical title lures the reader's eye, only the words FOURTH LEADER, as though to say 'Get ready to smile'.

Esoteric information of another kind the anthologist would dearly love to pass on, but cannot. Had he the time and the inclination (he has neither), he would sit down behind a breakwater of *Times* indexes and − working his way backwards − determine the date of the first letter from a 'Ms'. His objection to 'Ms' is mainly visual; besides, he doesn't know how to pronounce it. His regard for liberated ladies is so profound that he has resolutely refused to cuckoo-ise Sir Almroth Wright's 1912 letter on female suffrage: 'Sexually embittered women in whom everything has turned into gall . . . Women must give a willing subordination to the husband or father.' (To point out that Sir Almroth was married, and a close friend of Shaw's will avail us nothing.) But the anthologist does feel for *The Times* which occasionally dithers helplessly: see 4 February 1987 when the MP for Birmingham, Ladywood was Ms Clare Short on page 1, and Miss Clare Short on page 4. Had the same Member been Mrs Alexander Lyon on another page, *The Times* hat-trick must have been unique − and the target for female abuse. And what if Mrs Margaret Thatcher had chosen to be Ms Margaret Roberts, a question almost as significant as the identity of the first Ms letter to be published in *The Times*?

This Introduction was about to be rounded off in the same way that the Introduction to *The First Cuckoo* had begun many years ago, with a quotation from Max Beerbohm's essay, *A Letter That Was Not Written*.

Could not this outrage be averted? There sprang from my lips that fiery formula which has sprung from the lips of so many choleric old gentlemen in the course of the past hundred years and more:
'I shall write to *The Times*'.

8

Enter Mr J. R. Burg. As letters to *The Times* are the copyright of the senders, permission must be sought and given before they appear in book form. This is gladly given, though the odd correspondent will first deny ever having written to *The Times*; shown a copy of the letter, he will first congratulate himself on its quality, then the anthologist on his admirable powers of selection. So far, so good. The real problem rises when the correspondent approached gives his permission, then adds 'But my best letter appeared on . . .'. The anthologist blanches. Has he overlooked a classic? Enter Mr J. R. Burg who welcomed the choice of his letter on page 295. Clearing his throat, Mr Burg went on: 'What I thought my best letter to *The Times* of this particular kind was unfortunately not printed.' Really, this was too much. 'It was written a few weeks after the correspondence on foreign language phrase books had come to an end . . . I enclose a copy in case you have a place for "failed" letters.'

The Last Cuckoo opens with a sequence of 'perfect' letters. Here, surely, is another; one which proves beyond all doubt that Mr Burg graduated with honours from Stephen Potter's School of Gamesmanship.

From Mr J. R. Burg   *9 September 1985*

Sir,

Travelling in the Balkans before the war with one of my uncles, a botanist, we made use of various phrase books including a somewhat erratic English-Albanian one by George Nakos and Kamber Ali, the latter said to have been a near relation of King Zog. Some of the phrases included envisaged contingencies which might seldom occur to ordinary travellers, for example: 'Tell the Italian consul to fetch me an omelette.'

I am, Sir, your etc.,

J. R. BURG

This is probably the finest letter which *The Times* — for excellent reasons — never published. In two sentences, Mr Burg triumphed with at least half a dozen ploys: travelling in the Balkans was not common before the war (unless it was Richard Hughes, just down from Oxford and also in these pages, planning revolutions) but Mr Burg and his uncle were there; 'one' of Mr Burg's uncles implies that he had several, to have enumerated them would have invited comparison with P. G. Wodehouse's eleven aunts on his mother's side alone; a 'botanist uncle' has the reader asking 'what were the others?

9

Diplomat? Water-diviner? Professor of Sanskrit? Was the botanist uncle botanising or acting on behalf of British Intelligence? Mention of King Zog is a reminder that the British adore Royalty.

Mr Burg's final ploy is superb. He implies that he and his uncle were 'ordinary' travellers; we know they were not. We know that Uncle Burg went from restaurant to restaurant: 'Tell the Italian consul to fetch me an omelette.' History recalls what happened. The Italian consul protested vehemently to Rome so that on 7 April 1939 Mussolini invaded Albania, by which time Burg and nephew were safely back in England awaiting further instructions. A perfect note on which to end this Introduction if only Mr Burg had added some reference to the cuckoo's call in Albania. How does the Albanian cuckoo pronounce himself? The gravest doubts have entered the anthologist's mind since he re-read a Wodehouse story, *The Nodder*.

Mabel Potter was the private secretary of Mr Schnellenhamer, the head of Perfecto-Zizzbaum Corporation. Before going to Hollywood, she had been a bird-imitator in vaudeville, her cuckoo-calls acknowledged from the Palace, Portland, Oregon to the Hippodrome, Sumquamset, Maine. In Hollywood, however, Miss Potter disagreed with a director, explaining later:

They ask me as a special favour to come and imitate the call of the cuckoo for this new picture, and when I do it Mr Murgatroyd says I've done it wrong. He says a cuckoo goes Cuckoo, Cuckoo, when everybody who has studied the question knows that what it really goes is Wuckoo, Wuckoo.

Like Miss Potter, Beethoven and Mahler did cuckoo-calls but they are not here to help us. Cuckoo or Wuckoo? The answer may come in a *Times* Fourth Leader one Saturday morning.

10

Until 1922 *The Times* would seem to have dealt with its daily cascade of letters in a haphazard manner. In that year the editor, Geoffrey Dawson, set up a department to bring order to correspondence. Whether or not the senior person concerned was termed 'Letters Editor', those in charge were:

> 1922–31 James McInnes
> 1931–34 Francis Brewer
> 1934–39 Wilfred Gavin Brown
> and
> 1935–37 Roger Fulford
> 1939–53 Iolo Williams
> 1953–80 Geoffrey Woolley
> 1980– Leon Pilpel

To these gentlemen this book is gratefully dedicated.

The Perfect Letter

———◆———

Perfection — N. perfection; perfectness &c. *adj.*, impeccability.
   pink, beau-ideal, paragon; pink −, acme − of perfection; ne plus ultra; summit &c.
   model, standard, pattern, mirror, admirable Crichton; trump; very prince of.
   master-piece, -stroke, super-excellence &c....

Roget's Thesaurus

The perfect letter enlightened the cuckoo, made him sigh with pleasure − or, when describing the horrors afflicting a patron of the opera, prescribed helpless laughter.

Opera Buffa

From Mr Bernard Shaw   *3 July 1905*

Sir,
   The Opera management at Covent Garden regulates the dress of its male patrons. When is it going to do the same to the women?
   On Saturday night I went to the Opera. I wore the costume imposed on me by the regulations of the house. I fully recognize the advantage of those regulations. Evening dress is cheap, simple, durable, prevents rivalry and extravagance on the part of male leaders of fashion, annihilates class distinctions, and gives men who are poor and doubtful of their social position (that is, the great majority of men) a sense of security and satisfaction that no clothes of their own choosing could confer, besides saving a whole sex the trouble of considering what they should wear on state occasions. The objections to it are as dust in the balance in the eyes of the ordinary Briton. These objections are that it is colourless and characterless; that it involves a whitening process which makes the shirt troublesome, slightly

13

uncomfortable, and seriously unclean; that it acts as a passport for undesirable persons; that it fails to guarantee sobriety, cleanliness, and order on the part of the wearer; and that it reduces to a formula a very vital human habit which should be the subject of constant experiment and active private enterprise. All such objections are thoroughly un-English. They appeal only to an eccentric few, and may be left out of account with the fantastic objections of men like Ruskin, Tennyson, Carlyle, and Morris to tall hats.

But I submit that what is sauce for the gander is sauce for the goose. Every argument that applies to the regulation of the man's dress applies equally to the regulation of the woman's. Now let me describe what actually happened to me at the Opera. Not only was I in evening dress by compulsion, but I voluntarily added many graces of conduct as to which the management made no stipulation whatever. I was in my seat in time for the first chord of the overture. I did not chatter during the music nor raise my voice when the Opera was too loud for normal conversation. I did not get up and go out when the statue music began. My language was fairly moderate considering the number and nature of the improvements on Mozart volunteered by Signor Caruso, and the respectful ignorance of the dramatic points of the score exhibited by the conductor and the stage manager – if there is such a functionary at Covent Garden. In short, my behaviour was exemplary.

At 9 o'clock (the Opera began at 8) a lady came in and sat down very conspicuously in my line of sight. She remained there until the beginning of the last act. I do not complain of her coming late and going early; on the contrary. I wish she had come later and gone earlier. For this lady, who had very black hair, had stuck over her right ear the pitiable corpse of a large white bird, which looked exactly as if someone had killed it by stamping on its breast, and then nailed it to the lady's temple, which was presumably of sufficient solidity to bear the operation. I am not, I hope, a morbidly squeamish person; but the spectacle sickened me. I presume that if I had presented myself at the doors with a dead snake round my neck, a collection of blackbeetles pinned to my shirtfront, and a grouse in my hair, I should have been refused admission. Why, then is a woman to be allowed to commit such a public outrage? Had the lady been refused admission, as she should have been, she would have soundly rated the tradesman who imposed the disgusting headdress on her under the false pretence that 'the best people' wear such things, and withdrawn her custom from him; and thus the root of the evil would be struck at; for your

14

fasionable woman generally allows herself to be dressed according to the taste of a person whom she would not let sit down in her presence. I once, in Drury Lane Theatre, sat behind a *matinée* hat decorated with the two wings of a seagull, artifically reddened at the joints so as to produce an illusion of being freshly plucked from a live bird. But even that lady stopped short of the whole seagull. Both ladies were evidently regarded by their neighbours as ridiculous and vulgar; but that is hardly enough when the offence is one which produces a sensation of physical sickness in persons of normal humane sensibility.

I suggest to the Covent Garden authorities that, if they feel bound to protect their subscribers against the danger of my shocking them with a blue tie, they are at least equally bound to protect me against the danger of a woman shocking me with a dead bird.

Yours truly,
G. BERNARD SHAW

Long Distance Walking

[The following received the supreme accolade of being discussed in a *Letter from America*]

From Mr Mark Godding   *8 July 1977*

Sir,

Regarding the current enthusiasm for walking to extend one's life, may I point out that if one walked 10 miles a day, then having lived to the ripe old age of eighty, one would have walked for approximately nine years? It would also have cost a considerable amount in shoe leather. Is it worth it?

Yours faithfully,
MARK GODDING

['I put this letter,' said Alistair Cooke, 'in a file of human wisdom that contains such gems as Aristotle's "A play has a beginning, a middle and an end", Dr Johnson's "Much may be made of a Scotsman if he is caught young", Mark Twain's "The human being is the only animal that blushes, or needs to", and H. L. Mencken's definition of self-respect: "The secure feeling that no one, as yet, is suspicious".']

An appreciative Godding then wrote asking for Cooke's autograph, adding 'I am aged 15']

Police and Chewing Gum

From Millicent, Duchess of Sutherland   *3 July 1928*

Sir,

If I were to begin a letter on the subjects of the enforcements and non-enforcements on the actions of the London police, my pen might burn the paper. I will restrict myself to chewing gum!

Why in heaven's name are our police forbidden to chew gum? The steadying effect on the nerves, the calming of tiredness, the greater efficiency provided by chewing gum is a question of common knowledge. I have proved this on long motor runs and exhausting journeys. I encourage my chauffeur to chew gum: he is always fresher at the end of a long excursion than if he smoked cigarettes. Think of the hours a policeman is standing on his beat.

This perpetual interference in England in minor details with the liberty of the subject, whether he be prince or policeman, seems pretty absurd abroad. The English people are indeed strong in their submission, but whenever I come over I find them tiresome in their complaints about it. Please give the Metropolitan policeman back his chewing gun, and merely ask him to be careful where he emits it.

MILLICENT SUTHERLAND

[Her Grace's concern with the spot where chewing gum could be emitted shows she was resident on the Continent and not in the United States. There, as Bertie Wooster had recently observed, policemen park their gum against a rainy day].

Cows in St James's Park

From Mr E. W. Brabrook   *11 February 1905*

Sir,

It was with something like distress that, in coming here this morning through St James's Park, I missed the one piece of evidence of picturesque custom of which that park could boast.

Sixty or so years ago it was one of the 'delights of my youth,' passing through the park, to stop for a cup of milk and see it drawn from the cow; and I am sorry that it should now be 'the fallacious aspiration of my riper years.

To us city boys it was almost our only chance of seeing a cow in the flesh. It is now, or was till yesterday, the only remaining evidence of the 'Spring Gardens' that once were so famous.

I hope that the authorities will restore the cows to their wonted place. To remove them is a tyrannous action to others than their proprietors, and it does not mend the matter that it has been necessary to call in the prerogative of his Majesty to justify the doing of an act that a private proprietor could not have lawfully done.

I have the honour to be, Sir, your most obedient humble servant.

E. W. Brabrook

[This letter was sent from The Athenaeum]

'Anti-Cyclone'

From Mr Logan Pearsall Smith   *4 March 1911*

Sir,

The Times has won the gratitude of lovers of good English by its successful effort, not long ago, to supplant the uncouth word 'aviator' by the excellent and idiomatic compound 'airman.' May I suggest another verbal reform which no mere individual can effect, but which is not beyond the powers of your journal?

Every one will, I think, admit that another word, or at least an alternative name, for 'anti-cyclone' would be an addition to the language. Now that the facts of meteorology have become matters of common knowledge, it is surely regrettable that for so benign a phenomenon as the anti-cyclone, with its periods of windless calm, we should have no better name than this – a word which is somewhat pedantic in conversation, impossible in verse, whose end is stormy, while its prefix is loaded with suggestions of conflict, from anti-Christ to anti-vivisection.

Both 'cyclone' and 'anti-cyclone' are deliberate 19th century creations, and, although open perhaps to philological criticism, they have served their scientific purpose admirably, and will no doubt continue to do so in the future. But while popular speech has been able to adopt 'cyclone', it has found, as we might expect from its form, 'anti-cyclone' unsuited for its purposes. For a word to be popular must, as *The Times* recently stated, not only describe the thing itself, but also express our feelings about it. Such a word for anti-cyclone can probably be found: indeed, I should like to suggest that we already have one in English, the Greek word 'halcyon,' which was naturalized 500 years ago, and in the 17th century was used to describe periods of quietude and calm. It only survives now as an adjective: but the substantive might easily be revived as a description of those periods when

'Birds of calm sit brooding on the charmed wave.'

No doubt the word is at present somewhat too literary and poetic; but a little use would soon lower its flight to more prosaic levels; and we might before long read with no undue shock the statement in the morning paper that 'the Atlantic halcyon is approaching our shores, and is likely to extend its influence over the south of England.'

Very likely this suggestion can be improved upon. My main object in writing this letter is to show that some word is needed.

Your obedient servant,

L. PEARSALL SMITH

[Perhaps the rarest compliment ever paid a journalist came from Pearsall Smith. Writing to Robert Gathorne-Hardy on 13 May 1929, he referred to an account in *The Times* of the sun's eclipse as seen in Manila:

' "The weather was cloudless, the conditions were perfect. Acacia trees closed their leaves as for the night; dew fell, chickens roosted, and the peasants in outlying villages, terrified by the awful phenomenon, supplicated the Saints."

'Could this sentence, which Flaubert might have written with the help of Gibbon, be the chance product of a journalist's pen? I cannot think so.'

The Times archivist attributes the sentence to Sir Willmott Lewis, Washington correspondent from 1920 to 1948]

A Grey Wagtail

From the Chancellor of the Exchequer   *24 January 1933*

Sir,

It may be of interest to record that, in walking through St James's Park today, I noticed a grey wagtail running about on the now temporarily dry bed of the lake, near the dam below the bridge, and occasionally picking small insects out of the cracks in the dam.

Probably the occurrence of this bird in the heart of London has been recorded before, but I have not myself previously noted it in the Park.

> I am your obedient servant,
> NEVILLE CHAMBERLAIN

P.S. For the purpose of removing doubts, as we say in the House of Commons, I should perhaps add that I mean a grey wagtail and not a pied.

[On 30 January Adolf Hitler became Chancellor of Germany]

Reading in Bed

From Mr H. Malcolm Carter   *10 January 1962*

Sir,

I am surprised that none of your correspondents has proposed the obvious solution − the provision of a series of slits in the bedclothes through which the hands may be projected in the manner of the old-fashioned Turkish bath box. When not in use the slits may be closed by zips or buttons, or even by a handful of straw, barley for preference, as being softer than wheat or oats. It should, however, come from the binder, as the combine generally breaks it up and makes it rather untidy for indoor use.

> I am, Sir, faithfully yours,
> H. MALCOLM CARTER

The Secret of England's Fame

From Mr Colin MacInnes   *20 April 1967*

Sir,

The Times, in its new dispensation, has already published excellent articles and letters which all ask, basically, the same question, namely: what is the matter with England, and how can we extricate ourselves from our present predicaments?

May I suggest that the answer can be found if we all take five minutes off from our pressing worries and ask ourselves the following simple, basic question: which Englishmen, in our history, have *really* influenced not only England, but the world?

It seems to me that any short list will eventually reduce itself to three names: and these are Shakespeare, Newton and Darwin. The one a poet who helped to give shape and meaning to one of the most extraordinary languages the world has ever known. The next a young scientist of genius who, however much his theories have later been disproved, was one of the prime inventors of the modern world. And the third another scientist-philosopher who, more even than Karl Marx, has utterly altered almost everyone's ideas about everything.

If this diagnosis is correct, what might we have the intelligence to conclude? Surely this. When we pause to consider what our *real* genius is, is it not that of our artists and our scientists? And if we look around, even today, at who is really bringing credit to our country, will we not find that it is precisely these same people whom the world listens to, and respects, and admires?

Then what of that great procession of kings, generals, politicians and viceroys who have so much adorned our history? Have they contributed nothing?

They belong, it would seem to me, to our accidental period of imperial grandeur: which had certainly great will and courage in it, and earned us a lot of money, but also the unforgiving hatred of millions of human beings throughout the globe.

To the honourable list of our real heroes, Shakespeare, Newton, and Darwin, I would like to add the name of the eternal, anonymous Mr Smith. Mr Smith is a trader. Realizing, with his admirable common sense, that a basically poor island cannot live without commerce, and that these extraordinary poets and scientists would starve without him, he buys, and manufactures, and then sells.

And is that not, Sir, exactly what we really are: a people of artists and empirical thinkers and exporters? Are these not the people who have made our name respected, who have saved us a hundred times before, and who will do so again if we have the wits to recognize that they are what, at our best, we are?

Yours faithfully,

C. MACINNES

Oval or Intelligent?

From Mr B. Digby   *17 February 1915*

Sir,

A little light might be shed, with advantage, upon the high-handed methods of the Passports Department at the Foreign Office. On the form provided for the purpose I described my face as 'intelligent.' Instead of finding this characterization entered, I have received a passport on which some official utterly unknown to me, has taken it upon himself to call my face 'oval'.

Yours very truly,

BASSETT DIGBY

The Lady and Her Hat

From Miss Silvia Risolo   *29 June 1949*

Sir,

Please forgive my English. I am not English and have been in England for two months only. Two days ago I was in the London Bridge underground station. I went out of the train and began to go upstairs. Suddenly a gush of wind blew away my hat, and I ran downstairs to the platform, but the hat went down between the rails. Then I too went down between the rails and, since the hat stopped finally, I took it and climbed on the platform again. Nobody told me anything. Today a friend of mine told me that the rails are electrified and that I could die very easily. But why, if so, is there no advertisement near the rails? I did not know that the rails were electrified. I simply took my hat. Since I am in a rather difficult situation at present, some people might have thought that I had committed suicide – instead I was following my hat only. This story is comical and strange, but it is a little dreadful also.

Yours sincerely,

SILVIA RISOLO

The Cuckoo

On Hearing the First Cuckoo

From Mr Lydekker, FRS   *6 February 1913*

Sir,

While gardening this afternoon I heard a faint note which led me to say to my under-gardener, who was working with me, 'Was that the cuckoo?' Almost immediately afterwards we both heard the full double note of a cuckoo, repeated either two or three times – I am not quite sure which. The time was 3.40; and the bird, which was to the westward – that is to say, to windward – appeared to be about a quarter of a mile away. There is not the slightest doubt that the song was that of a cuckoo.

The late Professor Newton, in the fourth edition of Yarrell's 'British Birds' (Vol. II., p. 389, note), stated that although the arrival of the cuckoo has frequently been reported in March, or even earlier, such records must be treated with suspicion, if not with incredulity. And Mr J. E. Harting ('Handbook of British Birds,' p. 112) goes even further than this, stating that there is no authentic record of the arrival of the cuckoo in this country earlier than 6 April.

R. LYDEKKER

[The above incident occurred in Hertfordshire]

12 February 1913

Sir,

I regret to say that, in common with many other persons, I have been completely deceived in the matter of the supposed cuckoo of February 4. The note was uttered by a bricklayer's labourer at work on a house in the neighbourhood of the spot whence the note appeared to come. I have interviewed the man, who tells me that he is able to draw cuckoos from considerable distances by the exactness of his imitation of their notes, which he produces without the aid of any instrument.

R. LYDEKKER

[*On Hearing The First Cuckoo In Spring* by Frederick Delius, received its first performance in Leipzig on 2 October 1913]

The Cuckoo on the Keys

From the Reverend K. H. MacDermott   *25 May 1934*

[writing from Uckfield]

Sir,

For many years each spring I have tested the cuckoo's notes with a piano, and have found that they are always within a tone of D and B, or D and B flat (treble stave). It is of interest to observe that Beethoven, a great lover of birds, when he introduced the imitation of the cuckoo at the end of the second movement of his Pastoral Symphony, gave the two notes D and B flat, to be played by the clarionet. As Beethoven was at the time he composed that work (1808) completely deaf one wonders whether it was by chance he selected the correct notes, or merely because they fit in with the key of the movement, or whether his memory of the bird's song had survived after he had been unable to hear it for some years. If the latter, it is fascinating to realize that the cuckoo has not altered the pitch of his notes for over a century.

Yours truly,
K. H. MacDermott

[After taking holy orders Mr MacDermott became an Associate of the Royal College of Music]

Converted Cuckoo

From Dr H. Motz   *29 May 1959*

[Professor of Engineering in the University of Oxford, 1972–7]

Sir,

I know that it is rather late in the season to report on cuckoos; nor is it the usual story we have to tell. We have a cuckoo in the

Oxford University Engineering Laboratory, too young to issue its familiar call. It fell out of its nest — we can only think that the other young birds ganged up and threw out the false brother this time. The foster mother, a blackbird, comes dutifully down to feed him. Indeed, who could resist its desperate cries, not yet cuckoo-like but unmistakable in their purpose?

It fell into a basement in front of our high energy accelerator, out in the open, where we usually direct the X-ray beam. We dare not run the machine for fear of hurting the bird. Latinists or not, we are not inhuman, we scientists. But, who knows, maybe the X-rays would induce mutations which might make the wretched bird build its own nest in future?

Yours, &c.,

H. MOTZ

Their First Cuckoo?

From Mr David Mallon   *25 June 1977*

[writing from the Mongolian State University at Ulan Bator]

Sir,

I heard today the first cuckoo of this year. Is this a record for Outer Mongolia?

Yours faithfully,

DAVID MALLON

Disturbed

From Mrs Rosemary Samson   *14 June 1983*

Sir,

Last night (June 1), about midnight, shortly before the storm broke, my husband and I, and a friend who lives nearby, distinctly heard the cuckoo. The call came several times, apparently from a bird in flight.

I have never before heard a cuckoo at night. Was the bird disturbed by the impending storm? If so, why did we not hear others?

Yours faithfully,

ROSEMARY SAMSON

25

Duettist

From Dr Pamela Priest   *18 June 1983*

Sir,

Mrs Rosemary Samson's letter on the night cuckoo reminds me of my childhood in wartime Somerset, when anti-aircraft guns once set a cuckoo and a nightingale singing together.

Yours faithfully,
PAMELA PRIEST

[The credit shall go to Joseph Cooper who once commanded an anti-aircraft battery in Somerset]

Willing to Oblige

From Mr Douglas Vernon   *18 June 1983*

Sir,

Is Mrs Rosemary Samson not aware that the *Cuculus Canorus* (the cuckoo) has a marked tendency to behave in an eccentric manner whenever it senses the presence in the neighbourhood of a *Times* correspondence column contributor?

Yours faithfully,
DOUGLAS VERNON

Of a Different Feather

From the Minister of Foreign Affairs for Sierra Leone
29 August 1983

Sir,

I was able, in the course of my last transit through London in early August, to secure a copy of *The Second Cuckoo*, which I understand was only made available on the bookshelves a week or so before.

Though it was somewhat late in the season, it still reads and sounds (as my family is treated to *viva voce* rendition of some of the amusing selections) refreshing.

I beg to remain one of your no doubt innumerable cuckoo

supporters, or shall I say watchers in the tropics of the *Musophagidae* family.

Yours faithfully,
ABDULAI O. CONTEH

The Cuckoo's Finest Hour

[The Prime Minister had likened certain bishops of the Church of England to cuckoos]

From the Reverend Arthur Moss   *28 March 1985*

Sir,
The report of the first cuckoo of spring is always eagerly anticipated but less experienced bird-watchers frequently get it wrong, confusing the call of *Columba palumpus* for *Cuculus canorus*.

The good lady from Westminster, having heard several as widely apart as Canterbury, Liverpool and Durham, to mention but a few, as early in the year as February and March, might have had second thoughts and known that what she heard was the much rarer *Novum Testamentum*.

Yours faithfully,
ARTHUR MOSS

Cuckoos lead Bohemian lives,
They fail as husbands and as wives,
Therefore they cynically disparage
Everybody else's marriage.

Ogden Nash

27

The Cuckoo's Rekords

From Mr Graham Greene, CH   *24 May 1978*

[Order of Merit 1986]

Sir,

  May I suggest that the number of misprints per page in an English daily newspaper would be a worthy candidate for the *Guinness Book of Records*? Just to establish a claim I nominate page 4 of *The Times* of 12 May which contains 37 misprints. They include two well worth preserving: 'entertoinment' has a fine Cockney ring and 'rampaign' combining in one word the ideas of campaign and rampage in an article on vandalism, deserves to find a permanent place in the Oxford Dictionary. I was glad to note too the firm attitude taken to juvenile delinquency — two defendents aged 3 and aged 0 were committed for trial at the Central Criminal Court.

Yours truly,
GRAHAM GREENE

['Defendents' (*sic*) — was this the compositors' revenge?]

From Mr Patrick Drysdale   *4 September 1984*

Sir,

  On some days I think I take *The Times* for the pleasure afforded by the misprints. In today's (August 29) column by John Woodcock, who knows what to do with words, I read, 'Allott bowled one over before giong off'.

  While waiting for the opportunity to tell an irritating interlocutor to 'giong off', I find, a few lines lower down, 'England continued to dawdale'. Apart from the fact that it rhymes with my own name, I like the sound of 'dawdale'. It has a measured leisure to it, and I will always associate the summer of '84 with the memory of the England XI, her Majesty's government, and *The Times* proof readers all dawdaling on their way, giong towards imminent disaster.

Yours faithfully,
PATRICK DRYSDALE

[In 1984 England lost all five Tests to West Indies]

From Mr Gordon Martin   *11 September 1984*

Sir,

Whether, like Mr Drysdale, one should take *The Times* only
for the pleasure afforded by its misprints is perhaps
questionable. But there is no doubt that they can sometimes add
to the richness of the language.

Thus, on August 29, I was pleased to see your Labour
Correspondent's front-page report of 'confustion' at a Bristol
dockers' meeting in support for the coal-miners.

In a situation where combustion is at the heart of the matter,
and confusion is so patently widespread, confustion seemed to
me a particularly happy, albeit accidental invention by your
computer.

Yours sincerely,

GORDON MARTIN

From Mr Fritz Spiegel   *30 June 1984*

Sir,

Thank you for helping to revive attractive and apt old English
words, e.g. the miners' 'stoggage' (my – early – edition, June
27).

On checking with the OED I find that to be 'stogged' means
'to be stuck in the mud, mire, bog or the like'.

Yours faithfully,

FRITZ SPIEGEL

[Two academics now intervened from aery heights]

From Dr Kieran Flanagan   *20 September 1984*

[Department of Sociology, University of Bristol]

Sir,

The commentary on the *Alternative Service Book*, 1980, by
the Liturgical Commission, tells us that 'in communicating with
men, we have to accommodate our audience' according to class,
sex and age. Surely this advice has been taken to extremes at the
Royal Naval College Chapel, Greenwich, where, according to
the service list in *The Times* (September 15) for the Thirteenth
Sunday after Trinity, Tye's lovely anthem, 'Laudate Nomen
Domini', is to be rendered as 'Laudate Women Domini'.

Is this now to be the anthem of tokenism, the song of incorporation of the Anglican Church adaptable to all social groups as, for instance, 'Laudate Microbiologists Domini'?

I write as a distressed Roman Catholic sociologist with a passing interest in liturgy.

Yours faithfully,
KIERAN FLANAGAN

From Professor F. M. Fowler   *29 September 1984*

[Department of German, Queen Mary College, University of London]

Sir,

For a spirited defence of such New Alternative Anthems as 'Laudate Women Domini' Dr Flanagan and others in liturgical distress should contact the splendid la(d)y preacher who, according to your service lists, has – since the introduction of the mini-skirt – most frequently graced the pulpits of London churches. Her name and address: Miss A. Brevis (Palestrina).

Yours neofaithfully,
FRANK M. FOWLER

How long before Ms A. Brevis?

[*The Times*' first issue of 1985 began celebrations of the paper's bicentenary, a facsimile edition of itself (or *The Daily Universal Register* as it then was) for 1 January 1785 being included]

From Mr David Nathan   *4 January 1985*

Sir,

Would you kindly draw the attention of your head proof reader to an error in column three, page three, of the facsimile first edition of *The Times*, or *The Daily Universal Register*, as Mr Walter chose to call it.

There, under the heading 'Antiquities', is advertised a collection of 'the most remarkable runs and ancient buidings.'

Surely there is some mistake here. If it is allowed to pass uncorrected there is no knowing where it will end.

Yours faithfully,
DAVID NATHAN

From Mr John Goodchild *4 January 1985*

Sir,

I hope I am not too late in pointing out an apparent error in your issue of January 1, 1785. You describe the 'Ode for the New Year' as being by Paul Whitehead, though he died in 1774. Could this have been an early example of ghost writing or was it an error for William Whitehead, Poet Laureate, who died in April, 1785?

You may, of course, have printed a correction in the following issue, but I did not see it at the time.

I am, Sir, etc,

J. GOODCHILD

[The following correction appeared in *The Times* of 25 October 1984: 'The words "imported oil" in Woodrow Wyatt's article on Saturday should have read "imported coal" ']

Yesterday

West-End Imposter

From Oetzmann and Co.   *29 December 1900*

[a leading London furnishers]

Sir,

We think the following facts would be appreciated as a warning to West-end tradesmen and others:

A tall, well-dressed, gentlemanly man, age about 40, with dark moustache, wearing frock-coat and silk hat, has favoured our establishment with a visit, representing himself to be Lord Wilmington, and eventually giving as his town address No. 98, Carlton-gardens.

He selected several thousands of pounds' worth of goods, including some of our finest modern and antique furniture, &c., and informed our representative that he wished to furnish a large mansion in Glamorganshire.

He also made an appointment to call again with her ladyship, and desired to have all the goods he had selected placed in position in one of our show-rooms; the next day, however, we received a communication postponing this appointment and signed 'Wilmington.'

Being doubtful about this gentleman, we made inquiries, and find he has been proceeding in a similar manner with other large West-end establishments, giving an infinite amount of trouble, and passing under *aliases* of Lord Raeburn, Lord Manners, Lord Radcliff, Lord Brereton, Lord Wilmington, Lord Rauben, at a variety of addresses in London and the provinces, also castles in Scotland and Wales – at one establishment we know he made daily visits of considerable length spread over a week.

We have communicated with the Marquis of Northampton, whose eldest son is Lord Compton (now an Eton boy), and who was during the late Marquis's lifetime Lord Wilmington.

His lordship says that any one using the title of Lord Wilmington is an impostor.

We are, Sir, your obedient servants,

OETZMANN AND CO.

['Three addresses always inspire confidence, even in tradesmen,' said Wilde's Lady Bracknell. More than three apparently arouse suspicion]

Motor Cars and Horses

[Sir Edmund Monson, a former Ambassador Extraordinary and Plenipotentiary to the Emperor of Austria, and later to the French Republic, had pointed out that due to motor traffic it was becoming difficult to enjoy one's afternoon carriage drive in the Bois de Boulogne]

From Sir Henry Thompson   *5 September 1901*

[a distinguished surgeon, at this time aged 80]

Sir,

The single source of discomfort which I soon experienced as an alloy to the pleasure derived from the daily use of my motor-car during the last two months, in three adjacent countries, described in your issue of 17 August, was the hostility with which I was regarded by all the drivers of horses I met with. By not a few it was loudly expressed, sometimes in terms inadmissible in these columns. Hence my endeavour to bring about a better feeling between us, and an attempt to show what I felt was error, due solely to want of thought on their part; and I made it my business to show how much gentleness would achieve in the way of improvement.

Naturally, I have been pleased to see how much interest has been taken in the subject, and how many correspondents have expressed their hearty approval of the recommendations made. Others have made suggestions which indicate want of practical knowledge of the motor-car, and one at least has expressed in very strong terms views which demand from me a reply.

As an example of the first-named, one gentleman recommends that as the legal speed is said to be 12 miles per hour, a motor should not be capable of running faster. Had he known anything of the principles of motor construction and driving, he would have been aware that no car thus limited in power would ever ascend a hill. One cannot have less than 16 miles an hour in reserve, or the motor driver would, like a cyclist, have to push his machine up the hill. One requires exchange of speed into power, and in order to ascend a steep hill one often climbs at only four miles an hour, if less steep at eight or 12. But the *minimum* of speed in reserve for all purposes, and there are several, is about 20; and the rate at which I drive on a level, straight, roomy road, where I can see my way well, is a mile in four minutes, producing, with hill climbing, about an average of 12 miles an hour. My car is a 6½ h.p. Tonneau Daimler. With this power in reserve, one descends a hill by the simple weight of the car — no machinery going when all noise ceases, the latter fact being a considerable influence against disturbing horses.

Of the proposal to number motors with conspicuous letters, I need say no more than than if this were adopted it must be applied to carriages of all descriptions without distinction.

Lastly, I must be permitted to refer to the letter of Sir Edmund Monson, which appears in your issue of 31 August. Being old enough to have travelled before any passenger railway existed in this country, I also recollect well the period when railway trains were objects of intense fear to horses and the time it took for them to become accustomed to them; as it subsequently did to the ordinary bicycle. But the sketch of French automobile driving as practised even in the delightful 'Bois' and suburbs of Paris, including as it does such descriptive terms as 'monsters', 'excruciating noise', 'asphyxiating odours', with inmates 'enveloped in gowns, protected by hideous masks', like 'the demons of a travelling circus', giving 'the impression of a diabolical phenomenon', is, I hope, and have no doubt is, intentionally highly coloured. There are other terms of a similar kind, but the above suffice.

I wonder what Sir Edmund's Parisian friends will think of this picture of French refinement, which we in England have long learned to appreciate and esteem. I can assure him no such scenes are presented in the parks of London, and, I dare say without hesitation, never will be. I have traversed them quietly with my own motor, but no rate approaching to 'at least 40 kilometres an hour' would be attempted. No odour is ever emitted, and it is only exceptionally, as when dust and small fires are prevalent, that I wear any other than my ordinary spectacles. For example, I drove to Bedford from Hemel Hempstead yesterday, 35 miles out, in all 70, in about 5½ hours, about an average of 12 miles an hour, without any other glasses, as recent rains had laid the dust. And when I wear the 'goggles' they are faintly tinted neutral glasses with narrow, pale, coffee-coloured surroundings.

I am glad to see by *The Times* this morning that an English gentleman resident in Paris expresses his belief that Sir Edmund's opinion is hardly fair.

I have expressed myself as briefly as possible and trust I do not occupy too much space.

Your obedient servant,
HENRY THOMPSON

The French Pied

From Hachette et Cie   *2 May 1903*

Monsieur,

Dans une lettre publiée dans le *Times* du 15 Avril, un de vos correspondants fait remarquer que l'Almanach Hachette commet peut-être une erreur en attribuant à l'ancien 'pied de France' une longueur de 325 millimètres, alors que d'autres publications ne lui en donnent que 324.

Nous croyons cependant être dans le vrai. L'ancienne 'toise' de France était de 6 pieds et mesure exactement 1 mètre 949 millimètres ce qui donne pour le pied 0 mètre 32474, chiffre beaucoup plus rapproché de 325 que de 324. Votre correspondant dit en outre que Napoléon avait 5 pieds 7 pouces, c'est 5 pieds 2 pouces qu'il faut lire.

Veuillez agréer, Monsieur, l'expression de nos sentiments très distingués.

HACHETTE ET CIE

Experiences of a New MP

From Mr Alfred Davies, MP   *17 August 1901*

[Radical, Carmarthen District, 1900–6]

Sir,

I have collated a few of the striking epithets and characteristics descriptive of myself that have appeared in the newspapers during this my first Parliamentary Session, and I venture to hope that, as the experiences of a one-year Parliamentary recruit, they will not be uninteresting to your readers.

More than one recent newspaper has contained the startling statement that Mr Pickwick has come to life again, and that I am that gentleman resuscitated under another name, *minus* the tights and gaiters, which indispensable accessories, however, two illustrated journals have been kind enough to supply in cartoons bearing a greater or lesser resemblance to myself. Other newspapers have been good enough to say that I combine the best features in the character of Mr Pickwick and the Brothers Cheeryble, whilst I am also informed that, 'like Oliver Twist, I am always asking for more.'

Probably no two characters in Shakespeare form a more striking contrast than Fluellen and Dogberry. Yet I have been compared to the former for 'pertinacity,' and to the latter for 'artless directness.'

Again, whilst one journal calls me 'an excited Welshman,' another speaks of me as 'imperturbable,' and a third styles me 'a comfortable Welshman.' One critic speaks of my 'magisterial air,' whilst according to another I am 'meek and deferential.'

It is satisfactory to read that though I am an 'incorrigible Welsh member,' I am 'no laggard in the cause of "my" country and the Carmarthen Boroughs.' May I hope that my constitutents will note this last testimony, and bear it in mind at the next election?

It has fallen to my lot to be called, almost in the same breath, 'the charmer of the House,' 'the most polite of questioners,' 'a dogged Welsh member,' and 'an irreverent Philistine.'

My manner has been compared to 'the pompous air of a law Court usher,' and I have also been described as 'unctuous,' and 'the embodiment of the Welsh religious Radical,' as 'the indefatigable Mr Alfred Davies,' and, finally, as 'one of the most original characters and precious possessions of the House of Commons.'

A gentleman with a turn for poetical imagery styles me 'this son of the Red Dragon,' whilst a more prosaic contemporary states that I 'remind the old Parliamentary hands of Earl Granville.'

I fully appreciate the kindness of the genial journalist who writes that 'the House recognizes in "me" one of the quaintest and most delightful personalities that ever existed outside the pages of Dickens.'

Owing to the fact that I felt it my duty to put several questions to the Colonial Secretary in the House of Commons, I was on one occasion described as 'skimming to and fro in an absorbing and feverish desire to catch the Colonial weasel asleep, hoping that haply I may win a reputation by shaving the wily one's eyebrows'.

My personal appearance has also been noticed in such kindly terms as 'handsome,' 'dignified,' 'he looks grace, if not sweetness and light.'

Lastly, when I congratulated Mr Chamberlain on his recovery from his recent indisposition, it was humorously recorded that 'there was not a dry eye in the Strangers' Gallery.'*

As I am not only a raw political recruit, I highly appreciate the encouragements and the warnings of the Press, both of which are equally useful to me; and when the newspapers raise a good-humoured laugh at my expense I gladly laugh, too, because I feel that a little bright cheerfuness varies the monotony of political life, and neutralizes the bitterness of party strife.

Whilst I cling tenaciously to my Radical principles, I feel that a national advantage is to be gained from my course of action. I try to rise above the pettiness of faction, and I regard my political opponents as my friends. Liberal members have told me 'my bland, courteous, and natural ways are new to the House, and they have urged me to continue them.' Tory members have informed me 'that there is not a member on their side of the House who would do me an unkindly act.' The Irish party, although they know I am neither a pro-Boer nor a Little Englander, have shown me great kindness, and have convinced me that, if genuine good feeling exists anywhere, it can be foundin Irish hearts. One prominent Irish member said to me this week, 'If all members were as pleasant as you are the House would de much greater work.'

In conclusion, I may point out that I believe more ultimate good is effected in the world by courtesy and friendliness than by adopting the opposite course; and, whilst I have been told by a high authority I am acquiring a reputation by humour, I can truly say that I seek no reputation, but that I simply desire to do my duty to my constituents, and to strengthen the foundations of the Empire. If I have been at all humorous in the House of Commons, my reason is that I am of opinion that 'a merry heart doeth good like a medicine.'

I am, yours obediently,

ALFRED DAVIES

[* The Diary of Toby, MP, *Punch*, 3 July 1901]

Hedge Cutting

From Colonel Willoughby Verner   *13 July 1908*

[Inventor of the luminous magnetic and prismatic compasses; author of the *Military Life of Field Marshal HRH the Duke of Cambridge* (by command of HRH), and of *My Life Among the Wild Birds in Spain*; former Professor of Military Topography at RMC Sandhurst]

Sir,

Before any of your readers may be induced to cut their hedges as suggested by the secretary of the Motor Union they may like to know my experiences of having done so.

Four years ago I cut down the hedges and shrubs to a height of 4ft for 30 yards back from the dangerous crossing in this hamlet. The results were twofold: The following summer my garden was smothered with dust caused by fastdriven cars, and the average pace of the passing cars was considerably increased. This was bad enough, but when culprits secured by the police pleaded that 'it was perfectly safe to go fast' because they 'could see well at the corner', I realised that I had made a mistake. Since then I have let my hedges and shrubs grow, and by planting roses and hops have raised a screen 8ft to 10ft high, by which means the garden is sheltered to some degree from the dust and the speed of many passing cars sensibly diminished. For it is perfectly plain that there are a large number of motorists who can only be induced to go at a reasonable speed at cross-roads by considerations for their own personal safety.

Hence the advantage to the public of automatically fostering this spirit as I am now doing. To cut hedges is a direct encouragement to reckless driving.

Your obedient servant,
WILLOUGHBY VERNER

[Colonel Verner lived in Winchfield, Hampshire. On 8 December 1981, *The Times* reported that the Royal Borough of Windsor and Maidenhead had requested a householder to trim his hedge. Its letter began: 'Whereas a hedge situation at Altwood Road, Maidenhead in Berkshire belonging to you overhangs the highway known as Altwood Road, Maidenhead, aforesaid so as to endanger or obstruct the passage of pedestrians . . .']

May Day Celebrations

From Lady Macdonell   *3 May 1913*

Sir,

I have just read in *The Times* of today the very interesting article on the lost celebrations of May Day. The writer tells of many May Day rites now gone. May I tell you of one spot in England where some are still honoured, and have been for generations? Early this morning the children of Penzance were out in the fields gathering the 'May', or boughs of green. They will probably be cheered on their way by slices of bread and cream at the hospitable farmhouses. Yesterday the boys would bring out their May horns and be running about blowing them. If you asked them what they were doing, they would probably tell you they were 'scaring away the devil'. I have one of these May horns by me as I write. They are made of tin, varying from a foot to a yard in length and shaped like a herald's trumpet. They can evoke a tremendous blast. Some persons, only inured to the sound of motor horns, object to them.

It is a curious fact, though I have never heard attention drawn to it, that in the ancient carved chancel screen of the old church of Sancreed, a few miles from Penzance, there is a figure that recalls to one's mind the urchins in Penzance streets with their May horns. It is the figure of a youth with puffed-out cheeks, blowing a long horn, while before him a huge serpent writhes in graceful coils lifting a spiteful head with outstretched tongue. May this not be a medieval representation of a local – or perhaps not entirely local – custom of 'scaring the devil' before the coming of May? Perhaps someone better informed than I can answer the question.

Yours truly,
AGNES MACDONELL

Dancing and Manners

From Lady Middleton   *3 June 1913*

[Eliza Maria, wife of Digby Wentworth Bayard, 9th Baron Middleton, who had four addresses in England and one in Ross-shire, NB]

Sir,

I cannot quote 'fools rush in where angels fear to tread,' because, judging from the complicated correspondence on above subject, both have alike rushed – and trodden!

But I was reckoned 'good on the floor' since the days when a distinguished teacher of the Opera in Paris caught me, a naughty damsel, amusing my fellow-pupils by making a 'moue' at his back, and gently suggested that 'Mademoiselle oublie que la salle est garnie de glaces!'

So, as he called me his 'meilleure élève' afterwards, he was forgiving; therefore I may have as much right as many to suggest opinions.

First, I think very few dancers understand expressing the musical rhythm of, say, the valse – dancing it in tune as well as in time. Some few of one's partners did understand this; and oh! the joy of floating with them, down and round a big ballroom; now gently restrained in action, as the band softened or slowed down, now swinging into pace and vigour as the instruments broke forth into loudness, sweeping with a rush (guarded) through or round obstacles, singing in your heart, flying with your feet – then, curbing enthusiasm for a temporary relax into rest as you would restrain a high-spirited horse carrying you over a good country. It is the next best thing to that! But you must have the sympathetic partner to whom tune and time expression both appeal.

I have seen 'the Boston' danced by American *gentlemen* (I underline this term), and thought it clever, graceful, needing excellent steering, but reversing elegantly required a space not often found in ordinary London rooms.

Owing to illness and mourning I I have seen but little of these newly-brought dances; but at one country ball in recent times thought them dull and hideous, specially as danced by one man who appeared to be trying to tie himself into a knot, and who was called a South American.

They were made uglier by the sheathlike dresses of the ladies, revealing more of the 'human form' (rarely 'divine') than our grandmothers would have approved.

(N.B. – Our great-grandmothers did damp their India muslins to show theirs; one of mine received a shawl at the opera once from a Royal dame in kindly deprecation? But the said ancestress was the beauty of her day.)

The Times of 30 May quotes through a correspondent the *Spectator* of May 1710 in which is mentioned a dance called 'Hunt of Squirrel.'

It appears to resemble a charming Scotch dance of my early

youth, whose name has evaded my memory for the moment. A couple stand out on the floor, 'setting' to each other, and it soon becomes the duty of other lads and lasses to sidle up and, simply by adroit and nimble dancing, to oust the partner of either – girls turn away girls and men the men. A really good-at-the-game pair can show great sport trying to keep outsiders from separating them. The lady dancing backwards down the floor, now avoiding, now approaching her partner, can, if active and 'cannie,' keep the foe, whether male or female, at bay for a long time; while the gentleman can act with more persuasion towards one of his own sex by gently shouldering him aside while he himself dances gaily about.

I once in early days found myself *vis-à-vis* to a very great personage, who was quite resolved to keep the ground and chase away my cavalier. After flying round the room – a big one – at least twice – racing pace, despite much interference – at the bottom, I ventured, panting, to say, 'I am done, Sir!'

No lady being brave enough to come to my aid (though I glanced appeal at several friends looking on) and take possession of the future Monarch, his pitiless command. 'Go up to the top of the room again,' had to be obeyed. We both took a vast amount of exercise that evening.

I can imagine the above dance executed by roughs, when, of course, it could be made unsuitable for 'civil' society. One recalls with wrath the beautiful and coquettish Highland scottische, now romped off the floor, and the graceful visitant of a few years ago, 'The Washington Post,' vulgarized into obscurity; and now at one's servants' dances, when they and their friend mix with a young house party, as we frequently do for pleasant evenings, the so-called Kitchen Lancers, as pranced by the 'Salon,' scandalize kitchen, hall, and 'room' alike, and make the ladies'-maids next day spend all possible time in mending their ladies' rents and tatters. And the Lancers of old were such a pretty dance, showing graces and fine garments of all advantage. The old Scotch reel is rarely danced today, as the younger folk prefer eight-somes as more 'romping.' I hardly recall these in my child days in the North, I think they came from Perthshire. I would like to be informed on this point.

We know the cake-walk, which I have seen negroes dance, was the attempt of coloured folk to represent the grand and stately 'menuet de la cour'. The brilliant galop (how 'John Peel' cheered the most tired at the end of a good ball!) became feats of the 'bounding Bedouin'; the old polka with a sway and swing, was full of cheer and spirit; but all spoilt, as dances, by the dancers. The 'Tango' may be undesirable, the 'Turkey Trot' unsuited to polite society, but with all the afore-named wrecks of fine varieties on my mind, I query whether the *dancers* and not the *dances* are to blame, and should be forbidden ballrooms as misinterpreting a high art, even used as expressing religious joy, in those spirits that know worship. But we live in a motor and irreverent age, rude and uncouth in many ways, and 'gone from beauty.'

I am, Sir, yours, &c.,

E. MIDDLETON

[Lady Middleton died on 27 April 1922. Two days later *The Times* reviewed a production at the old theatre, Stratford-on-Avon, of *The Taming of the Shrew*, played by the All Saints Choir School, Margaret Street, W1. An anonymous fourteen-year-old actor gave a virtuoso performance as Katharina. His name was Laurence Olivier]

A Drain on the Family Removed

[On 16 March 1914 the price of *The Times* was reduced to one penny]

From Mr Alfred de Rothschild   *17 March 1914*

Sir,

I hope I may be allowed to send you my most heartfelt congratulations. *The Times* has hitherto been a luxury, but now it will become a household word.

Yours very sincerely,

ALFRED DE ROTHSCHILD

[The word 'luxury' had been used impersonally; prior to 16 March 1914 *The Times* had cost something like £2 11s 8d a year, subscriptions to Mr de Rothschild's six clubs £61 19s]

Dogs during the Season

[Insisting that 'most people worth anything love dogs', a correspondent had deplored the banishment of her dog ('better behaved than most children') to the guard's van while she travelled first-class]

Sir,

I am glad to see Lady Alderson's impartial, sensible letter in *The Times* of yesterday on the travelling dog owner's grievances and rights. If the travelling dog owner has rights so have householders – and for the sake of London dog owners I would ask the same question of those representatives of what Lady Alderson rightly calls a 'cross minority of nervous, fussy people', who, as chairmen and members of squares and gardens committees, rule out dogs, even when led, from the use and enjoyment of those air spaces.

Householders having access to such gardens on a South Kensington property (and there are others equally inhumanely treated) pay two guineas or more per annum for the privilege of sitting under the besooted shade of a plane tree on a hot summer's day. Yet, if they avail themselves of this privilege they must leave their panting little companions indoors – for no better reason than some old ladies 'cannot bear dogs' and are 'terrified' of them. Surely London must be unsuitable for such sufferers. In any case, when the gardens are left in sole possession of hundreds of cats and frozen solid during winter, seats unoccupied by nervous ladies or nursery-maids in charge of perambulators, might not the poor dog have 'his day'?

House agents in these district know well that this is one of the many causes which lie behind the too obvious board notices of 'This house to be let or sold', 'Apply within' – to find, often, only the cat in charge. I plead for dogs obliged to remain in town during the season.

Yours, etc.,
CONSTANCE H. EMMOTT

[A male correspondent counterattacked Lady Alderson: if she dared to travel with her dog as companion, he would bring his monkey]

1815–1915

From Canon W. Wood   *15 January 1915*

Sir,

May I add another illustration to those which have already appeared in your columns, showing how near two lives can bring together events which seem so far apart? I remember my father telling me how, when he was attending a country grammar school in 1805, one day the master came in, full of a strange excitement, and exclaimed, 'Boys, we've won a great victory!' Then he stopped, burst into tears, and added, 'But Nelson — Nelson is killed!' When I was myself a boy Waterloo was a recent event, and even 'the '45' was remembered and talked about.

In a few weeks I shall be 85, but can still ride my bicycle.

WILLIAM WOOD, DD

Leeches

From the Master of Christ's College, Cambridge
28 January 1915

Sir,

Our country has been for many months suffering from a serious shortage of leeches. As long ago as last November there were only a few dozen left in London, and *they* were second hand.

Whilst General Joffre, General von Kluck, General von Hindenburg, and the Grand Duke Nicholas persist in fighting over some of the best leech-areas in Europe, possibly unwittingly, this shortage will continue, for even in Wordsworth's time the native supply was diminishing, and since then we have for many years largely depended on importations from France and Central Europe. In November I made some efforts to alleviate the situation by applying to America and Canada, but without success. I then applied to India, and last week, owing to the kindness of Dr Annandale, Director of the Indian Museum at Calcutta, and to the officers of the P. and O. Company and to Colonel Alcock, MD, of the London School of Tropical Medicine, I have succeeded in landing a fine consignment of a leech which is used for blood-letting in India. It is true that the leech is not the *Hirudo medicinalis* of our pharmacopœias, but a different genus and species, *Limnatis granulosa*. Judging by its size, always a varying quantity in a leech, we may have to readjust out ideas as to a leech's cubic capacity, yet I believe, from seeing them a day or two ago, they are willing and even anxious to do their duty. They have stood voyage from Bombay and the changed climatic conditions very satisfactorily, and are in a state of great activity and apparent hunger at 50, Wigmore-street, London, W.

45

It is true that leeches are not used to anything like the extent they were 80 years ago — Paris alone, about 1830, made use of some 52 millions a year — but still they are used, though in much smaller numbers.

It may be of some consolation to my fellow-countrymen to know that our deficiency in leeches is more than compensated by the appalling shortage of sausage-skins in Middle Europe. With true German thoroughness they are trying to make artificial ones!

I am yours faithfully,

A. E. SHIPLEY

[Sir Arthur Everett Shipley published nearly fifty papers on parasitic worms]

From Mr D. Dencer   *23 March 1982*

Sir,

Your recent news item on leeches (17 March) interests me because I have been using these little creatures in my practice of plastic surgery for 30 years.

The bugbear of skin flaps is that blood stagnates in them and destroys them. The leech, with his two-fold skills, combats this, first of all by sucking out the sluggish blood, and secondarily by injecting an anti-clotting agent called hyalurodinase into the wound. This means that the wound made by his bite will still drip blood perhaps two days later. All of this helps the plastic surgeon very considerably.

Reasonably, therefore, one must be kind to leeches. They don't come from Hungary, as your informant suggests; they come from Africa. Don't you remember Humphrey Bogart climbing back into the African Queen with his back covered with leeches? Therefore they must be kept warm. We keep our leeches in a warm cupboard and periodically they are taken into the sunshine.

Long ago I knew a pharmacist who felt very keenly about his leeches. He would roll up his sleeve and feed them off his arm as a special treat. I remember, still, watching the sensual peristaltic movements of these gleaming dark-green bodies as they engorged themselves, it would seem in a sort of haemorrhagic orgasm.

You have to be very careful with leeches, because each end is very alike. When you want a leech to bite you must present the right end. They like to sit on their bottoms and bite with their mouths. If, through anatomical ignorance, you try to reverse the process you will end up with a resentful, sullen and dispirited leech.

My ward sister starts them off with milk or jam. She tells me that a little jam on the skin will start them off with enthusiasm, and many a skin flap in peril has been saved by these small, little-known creatures.

Yours faithfully,

D. DENCER

The Hibernation of Flies

[Sir George Birdwood, a former Professor of Anatomy and Physiology at Grant Medical College, Bombay, was an authority on incense and carrots.

From Sir George Birdwood   *4 January 1916*

Sir,

The question of the hibernation of flies having swarmed in the correspondence columns of *The Times* from before St Thomas's Day, as if we were still in 'Bartholomew tide', it may interest some of your readers, if, by your kind favour, I am allowed to place on public record the following instance of the habit, in a particular fly, that came under my own close observation − not scientific, but simply sympathetic; for being half-Hinduized in my philosophy of life, I fully recognize flies as fellow human creatures, and comparatively high up in the scale of 'the 84 millions of millions of transmigrations' through which the soul of Nature gradually ascends from atoms up to man.

In November 1912, a lady taking tea, letting a drop from the cup fall on the back of her left hand, a half-starved fly, that had been warming itself on the shade of an overhanging lamp, at once flew down to sip of it; and was left so to do, until 'well fed up', and with a blessing on its head, it flew back to its hiding-place behind, as was afterwards found, the pier-glass above the mantelpiece. The fly repeated its visits every night of that winter; and after the following spring and summer had passed, repeated them in November of 1913, but for 14 nights only, after which it disappeared for ever.

One of the most humanizing sights of Old Bombay was of the stricter Hindus, of certain castes, feeding with sugar the insects, chiefly ants, among the grass of the 'Esplanade', stretched flush

47

with the sea along the spacious breezy curve of Back Bay; and
that notwithstanding their familiar proverb: 'The scorpion bears
poison in its tail, the fly in its head.'

I have the honour to be, Sir,
your most obedient servant,
GEORGE BIRDWOOD
St Sylvester's Day, Patron of the Hon East India Co

A Poltergeist

[On 8 August 1919 explosions shook Swanton Novers
Rectory, near Melton Constable, Norfolk. Soon oil began
to pour from the ceilings and gush from the floors. The
week ending 30 August saw various spirits: Monday water,
Tuesday petrol, Wednesday pure paraffin, Thursday petrol
and paraffin, Friday water. 'Inexplicable,' said the experts]

From Sir Sydney Olivier   *3 September 1919*

[Civil servant; Fabian; as Baron Olivier Secretary for India
in MacDonald's first Labour government 1924; uncle of
Laurence Olivier]

Sir,
These manifestations of unction at Swanton Rectory have all
the characteristics of a case of *Poltergeisterei*. In such cases, as
the records of the SPR [Society for Psychical Research] bear
witness, there may almost invariably be found 'a little 15-year-
old girl' about the place, or sometimes an equally ostensibly
innocent boy. It seems that such young creatures serve the
Poltergeist as a *nidus or point d'appui* for his (or her) diversions.
It is therefore probable that if the 'little girl' mentioned is
removed from the Manse the energies of the mysterious agent of
these exudations may languish and shortly cease.

Yours faithfully,
SYDNEY OLIVIER

[In Noel Coward's *Blithe Spirit* (1941) there was found a
little 18-year-old (?), the maid Edith. Admirers of the
Master's sublime farcical masterpiece will not need to be
reminded of:

MADAME ARCATI: That cuckoo is very angry.
CHARLES: How can you tell?
MADAME ARCATI: *Timbre.*]

All Must Work

From Admiral of the Fleet Lord Fisher, OM
5 January 1920

[During the 14 months prior to his death in July 1920, the greatest British sailor since Nelson had 36 letters in *The Times*. Their style was unique]

Sir,
A friend tells me in Canada a policeman can ask any saunterer, even in a glossy silk hat and white spats, if he is idle, and can hale him there and then before authority to be made to work. My friend may be lying, but it's a righteous lie. Elisha lied to the hosts of the Syrians and said: – 'This is not the way, neither is this the city – follow me, and I will bring you to the man whom ye seek' (being himself!). By the way, I've never read any episcopal or ecclesiastical remonstrance about Elisha's lie – I suppose it's the origin of 'All is fair in love and war'!

To resume: – The only escape from national ruin is by *increased production*, and to this end the object of these few words is not to saddle the 'working man' alone with this vital necessity, but to lay that vital necessity on the whole nation. A huge co-operation of all classes is imperative. 'Co-operation in profits' being the first article in the new Magna Charta. Some have brains, some have money, some have physical aptitude. All lend a hand. This is the only way to get rid of class antagonism, nationalization, and all the ohter funny systems of getting something out of nothing, or 'eating your cake and drinking it' (as someone said I said – another Elisha lie!).

According to recently disclosed departmental facts (I own also these may be lies) the United States dollar is scooping us out, and the United States mercantile marine (at zero before the war) possesses now 12 million tons of shipping, as against our corresponding 18 millions – not that I think England will succumb – *she never does* – but *Production is the one word*. The artisan must be encouraged and be made free by becoming a partner. That's the way out. To be a *flaneur* in Bond-street does us no good in production. Such must 'pay up' for that

49

luxury or go to prison (as in Canada). *Every one must work.*

Yours,

F<small>ISHER</small>

P.S. Soon it may be once more 'too late'. Read Ludendorff's epilogue that 'Workmen's Councils' brought about the Revolution and the Revolution stopped the war. I don't agree. That same bevy who won the war for Elisha (when he lied) won the war for us. We prayed — the others didn't! Kitchener said to Lord Roberts at the Marne, 'Someone has been praying'! there was no other way of accounting for the miracle.

'Ca Passe'

[A leading article had discussed Emile Coué whose clinic at Nancy had become a place of pilgrimage for those in search of cure by auto-suggestion; his other formula was 'Every day, in every way, I am better, and better, and better'.]

From Captain C. Scott Moncrieff   *31 March 1922*

[now engaged on his translation of Proust's *A la recherche du temps perdu*]

Sir,
The Nancy formula which you commend in a leading article this morning is not without a precedent, 10 or 12 centuries old, in our own tongue. Our earliest lyric poet, whose name was, he tells us, Deor, bases his one surviving work (a poem which would extend to 42 lines were not some of them dismissed as suspect by modern scholarship) upon the same two words. As Theocritus, at the end of his Third Idyll, makes the goat-herd envy three of the fortunate ones of the past, Hippomenes, Melampus, and Adonis, and resolve to die, so, conversely, Deor recalls the classic examples of misfortune and suffering, comparable to his own, and resolves to live, ending each verse with the simple refrain: —

'*thæs ofereode, thisses swa mæg'

Which may be interpreted, in modern French, *ca passe*.
I am, Sir, your obedient servant,

C<small>HARLES</small> S<small>COTT</small> M<small>ONCRIEFF</small>

[*That was surmounted, so may this be]

50

Women Medical Students

From Dr Charles H. Pring   9 March 1922

Sir,

The majority of your correspondents – the ladies in particular – wholly miss the essential objection to mixed medical classes, whether at the London Hospital or elsewhere. Whether a particular lady lecturer feels 'no embarrassment' when dealing with nauseating subjects in her class of boys and girls is beside the mark, save that such absence helps the argument. There is no desire to 'ban' women doctors, nor to bid them keep to their obvious duties in the home, still less to hinder their 'occasional flirtations', the golden opportunities for which are to be found in the mixed schools.

No, the objection is that when young women consort with young men under conditions where ordinary delicacy and modesty are necessarily absent, the normal high standard of conduct is lowered. No matter how choice the demeanour and character of the feminine neophyte, after a few months of the students' common room she becomes coarse, immodest and vulgar. It is because mixed classes have *not* 'put a stop to the reiteration of salacious stories' that such stories are passed on to and readily absorbed by 'the boys in gowns'; that all sweetness and refinement is repudiated; that death itself is made the subject of jest. It is because of these things that those of us who have daughters view the prospect of their possible association with the advancing sisterhood with misgiving and dismay.

Yours, etc.,
CHARLES H. PRING, MA
(Fellow of the Royal Society of Medicine)

Outbreak of the Russian Revolution

From the Reverend B. S. Lombard   9 March 1925

[late British Chaplain at Petrograd]

Sir,

Saturday was the anniversary of the outbreak of the Russian Revolution. No one who was present in Petrograd at the time is likely to forget it. During the morning and early afternoon, sullen crowds thronged all the main streets. Mounted police moved quietly among them. There was no disorder, all seemed to be waiting for something; they might have been workmen outside the gates of a factory before opening time. Nevertheless one felt instinctively that the atmosphere was charged. It reminded one of the strange, gloomy silence that so often comes before a storm.

I boarded a tramway car to visit some people near the Nikolai Station. It was very crowded, but I was able to stand in front near the driver. As we proceeded up the Nevsky Prospect I became aware that a lady I knew was a fellow-traveller. I suggested that she should stay with the friend she was on her way to visit, and not attempt to return, as I felt there was going to be trouble.

I had hardly spoken the words when there rose a dull murmur, and one caught snatches of 'Give us bread, we are hungry.' The tramway car was not travelling fast owing to the crowds. A university student jumped on to the footboard, said something to the driver, and then turned to the control lever, and the car came to a standstill. This held up all the rest, so my friend and I got off and walked. I took her to her destination, and begged her friends to keep her for the night, and then returned to Nevsky.

There I found everything changed. The placid dullness of these sullen crowds was replaced by alertness and excitement. As I neared the statue of Alexander III, a workman ascended to the plinth, and began to address the people. A policeman approached and remonstrated. The speaker refused either to get down or stop talking, whereupon the policeman drew his revolver, and shot him. It was the match to the fire; the smouldering fuse had reached the powder, and it went off. The Revolution had begun. In 20 minutes there was hardly a vestige of that unfortunate policeman left. Men, women, and even children fell upon him and literally tore to pieces. One could hardly believe that those sad, silent people of half an hour before could have been suddenly transformed into such savages, lusting for the blood of the wretched man.

After this the crowd moved down Nevsky in one solid mass, were met by police, and were fired on. Every one knows the rest: innocent and guilty alike were shot down until the troops joined the people, and the so-called 'bloodless Revolution' began.

I am, etc.,

B. S. LOMBARD

The Nightingale

[The British Broadcasting Company would not become a Corporation for some months]

From Dr Adolf Antusch   *29 May 1926*

[Writing from Prague]

Sir,

On the eve of Whit Sunday, May 22, I heard the English nightingale in Prague. By chance I was listening to the London concert [the Grand Hotel, Eastbourne Orchestra], using an ordinary three-valve set, some minutes before midnight, as it was interrupted. After a short announcement, which I did, not understand, following a song I recognised at once as the often-praised nightingale song. At the beginning we also heard at the same time the deep-sounding strokes of Big Ben. You can imagine our surprise and joy to hear for the first time the sound of the nightingale. This wonderful event will be an everlasting impression for my whole life. Many thanks to the BBC.

                Yours faithfully,

                ADOLF ANTUSCH

[Later Beatrice Harrison would take her 'cello into the garden of her Surrey home and persuade nightingales to take up the treble – BBC engineers in attendance]

Kitchener's Army

From Sir Arthur Conan Doyle   *15 February 1927*

Sir,

One could not read the last paragraphs of Mr Winston Churchill's accounts of the Somme Battles, as given in your issue of February 12, without rejoicing that Kitchener's Army has at last received a worthy panegyric. Personally, I have long recognized that Winston Churchill had the finest prose style of any contemporary, and it is indeed a splendid thing that he should use it to do that which seemed impossible – namely, to give an adequate appreciation of that glorious Army of patriotic volunteers who gave themselves so ungrudgingly to their country's service.

Yours faithfully,
ARTHUR CONAN DOYLE

[The last sentence referred to by Doyle in *The World Crisis* ran: 'Unconquerable, except by death, which they had conquered, they have set up a monument of native virtue which will command the wonder, the reverence, and the gratitude of our island people as long as we endure as a nation among men.']

Sleeping Out of Doors

From Dr H. Wynne Thomas   *21 July 1928*

Sir,

I was much interested in your article 'Sleeping Out of Doors.' As I have myself slept out of doors every summer since 1912, perhaps some personal experience may be of use to others. My house is just ten miles from London Bridge, and fortunately, my garden is not much overlooked, although I live in the centre of Bromley, in the High-street.

I first tried sleeping in a hammock, but found it draughty and difficult to turn over, so I soon took to sleeping on a canvas Army bed, which is easy to pack up if required. If the weather is fine, I always sleep under the stars, with no covering on my head, in a sleeping bag, with an extra rug if necessary. If the weather is cool or likely to rain, I sleep in a wooden shelter I had made facing south-east, just large enough to take the bed. I begin sleeping out when the night thermometer is about 47 deg. to 50 deg., that is, as a rule, early in May. This year I started on 20 April. Having once started, I go on through the summer till October, and have even slept out in my shelter on into November, when the temperature has fallen as low as 25 deg. during the night. If it should be a wet night I stay indoors, but then usually feel the bedroom stuffy, although the windows are wide open, and not refreshed as I do outside. If it rains when I am in my bag, I do not mind, and have often slept out in a thunderstorm. This last week I slept six hours without waking and got up feeling fresh and keen like a schoolboy, though I am well past 60.

Friends say, what about midges and insects? Well, all I can

say is that in 16 years I have only been bitten once by a mosquito. As to midges, they are very busy up till 10, but evidently go to bed before I do. As to other animals and insects, they have never worried me, and the secret, I believe, is that my bed stands 1ft. from the ground. I hate the cold weather, and look forward to the spring that I may sleep out; and to hear the 'birds' chorus' in the early morning in May is worth waking up for; it only lasts about 20 minutes, but must be heard to be appreciated. In June it dies down, and few birds sing after Midsummer Day.

When sleeping outdoors I never get a cold. I do not require so much time in bed, and wake refreshed in a way I never do indoors, with such an appetite for breakfast as no tonic can give. I enjoy the best of health, and wonder more people do not try it. During this summer whether I have never had any difficulty in keeping my rooms cool. My study has never been higher than 70deg., while outside in the shade my thermometer is 84deg. and 88 deg., simply because I shut my windows at 9 a.m. and pull down the blinds, and open them at 8 p.m. and leave them open all night. I bottle up the cool night air and shut out the air which is baked by the hot road and pavement. My study faces due west and has the sun streaming down nearly all day. Bedrooms must be kept cool in the same way.

Yours faithfully,
H. WYNNE THOMAS

[An ex-President of the British Homoepathic Society, Dr Thomas had written on 'Nocturnal Emissions in Children' – Jl. Homoeop. Soc. 1899]

The Georgians

From Lady Cust   *3 November 1930*

[writing from The Cloisters, Eton College; her husband, Sir Lionel Henry Cust, was surveyor of the King's Pictures and Works of Art 1901–27]

Sir,
Is it not time that certain of the Victorians stood aside for a little while and stopped finding fault with the present generation? We can hardly pick up a paper nowadays without reading the lamentation of pessimists over England's wretched state. A few days ago, someone writing to

The Times quoted 'a middle-aged masseur' who considered there was no one left in the country to be trusted. Now another has been bewailing our vanished dignity and the golden days that will never return. Well, were they so very golden? For the comfortable classes in their great houses, yes; but what of the Crimean heroes who walked the streets and lanes destitute and hopeless, and the great gulf fixed between rich and poor; derelicts for whom there was nothing save haphazard charity between starvation and the workhouse; and the jerry-built homes that directly caused the slum problems of today?

It is true that the young are not easily discouraged. But it is scarcely helpful to be constantly reminding them that the country is completely decayed, and that they can never hope to do as well as those who have gone before them. When a great life is closed the usual wail is raised about 'the last of his kind' and 'a torch gone out in the dark', and so forth. It is not true. Let our pessimists stop their croaking and watch the glorious achievements of this generation; things unheard of, undreamt of, in their day.

Yours obediently,

SYBIL CUST

A Wife for Sale

From Dr Cloudesley Brereton   3 May 1932

Sir,

The extract on the sale of a wife from *The Times* of 100 years ago, in your issue of today, reminds me of what the late George Danby Kerrison once told me. As a small boy he was riding one day with his uncle down one of our Norfolk roads, when they came across a farmer standing by the wayside with a woman 'with only her shift on' and a rope round her neck, as if she was an animal for sale. She was his wife, and he was offering her to the passers-by for 10s. Another farmer bought her, and the curious thing is that the woman, who lived several years with her second 'husband', was treated by the neighbours with exactly the same consideration as if she had been his lawful wife. Judging by my friend's age, this must have happened much later than 1832 – round about 1840, in fact.

Yours faithfully,

CLOUDESLEY BRERETON

The Abhorred Shears

From Mr F. Warren   *17 October 1932*

Sir,
   In the Rhineland two or three years ago, driven to risk even
the Prussian haircut, I sat in the barber's chair. After the
universal formalities, the operator pushed home a wall plug
connected by a length of flex to some gadget in his right hand
and prepared to attack from the rear. Before I had time to co-
ordinate impressions a hornet, or so it seemed, with power
amplifier burst into full song behind my left ear, but any
reaction that might have been induced was suppressed when the
buzzing atrocity began to crawl and browse about my scalp.
   Pride of race gave me self-control. Thought, so far as thought
was possible, toyed with short circuits, Sing Sing, voltages, and
reaping machines. The ordeal ended with an intimate
exploration of the inner ear by the buzzing horror and a query
from the barber as to whether we had the instrument in England.
With an involuntary 'No! thank Heavens!' I left.
   Returning home soon afterwards and visiting the barber I
found the Terror to be among us; now one cannot evade it, and
I am haunted by the guilty fear that my thoughtless exposure of
our immunity may have led to the subsequent invasion. Man is
traditionally impotent when in the barber's chair, but now that
the type and War Loan conversion schemes are disposed of
perhaps *The Times* could voice a protest against the adoption of
sheep-shearing apparatus as an aid to hair dressing and restore
to the operator his outlet for vocal and muscular expression.
                              Yours faithfully,
                              FRANK WARREN

['The Terror' had been introduced into England from the
United States soon after 1910; it is even possible that editor
of *The Times* had endured it]

Plus a Little Something

From Mr Walter B. Harris   *1 February 1933*

[Commander of the Ouissam Alaouite of Morocco;
correspondent of *The Times* in Morocco]

Sir,

A Berber chieftain who has installed a radio set in his castle in the Atlas Mountains asks me to obtain through *The Times*, which he describes as 'the origin and source of all knowledge, the following information.

He is anxious to know where he can obtain one of those small and inexpensive machines, to be affixed to the loud-speaker, which interpret into Arabic all air commnications that are received from abroad in foreign languages. Perhaps some readers of *The Times* would kindly let me know.

I am, Sir, your obedient servant,

WALTER B. HARRIS

Hint to the Kremlin

[In his later years Count Leo Tolstoy prepared an anthology, *The Circle of Reading*, which sold freely until his death in 1910. Thereupon the book was seized and the publisher Posadov Gorbunov prosecuted. On 5 February 1912 a devastating letter from Mr Charles Hagberg Wright appeared in *The Times*]

From Sir Charles Hagberg Wright   *9 January 1935*

[Secretary and Librarian, the London Library]

Sir,

On February 5, 1912 a letter appeared in *The Times* condemning in strong terms the prosecution of Mr Posadov Gorbunov, the Russian publisher of Tolstoy's popular stories.

In 1928 I was a public meeting in Russia during the Tolstoy centenary celebrations, where I again met Mr Posadov Gorbunov, and found him full of vigour and ready to issue a new series of tales for the people.

He related how in 1912 he was condemned to twelve years of exile by the Appeal Court in Petrograd, when a Senator named Michael Stahkovich rushed into Court flourishing a copy of *The Times*. Holding it up before the Judges, he exclaimed:

'Your Excellencies, you cannot convict Mr Gorbunov; listen to what *The Times* says.'

'You must not interrupt the proceedings, Mr Senator, the sentence has been pronounced and it is final.'

But the Senator, undaunted read out loud an extract from *The Times*, which was heard in silence.

When he had finished there was a brief consultation between the Judges, after which the President of the Court declared that they could not revoke the sentence, but a rider would be added that it was not to be carried out. Mr Gorbunov was set free.

I am, etc.,

C. HAGBERG WRIGHT

Beards and Bicycle Chains

From Mr N. R. Davis   *5 May 1937*

Sir,

It is curious that there should be a (Reuter) news paragraph in your issue of April 29 about a man at Holsted who caught his beard in a bicycle chain while adjusting the mechanism, for when I was there in the spring of '92 there was a very popular rhyme which went something like this:

> At Holsted an elderly Dane
> Caught his beard in a bicycle chain.
> It's hoped if it grows
> Till it reaches his toes,
> He'll be able to cycle again.

Yours, &c.,

N. R. DAVIS

After the Fires

From Mr Clough Williams-Ellis   *3 January 1941*

[the creator of Portmeirion]

Sir,

A major architectural disaster has befallen us in the mutilation or destruction of many of Wren's City churches, little masterpieces of English Baroque that we all saluted with affectionate respect even if we failed to know them intimately or learn to love them for their innate intelligence and charm.

One of our aims in this war, a basic and uncontroversial one, is so to contrive things that apparent calamities may, wherever possible, be turned to our ultimate advantage. Not long since, the ecclesiastical authorities themselves proposed to make away with a number of these churches as 'redundant' and profitably to exploit their sites for secular uses. Now that rebuilding is anyhow thrust upon us − (the supine acceptance of a 'total loss' in this matter is surely unthinkable) − and now that some rationalization of the City's plan will presumably be called for, is there not something to be said for resurrecting these lovely buildings where they will be certain of a welcome, secure of an honoured future, and where their lustre may best illumine our pervading architectural gloom?

Briefly, where a City clearance really does seem justified, let the old church site be profitably secularized, on the one condition that an adequate sum be set aside for, or towards, the rebuilding of the church itself in some provincial city or town that has honourable scars to be healed, and where a worthy and permanently secured island site can be made ready for it. There could be few towns where the authentic Pheonix-Wren church would not be the most gracious, notable, and revered building in the place, so giving a more general pleasure and exercising a wider civilizing influence than ever it did as an obscured member of a congested galaxy. Decentralization, diffusion, democratization . . . If the enemy's bombs serve to disperse this cultural heritage more widely and more effectively over our country at large, there will at least be a credit side to the account. The antiquary may object that our reconstructions will not be 'authentic.' I doubt the validity of their obvious arguments.

Apart from original Wren drafts, I believe that pretty well every one of his buildings has been accurately surveyed, measured, and recorded in complete detail, so that, with photographs, far more exhaustive working drawings could probably be handed to the reconstructor than were given to the original builders. All the architect's designs (as always) had to be interpreted, well or ill, through the medium of a multitude of contractors and craftsmen, often with little or no effective supervision from the chief himself. Where parts of the original Wren fabric survive in usable condition, obviously one would piously incorporate them in the new Phoenix, but it seems to me that a stone now hewn faithfully to the master's design is not 'unauthentic' merely because it takes shape posthumously. If that pedantic test be applied to other cooperative arts, then there has been no true Beethoven symphony for over a century, no genuine play of Shakespeare's for over three.

I am, Sir, your obedient servant,

CLOUGH WILLIAMS-ELLIS

[Sir Clough Williams-Ellis recalled (29 July 1974) that his letter provoked considerable reaction, 'some averring that the redundant churches shanghaied into alien surroundings would look ridiculous — many having been most ingeniously designed by the Master to fit into and exploit exceedingly cramped and awkward sites. True, but my retort was that in such cases the new surroundings should be course be modified and adapted to pay due respect to the so distinguished new-comer. Jack Squire — founder of The Architecture Club and then editor of *The London Mercury* was on my side and I recall a poem of his in which he administered a stinging rebuke to the then Bishop of London for his indifference to the fate of Wren's churches. I wish I could remember it — or better — recover it — but I seem to recall the lines:

"An eloquent witness in every street
That the worship of money was not complete."
Or something like it.']

An Old Soldier Remembered

From Field Marshal Lord Wavell   *12 April 1944*

[writing from The Viceroy's House, New Delhi]

Sir,

In reading *The Times* of March 16 I saw an obituary notice of Mr Tom Byrne, VC, I do not know whether it would interest any of your readers to know that one of his last jobs in the Army was as groom to my father in Dublin about 1901–02.

I had just joined the Army then, and remembered him well as a dignified old soldier with whom I had many talks in the stables at Dublin Castle. He liked especially to speak of Captain De Montmerency to whom he had been batman and to whom he was entirely devoted. I remember him showing me his Victoria Cross and telling me of his experience in the 21st Lancers' charge at Omdurman. He was typical of the best type of old soldier.

Yours truly,

WAVELL

[Captain De Montmorency also won the VC at Omdurman, where Byrne saved the life of a Lieutenant

Molyneux. Shot in the right shoulder and wounded in the chest, Byrne nevertheless charged three Dervishes. Winston Churchill described Byrne's act as the bravest he had ever seen performed]

The Charge of the Light Brigade

From Sir Lenthal Cheatle   *9 March 1946*

[a consultant surgeon]

Sir,

With your authoritative permission may I be allowed to place on record, before I die, a conversation that was indelibly fixed in my memory five decades ago? Dr Ligertwood was then in medical charge of the Chelsea Pensioners, and after taking me to see an old bed-ridden Balaclava hero who was in hospital after being 'knocked about by his wife' told me the following story. He was on the staff of Lord Raglan and saw the charge of the Light Brigade. He saw Lord Raglan write the despatch and Nolan deliver it. Lord Cardigan after reading spoke to Nolan, who waved his arm in the direction of the Russian lines. He then saw Nolan killed on his return ride, and was present when Lord Cardigan rode up to Lord Raglan after the charge and heard him say, 'Those fellows have been pulling me about.'

Dr Ligertwood then told me the despatch in question stated, 'The Light Brigade will advance,' saying nothing about a charge. When Lord Cardigan had read the despatch he said to Nolan, 'The Light Brigade will advance, but where to?' and Nolan, waving his arm towards the enemy said, 'Well, my Lord, if you don't know where the Russians are, they are over there.' Lord Cardigan may have been piqued by Nolan's behaviour, for they were on unfriendly terms. Dr Ligertwood told me finally it was afterwards learnt from the Russians that the officer on the chestnut horse had his steed to thank for his escape. That officer was Lord Cardigan.

I am, Sir, your obedient servant,

G. Lenthal Cheatle

[Sir Lenthal died in 1951 aged 85]

Ordeal for Sentries

From Mr Henry Maxwell   *9 May 1951*

Sir,
    While it is natural that tourists and visitors to London should take an interest in the sentries at Buckingham Palace, it is surely unnecessary for them to gather in groups in front of these boys to gape and stare at them at the range of a few feet, as though they were wild animals. Not infrequently visitors come right up to a sentry and proceed to photograph him at point blank range, whil sometimes, amidst much amusement, the girl friends of the visitors will station themselves at either side of the sentry to be photographed with him.
    All of this must be extremely embarrassing and annoying to the sentries, though they bear the bad manners of the visitors with exemplary patience. I cannot help thinking that police should be instructed to move people on when their attentions are likely to prove an embarrassment to soldiers on duty.

                              Yours faithfully,
                              HENRY MAXWELL

A Vanishing Craft

From Mr J. G. Strachan   *9 April 1954*

Sir,
    It has been brought to my notice that the once flourishing craft of swaging is rapidly becoming forgotten. In my grandfather's lifetime the swager was a familiar figure in the West Country, mentioned several times in his diaries. Workshops like the one he describes as Chetnole must have continued to fascinate, while such individual crafts were still scarcely affected by nineteenth-century industrialism. Today a swaging iron is something of a curiosity, and the old swagers, still working with scud and fossick, are few and far between. Cannot something be done to preserve this craft from extinction?

                              Yours faithfully,
                              J. G. STRACHAN

† 'Swaging' is the shaping or working of cold metal, wrought iron, &c., by hammering it on a suitably grooved or perforated block.

Glimpse of Philately

From Miss V. Sackville-West, CH   *31 January 1956*

Sir,

I am no philatelist, but if pre-natal influence counts for anything I ought to be. My mother amused herself during the months before my birth by papering a small room at Knole with stamps arranged in strips and patterns. As the date was, I regret to say, 1892, many of those stamps must now be of some interest and value. I remember that there were many Russian stamps of the Tsarist régime, and there were some early Victorian stamps also.

       Yours, &c.,
       V. SACKVILLE-WEST

Hip Baths

[THAMES HARE AND HOUNDS desire to purchase silver running figure for trophy; also Victorian hip baths. – Secretary, 48 Pont Street, SW1]

From Mr A. Fletcher   *21 February 1957*

Sir,

As the unwilling author of the advertisement for hip baths that appeared in ther Personal Column last week, I must make plain the fact that this outmoded form of ablution is retained in Thames Hare and Hounds by members who know of none other. Those of us who yearn for the trickling warmth of the modern shower-bath are not comforted; there is a shower but it is cold.

The snug and soothing picture described in your leading article of 18 February is but a sop to reaction, for while our seniors find the hip bath scandalously enjoyable, the younger members think only of the bathrooms in their homes. The hip bath is good for wallowing, not for washing, and after it one remains all spattered with dirt. Tom Brown and his friends thought hare-and-hounds the most delightful of games, but they had buttered toast in the housekeeper's room; for us the only reward is a second bath at home.

       Yours faithfully,
       ANTHONY FLETCHER

Navigating the Greek Trireme

From the President of Wolfson College, Cambridge
4 October 1975

Sir,

   Thank you for giving space to such a fascinating and instructive correspondence. May I try to cast the account? All good men seem to agree to the following:

   1. That oared ships did not go into battle under sail;

   2. That the Greek trireme used full oar power, to produce up to 11½ knots in short bursts, only in battle or in emergency;

   3. That oared ships did not put to sea when the wind was unfavourable, rowed out of harbour and then either hoisted sail or continued rowing according to the state of the wind;

   4. That a trireme's speed in still water under oar can be credibly calculated to have been five to six knots with one division rowing, a little more with two;

   5. And that this calculation does not conflict with Xenophon's '120 nautical miles under oar in a long day.' The word he uses can only mean the hour of daylight. So, with 15 hours of daylight plus one hour of twilight at latitude 42° on midsummer day, the speed works out of seven knots and a half, but there would have been little help from the current for the last 103½ miles. According to the Navigation Department of the National Maritime Museum, Black Sea currents run counter-clockwise, but through the Bosphorus there is a north-south current because of the 17in difference of levels at each end. The later MSS of Xenophon have a variant reading 'a *very* long day', which suggests that the scribe shared your correspondents' feeling that Xenophon was exaggerating a bit. Etesian winds blowing with the current through the Bosphorus would have kept a galley in port.

   Lord St David's galleys were the *a scaloccio* type of the second half of the sixteenth century with gangs of men pulling and in some cases also pushing, very long sweeps. A contemporary admiral reported them slower, in spite of greater manpower, than the earlier *a zenzile* galleys in which three or four men sat at benches set herringbone fashion, each rowing an oar of 30ft or so. Dr Tarn was rightly impatient of the theory then current that the ships of high numerical denominator in the Hellenistic navies had many banks of oars; and suggested instead that the Greeks must have a had an *a zenzile* system for triremes and *a scaloccio* systems for the rest. The first part of this suggestionn has been rejected because:

   1. The Greek trireme's oars were 12⅔ long (the longer oars

65

amidships and, surprisingly, no difference between the levels);

2. an *a zenzile* galley rowing 170 men would have been far too long to fit into the known length of the Piraeus trireme sheds, the three-level system being (obviously) more economical of space.

There are other more detailed, equally cogent, reasons but these two are conclusive. Tarn was quite right about the ships of numerical denominator higher than three. They must have rowed more than one man to an oar at no more than three levels, usually, to judge from the monuments, at two. And the numerical denominator has nothing to do with levels, as people still tend to think; but indicates the power to which the original rowing unit had been raised by the various developments (i.e. 3, 4, 5, 6, etc. men to the oar-room, the space between the rowlocks, irrespective of level). A three-level trireme does not imply a four-level quadrireme.

Two final points:

1. The men who rowed the Athenian galleys in the fifth century were not slaves, indeed the slaves who rowed exceptionally at Arginusae were given their freedom for it.

2. If the hashish-carrying Punic warship reported in your columns is the one about which Miss Honor Frost has recently published excavation reports, it is too small to be trireme.

Yours faithfully,
JOHN MORRISON

Metternich's Journey

[A politician's downfall had been described as the most undignified since Metternich left Vienna in a laundry basket]

From Dr C. A. Macartney, FBA   *16 April 1977*

[sometime Fellow of All Souls College, Oxford]

Sir,

Your second leader of April 12. Metternich did not leave Vienna in a laundry basket. From his office in the Ballhausplatz he walked across on the morning of March 14 to the nearby palace of Count Ludwig Taaffe. Prince Karl Liechtenstein then provided him with a carriage, in which he was driven to the Prince's castle of Feldsberg. The later journey to England (for which Baron Rothschild paid) was uncomfortable, but not humiliating. Metternich travelled by train, under a false passport.

I have the honour to remain, etc,

C. A. MACARTNEY

Where in the World?

From Mr Herbert C. Tobin   *25 July 1977*

Sir,

There are doubtless many who, like myself, deplore the habit – which unfortunately is becoming increasingly common – of referring to foreign countries not by the names by which they have been known for generations and indeed for centuries to the English-speaking world, but by the local usage of the countries concerned. I may instance the abandonment of the ancient and famous names of Ceylon, Persia, and Siam in favour of Sri Lanka, Iran, and Thailand, or the increasing use of Romania instead of Rumania (or Roumania).

If it be objected that the countries concerned wish to be known abroad by the names familiar to their nationals, we can with equal logic start speaking and writing of Sverige, Suomi, Espana, Hellas, Shqiperi, Misr, Bharat, and Nippon instead of Sweden, Finland, Spain, Greece, Albania, Egypt, India, and Japan, among many other examples.

Further progression along this fashionable but undesirable path will no doubt lead us in due course to speak and write of Bruxelles, Den Haag, Köln, Firenze, Venzia, Napoli, Wien, and Praha instead of Brussels, The Hague, Cologne, Florence, Venice, Naples, Vienna, and Prague – also among many other examples. And if we are to be guided by strict logicality we should speak not of Persian and Siamese cats but of Iranian cats and Thai cats, whilst Persian rugs and carpets will have to give place to Iranian ones.

Sir Winston Churchill, when wartime Prime Minister, sent a minute to the Foreign Office in April 1945 (it can be found among the Appendices to the sixth volume of *The Second World War*) worded as follows:

'I do not consider that names that have been familiar for generations in England should be altered . . . Constantinople should never be abandoned, though for stupid people Istanbul may be written in brackets after it. As for Angora, long familiar

67

with us through the Angora cats, I will resist to the utmost of my power its degradation to Ankara. . . . If we do not make a stand, we shall . . . be asked to call Leghorn Livorno, and the BBC will be pronouncing Paris "Paree".'

Four years earlier, amidst many other preoccupations, Sir Winston on two occasions asked the Foreign Office in 1941 to inform him why Siam was 'buried under the name of Thailand' and what were 'the historic merits of these two names'. I believe also that during his post-war Premiership in the 1950s, Sir Winston gave instructions that (except in intergovernmental communications) the designation Persia was to be used, and not Iran.

With that illustrious example before us, may one make a plea that, where a recognized English form exists for names of foreign countries, cities, or geographical features, it should not be departed from except for very good reasons.

Yours faithfully,
HERBERT C. TOBIN

Olympic Spirit

From Miss Bridget Boland   *12 May 1984*

Sir,

My father, J. P. Boland, won two events in the 1896 Olympic Games. He was in Greece because his tutor at Oxford had given him an introduction to the archaeologist, Schliemann, and in Athens he chanced to meet an Austrian fellow undergraduate who was entered for the tennis in the games and who persuaded him to take the place of his doubles partner, who had fallen ill.

When they won and an official was putting up the Austrian flag and the Union Jack, my father said to him with a grin: 'Actually, I'm Irish.'

The apologetic official looked anxiously at his array of flags and my father said: 'It's a gold harp on a green ground, we hope, but that one will do to be going on with.'

When he went on to win the singles the official was even more apologetic, but he soothed him, saying: 'It's a difficult flag to make in a hurry and I'm afraid I'm now entering for putting the weight as well, so why not make one just saying J.P.B.?'

Unfortunately he lost, or he might have started a trend more in keeping with the intentions of the originator of the modern games.

Yours truly,
BRIDGET BOLAND

The Menu

[Jonathan Meades, who eats out for *The Times*, discovered –
3 January 1987 – 'the London restaurant by which all others
will come to be judged'. The Cuckoo read on. 'Sumptuousness,
culinary brilliance, commfort, congeniality . . . With half a glass
of Clos du Val Chardonnay, a half of a serviceable Clos des
Roches Sancerre, one Kir and a glass of Muscat de Frontignan,
the bill for the two of us came to £53.'

But that was only lunch, paid for – presumably – by *The
Times*. What of dinner, the main meal of the day? The two letters
which follow will surely awe Mr Meades, one may convince him
he should be doing field work in Mitcham. Readers seeking some
sort of connection between the letters are reminded that the Sir
Frederick Keeble referred to was not only a former Oxford
Professor of Botany but also the husband of Lillah McCarthy
who had created Ann Whitefield in *Man and Superman*. It is
possible that Keeble lunched with GBS and observed the sage
eating a nut cutlet. However, it is unlikely that even Shaw would
have followed the example set by the remarkable Mr Branson.

Doubtless the Branson menu – though not sumptuous by the
standards imposed by Mr Meades – ensured that our hero
lunched and dined alone.]

Ideal

From Sir Nicholas Grattan-Doyle　　　　　*4 November 1935*

[Unionist MP for Newcastle-on-Tyne (North) 1918–40]

Sir,

In these days of wars and rumours of wars, much that would
otherwise be of moment passes unnoticed. But food is always of
interest, so I crave courtesy to propound this question to those
among your readers who are still, in spite of vitamin fiends and
slimming devotees, among that rapidly diminishing band once
known as gourmets – what is the ideal meal?

Sir Frederick Keeble has just told us that no one has enjoyed a perfect meal since our first parents were expelled from the vegetarian bliss of Eden. On the other hand, two notable banquets – 'dinners delectable' I have seen them called – have just been held in Bath, the first in memory of the author of 'Notes on a Cellar Book,' George Saintsbury, the second the annual dinner of the Wine and Food Society, which would indicate that fine feeding, which the two societies exist to encourage, is not yet a lost art. I append the menus for the information of the gastronomically inclined.

Is either the ideal meal? Is there an ideal meal? In what meal, if any, can the succulent steak and the Roast Beef of Old England claim to be included? And when, if ever, may we expect to see the menu of even the 'posh' dinner – the idiom of the younger generation inevitably creeps in – written in English?

I am, Sir, your obedient servant,

NICHOLAS GRATTAN-DOYLE

WINE AND FOOD SOCIETY DINNER	SAINTSBURY CLUB DINNER
La Veloute de Tomates Le Consomme Madrilene Manzanilla Sherry	La Tortue Royale Harvey's Sherry
Les Blanchailles Diablées Le Suprème de Turbotin Florentine Liebfraumilch Imperial Silver Jubilee, 1929	Les Filets de Sole Nantua Berncasteler 1921
	Le Ris-de-Veau en Cocotte Château Cheval Blanc, 1923
La Selle d'Agneau, persillée Les Haricots Verts Château Clos Fourtet, 1917	Le Perdreau roti sur canape La Salade Parisienne Clos de Vougeot, 1911
Le Faisan Roti à la Périgourdine Aloxe Corton, 1919	La Bombe Nesselrode Château d'Yquem, 1921
	Les Délices Edenmore Cockburn, 1912
La Bombe Arlequin Les Friandises Martinez, 1908	Dessert Sercial Madeira, 1850

[The two dinners were held in the Banqueting Hall of Bath's Guildhall on 23 and 25 October 1935. Guests at the Saintsbury dinner included Sir John Squire, André Simon and Vyvyan Holland, the son of Oscar Wilde.

A Bath hotelier with a long memory costs the Saintsbury dinner at £3 15s, a figure which encourages a glance at weekly earnings in 1935 – Norman Birkett, KC £577, Prime Minister £100, Permanent Under-Secretary civil service £60, average solicitor and general practitioner £20, Royal Navy captain £15 10s, industrial worker £2 16s.]

Ideal, if not for Horses

[*The Times* heard that a correspondent's name had become ill after eating grass-mowings]

From Mr J. R. B. Branson   *2 May 1940*

Sir,
    In view of the publicity you have accorded to Mrs Barrow's letter, I hope that you will spare me space to say, as an advocate for the consumption of grass-mowings, that I have eaten them regularly for over three years, and off many lawns. The sample I am eating at present comes off a golf green on Mitcham Common. I have never suffered from urticaria or any of the symptoms Mrs Barrow mentions. Nor did any of the many of my horses to which I have fed grass-mowings, freshly cut and cleaned from stones, &c. For my own consumption I also wash them well.
                        Yours faithfully,
                        J. R. B. BRANSON

[A typical meal *chez* Branson: lawn mowings mixed with lettuce leaves, sultanas, currants, rolled oats, sugar, and chopped rose-petals, with uncut rose-petals sprinkled over the whole.
    On 13 May Winston Churchill augmented Mr Branson's diet with the promise of 'blood, toil, tears and sweat'.]

The Ideal Waiter

From Mr W. Mumford   *5 April 1930*

Sir,
    That the true waiter should receive his accolade, if not a step

71

in the peerage, has long been my conviction. Consequently, although I have not the honour to be a waiter myself, I read your appreciation in *The Times* this morning with profound satisfaction, even while deprecating somewhat a touch here and there of a frivolous in treating a subject so inherently serious. Permit me, Sir, to assert, and I do so without hesitation, that the true waiter, in order to live up to the high standard of his calling, must be possesed of a greater variety of gifts and acquirements than the representative of any other profession. There are unquestionably today more good lawyers in Great Britain than there are good waiters – due to no other cause than the less exacting requirements of the Bar.

The waiter, as he should be and as he is expected to be, must have outward details such as the setting of the table or the pouring of the wine – matters of form as distinct from those of content – so completely mastered that at no time can there appear any flaw in his technique. He should have such knowledge of the viands and wines he has to offer as will command the respect of the most fastidious gourmet. He should be able to command at least two languages besides his own. He should be able so to control his temper as to receive even insults in accordance with the high and honourable traditions of his class rather than to attempt to compete with the lower standards of other classes.

But there are qualities less self-evident, which he is expected to display. He must have infinite tact, so as to enable him to handle appropriately any human situation or disposition, a knowledge of character such as to give him to read promptly that of the guest of the moment and shape his course accordingly, as well as a sixth sense, which I shall call 'anticipatory,' informing him what the guest wants before the guest knows himself, that he my supply it unobtrusively. He should have true, not assumed, kindliness and sympathy, but with an insight that will enable him to display it in the manner most acceptable to the case in hand. In fine he should have the will, education, and natural gifts to produce in each patron, however trying and diverse the circumstances, a pleasant feeling of well-being, which alone can give food the final touch of the delectable that makes a perfect meal.

These qualities are rare. The combination of them is so unheard of that it is expected from no other calling. We do expect it from a waiter, thus rendering him an unconscious tribute.

I am, &c.,
WILLIAM MUMFORD

Ideal for the Winners

[The Allied leaders Truman, Stalin and Churchill (replaced by Attlee after the general election results announced on 26 July) met for the last time from 17 July to 2 August 1945]

From Mr C. B. Acworth   *20 July 1945*

Sir,

One of the avowed aims of the Potsdam meeting is the parcelling out of the world's food supply to avoid Europe facing famine this winter. That being so one can only marvel at the tastelessness of the propaganda which announces that delegates will be fed on 'every luxury' in the way of food, that air transport has been given to wines from France, angostura from the West Indies, &c. Concern about the supply of game and strawberries-and-cream hardly seems worthy of a conference concerned with providing wheat for the elementary need of bread, nor does it make an agreeable pendant to the fact that our troops in Berlin have up till now been subsisting on compo rations.

Yours faithfully,

C. B. ACWORTH

[On 17 July the evening meal consisted of caviare, cold meat, turkeys, partridges, salads of all kinds, vodka and wines. Sir Alexander Cadogan, Permanent Under-Secretary at the Foreign Office, thought it 'rather disgusting in the midst of a starving country']

Cheese . . .

From Mr Ivor Back   *24 December 1945*

Sir,

I want to ask a simple question. In what way did the substitution of the monotonous 'mousetrap' cheese for the splendid native cheeses of this country help us to win the war? In what way does it now help our return to prosperity? Whenever I have had the opportunity I have put this question to economists, but not one of them has been able to give me a satisfactory answer. More than anything else the people of this country are crying out for variety in their diet. It is understandable that in the case of food imported from abroad this cannot be readily achieved; but native products like cheese could surely be made accessible to them.

Good cheeses like the Stilton and the Wensleydale and the lesser known Blue Vinney (whose very names now make one's mouth water) are not luxuries; they are within the reach of even a modest purse and they are also an important item in a balanced diet. I do not know whether their manufacture has been suppressed by some high authority, but, if this is the case, I do earnestly hope that they will soon be restored to us.

I have the honour to be, Sir, your obedient servant,

IVOR BACK

[On 25 February 1947 Dr Edith, later Baroness, Summerskill, Parliamentary Secretary, Ministry of Food, informed the House of Commons it was not the function of her Ministry to pander to acquired tastes but to ensure that those who had had no time to acquire those tastes had suitable food; the nation liked mousetrap cheese. For the Conservative Opposition Mr Lennox-Boyd said the lady had brought class consciousness into cheese]

. . . and Chianti

From Mr John Longrigg   *28 January 1947*

Sir,

The other day I bought half a pound of Blue Danish cheese and some white Chianti. The purity and intensity of the pleasure they produced were so disproportionate to the simplicity of the arrangements involved that I am almost led to believe that it is worth being confined for months to mousetrap and beer. Are chocolate biscuits only exciting when they are produced only occasionally? And are we to sympathize with the man who beat his head against the wall because it was so nice when he stopped?

I remain, Sir, your obedient servant,

JOHN LONGRIGG

Grey Squirrels

[On 2 December 1946 *The Times* heard that not only had a grey squirrel been murdered − but also eaten.]

[an eminent civil servant whose interest included the collection of thistledown for pillows and the science and art of scything]

Sir,

May I, as an executor of the grey squirrel whose fatal crossing of my lawn and successful emergence in a casserole you recorded on 2 December, thank you for the posthumous fame which your obituary notice has brought to the deceased?

Its canonization began with telephone inquiries from several of your London contemporaries and a local paper's request for a biography of our cook. Then, with some appeals for advice, recipes began to arrive. Some of their kindly senders drew from American cookery books: others recorded personal experiments, and the Ministry of Agriculture and the Wine and Food Society both contributed. One correspondent registered on an anonymous post-card contempt for the 'clodhopper' who would take a gun to a squirrel. Another reported more than 150 Chiltern squirrels stalked and shot within a few months by a man with a .22 rifle. Yet another experienced hunter advised the sinking of a baited barrel in the ground. From Surrey I heard of Canadian troops astonished at our neglect of squirrel meat. Was I wrong in detecting an echo of the saga when Lord Marshmallow's heir, at the high point of his Christmas shooting party, located two squirrels in the home covert (ruthlessly exposed by Mr Gillie Potter as 'the holly bush behind the wood shed')?

A resident of the Channel Islands told how during the occupation he tricked a *Gestapo* man, in return for hints about the stalking of inferior prey, into giving him the grey squirrels he shot. A British officer, writing from Seremban, in Malaya, described how a growing queue of villagers, begging him in four different tongues to kill for their supper the pest that was damaging their coconut trees, embarrassed his shooting. A handsome private Christmas card was sent me, which had chanced to include a quotation from Brillat-Savarin commending these squirrels as 'highly prized' in Connecticut, and describing how six or seven of them, which his party shot, were stewed in Madeira and served at a 'distinguished reception.' A correspondent in Lyons sent me independently the precise reference of this quotation. Several writers recalled nostalgically feasts of fried or roasted squirrel in the hill-billy country of the Southern States. An admirably vivid letter from the editor of the *Talladega Daily Home* reported that the creature was still regarded in the woods of Alabama as 'one of our major game animals' and 'something of a delicacy.' The country folk there cherished their 'squirrel dogs,' the best of them often mongrels, trained to ignore all other breeds of game.

I am today the richer by much new knowledge and several good dinners. I needed no such proof that, to students of an obscure subject, a letter published in *The Times* was as good as a travelling scholarship. It had not occurred to me, till a puzzled railwayman delivered at our door a timely bunch of grey corpses from a Sussex shoot, that it could also be an insurance against meat ration deficiencies during a lorry-drivers' strike.

Yours, &c.,
STEPHEN TALLENTS

[Mr Gillie Potter was one of the BBC's most civilised entertainers. Lord Marshmallow — and his heir Twister Marshmallow — lived at Hogsnorton, an estate not unlike Blandings.]

Stilton

From Mr T. S. Eliot   *29 November 1935*

Sir,

May I be allowed the pleasure of supporting Sir John Squire's manly and spirited defence of Stilton cheese? At the same time I should like to add, before it is too late, a few reflections on the project of a statue.

I do not suggest for a moment that the inventor of Stilton cheese is not worthy of a statue. I only criticise the proposal on the ground of the transitory character of the result. Certainly, all the business of public subscriptions, speeches, broadcasts, the wrangling over designs, the eventual unveiling with a military band, and the excellent photograph in *The Times* — this is all exciting indeed. But once a statue is erected, who in this country ever looks at it? Even the work of Mr Epstein is now so familiar to the common man that he no longer stops to ask what it is all about. In a few years' time the Stiltonian monument would be just another bump in a public place, no more inspected than the rank and file of Statesmen, warriors, and poets.

No, Sir, if cheese is to be brought back to its own in England, nothing less is required than the formation of a Society for the

Preservation of Ancient Cheeses. There is a great deal of work which such a society, and its members individually, could do. For instance, one of its first efforts should be to come to terms, by every possible persuasion, with the potteries which supply those dishes with three compartments, one for little biscuits, one for pats of butter, and one for little cubes of gorgonzola, so called. The production of these dishes could be stopped by a powerful organization of cheese-eaters. Also troops of members should visit all the hotels and inns in Gloucestershire, demanding Double Gloster. (On two occasions I have had to add the explanation: 'it is a kind of cheese.')

On one other point I disagree with Sir John. I do not think even the finest Stilton can hold the field against the noble Old Cheshire when in prime condition − as it very seldom is. But this is no time for disputes between eaters of English cheese: the situation is too precarious, and we must stick together.

Your obedient servant,

T. S. ELIOT

[*Murder in the Cathedral* was running at the Mercury Theatre.]

Finding Wasps' Nests

From Major C. J. L. Lewis   *16 September 1967*

Sir,

Many years ago I recall being shown a certain method of finding wasps nests by the late General Prescott-Decie. The General caught a wasp on the window pane, covered it with flour and released it out of doors, saying that it would immediately return to its nest. This it did, zooming in a straight line to the local river bank, with myself and a friend running underneath the flour-coated insect.

Today, 40 years later, I tried the same method. The wasp flew some 30 yards and disappeared into its nest. Possibly some of your country readers, plagued by wasps, may care to try this. It's a certainty.

Yours faithfully,

C. J. L. LEWIS

[General Prescott-Decie was also expert at pig-sticking]

From Mr Andrew Hall   *19 September 1967*

Sir,

Major C. J. L. Lewis reveals in his letter that a country wasp, when covered with flour, will go 'zooming in a straight line' to its nest. Clearly town wasps enjoy being taken for a ride.

I caught one just now, devouring an expensive peach. I covered it, and myself, with large quantities of flour. I descended from a great height to street level and released the insect. It did not return directly to its nest. It rose vertically and vanished towards the sun. I returned to my flat.

That same white wasp was once again lunching on that same peach. How can one destroy a creature with a sense of humour?

Country wasps are just plain stupid.

Yours faithfully,

ANDREW HALL

From Mr Norman Williams   *19 September 1967*

Sir,

I was fascinated when I read the method for finding wasps' nests. I at once tried it out, for we have many wasps here in Bath.

I caught my wasp and coated it with flour. Then I ran down the garden beneath the whitened creature. Unfortunately it soared over a ten foot wall. I was not so agile. When my bruises are healed I shall try again, but this time will use self-raising flour, on myself as well as the wasp.

Yours faithfully,

NORMAN WILLIAMS

From Mr Anthony Parkin   *20 September 1967*

Sir,

I wonder how many of your readers spent Sunday morning catching wasps and covering them with flour. The first one we caught and treated spent several minutes wiping the flour out of its eyes, then flew off vertically at great speed until it was out of sight. Needless to say, we experienced some difficulty in following.

We caught another one, dipped it, and released it in the garden. After revolving several times on the bird table, presumably to get its bearings, it flew to a nearby rose bush. On being shaken off it flew to another rose bush and we got bored with waiting for it to lead us to its nest.

Half an hour later my wife swatted a wasp in the kitchen. When she picked it up to throw it out she found it was covered in flour!

Yours faithfully,

ANTHONY PARKIN

From Mr Timothy Simon   *20 September 1967*

Sir,

Much plagued by wasps, we fell upon the remedy proposed by Major C. J. L. Lewis, consisting of flouring the wasps and dashing off in pursuit, in order to find the nest. I lined up the children, two mounted on bicycles. Unfortunately the wasps selected insisted on cleaning themselves before taking to the air.

Should we, perhaps, have used self-raising flour?

Yours faithfully,

TIMOTHY SIMON

Sir,

My letter was about finding wasps' nests rather than catching wasps.

Messrs Parkin, Simon, Hall and Williams were all singularly unfortunate in their efforts. If the flour-coated wasp is released *out of doors* it will fly straight though possibly high to its nest. This certainly applies to Radnorshire wasps, which admittedly have no sense of humour, Mr Hall.

Self-raising flour should not be necessary!

I am prepared to wager that many nests throughout the country have been found by the method described. Selah.

Yours faithfully,
C. J. L. LEWIS

[After the wasps of Radnorshire and elsewhere had been able to reconsider their tactics, the problem lingered in the mind of one correspondent]

From Mr Norman Williams   *31 January 1970*

Sir,

Sometimes a letter to *The Times* brings unexpected results; for example, would anyone imagine that such a letter would result in vast quantities of flour being delivered at the home of the innocent writer? Yet this happened to me, after a letter of September 19, 1967, in which I replied to a military gentleman who had informed your readers that an infallible cure for the wasp nuisance was to catch a wasp, presumably of a gentle disposition, coat it with flour and then trail it to its nest which could then be destroyed. I tried this, but unfortunately collided with a wall while running. So, in a letter to *The Times*, I suggested the use of self-raising flour.

I do not know if the military gentleman adopted these tactics, but I do know that several firms sent me large bags of self-raising flour to try. That was not all. A famous firm of publishers asked my permission to include my letter in a 'Resources book for teachers', with what effect on the wasp population I have never known.

Might I also add that years ago I wrote you a letter suggesting that possibly Robert Burns was not the greatest poet who ever lived. An irate Scotsman challenged me to a public debate in the Free Trade Hall, Manchester, where I then lived.

Being of a cowardly nature I declined his offer and came to live in Bath.

Yours faithfully,
NORMAN WILLIAMS

[The residents of Bath are not cowardly; some, like Richard Brinsley Sheridan, fight duels. Besides, they have more important things than wasps to think of. Consider the headline in the *Bath Evening Chronicle*

MAN FOUND DEAD IN CEMETERY

which caused no concern, and the report in October 1976 about a woman who admitted handling stolen goods. 'The judge said that but for her two children and her previous good character, she would have gone straight to bed.'

Meanwhile wasps, having recovered from copious flour-coverings, revised their timetable of aggression]

From Mr James W. Gillett   *12 December 1986*

Sir,

On December 3, within minutes of seeing the first snowdrop in bloom, my wife was stung by a wasp!

Yours faithfully,
J. W. GILLETT

Information — 1

Quiller-Couch, Gardner . . . .

[Behold her, single in the field,
Yon solitary Highland Lass!
Reaping and singing by herself;
Stop her, or gently pass!]

From Mr Rob Thomson and Mr William Palmer
22 November 1982

Sir,
Encouraged by the general response to *Hymns for Today's Church*, we intend to convene a working party to render into non-emotive, non-sexist, modern language, *The Oxford Book of English Verse*.

We have been concerned by the way in which poetry has been much neglected in recent years and can only assume that the old-fashioned language of Milton and Shakespeare has ceased to be meaningful or relevant to modern readers. So far we have confined our efforts to improving the poems of Wordsworth, and offer as an example the opening lines to "The Solitary Reaper":

> Look at solo Ms McPherson,
> In her field, a single person,
> Cutting corn with vocal tune,
> Stop, or leave her all alone,
>   Hitherto mute and inglorious.

Yours,
ROB THOMSON
WILLIAM PALMER

[The non-emotive, non-sexist gentlemen might at least have started on Summer is y-comen in, Loudé sing, cuckoo!]

Death of a Mouse

From Sir Charles Jeffries   *31 October 1949*

[Joint Deputy Under-Secretary of State, Colonial Office, 1947–56]

Sir,

Several years ago I bought a very ingenious mousetrap which actually caught one mouse. The cheese was placed in a cage approached through a small doorway. When the mouse had entered, the door automatically closed behind him. When, bored with trying to get at the cheese, he sought to depart, the only way open was up a sloping tunnel. At the top he came out on to a platform, which tipped over under his weight and deposited him in a tank of water. As the platform returned to level, it released a catch which opened the front door for the next victim. It is only fair to the mice to say that the one caught by this apparatus was too young to know any better.

Yours faithfully,

C. J. JEFFRIES

Time Warp?

From Mr C. P. Bockett-Pugh   *23 April 1985*

Sir,

You have recently reported Albert Einstein's date of birth as April 14 and March 14. Only the latter is correct. The special theory of relativity does not allow multiple anniversaries.

Although Einstein's so-called clock hypothesis suggested that one travelling at 100 million miles per hour for seven and a half years would appear to become one month younger than one's fellows, this would not alter one's birthday. There is no evidence that Einstein made such a trip anyway.

Yours faithfully,

CHARLES BOCKETT-PUGH

Arrival of the Scaup

From Mr C. J. Purnell   *19 December 1945*

Sir,
   In your issue of 5 December 1944, you recorded the arrival of
the scaup on its annual visit to St James's Park late. This year
he has come nearly a fortnight later.
                              Yours faithfully,
                                   C. J. PURNELL

A Lesson for Pavlov

From Dr William Sargant   *18 May 1960*

[honorary consulting psychiatrist to St Thomas's Hospital,
London]

Sir,
   With the Summit Conference now upon us, and because of
the state of disturbed judgment to which Mr Khrushchev's
propaganda exploitation of the recent air spy incident reduced
at least some sections of both the public and the press in Britain
and America alike, it is becoming more and more important that
we should all start to get a better understanding of Russian
methods of psychological warfare, otherwise the battle for
men's minds being waged so intensively at the present time will
result in a resounding defeat for the western nations, and this
could be far more devastating in its subsequent effects than the
outcome of the present race for rocket supremacy.
   Obviously, Russian propaganda methods, like others, are
based to a large extent on past experience of what works, but,
if any expert advice is taken on methods of psychological
warfare, it has to come in Russia from scientists versed in
Pavlovian theory and practice. This is because in general
medicine, and especially in psychological medicine, no other
scientific approach is generally considered valid, apart from a
Pavlovian one. And it has also, after all, paid some very
valuable dividends in recent years in the political field.
   Now, Pavlov showed long ago – and this work has been
confirmed time and again since – that one of the surest ways
of breaking down the nervous stability of the dog and of other
animals, and producing in them states of uncontrolled neurotic

excitement, which may later lead on to hysterical and submissive behaviour, and finally even to depressive apathy, is to give a trained, cooperative but anxious animal a random series of positive and negative conditioned stimuli or signals. A hungry, tense animal, for instance, who has been used to an orderly laboratory existence, in which certain given signals are followed by food, and others by no food, can quickly become neurotic and confused when he tries to sort our a sequence of positive and negative food signals, followed indiscriminately by food or no food, which do not, and were never intended to, make sense to him from the beginning.

This quite simple physiological technique, taken from Pavlov's laboratory, has been found just as applicable to man and has been repeatedly used on British and American politicians, press, and public alike in recent years. For instance, when the original sputnik was launched amidst world excitement, we were first of all told that it had no military significance and was merely an interesting scientific experiment. Then, soon afterwards, we were reminded that it meant that any part of the United States could be wiped off the face of the earth at will. Again we were quickly reassured of its purely pacific intent, and yet later again of the devastating effects of this developing on any future war.

Then a dog was dramatically sent up in another sputnik to keep tension at a high level. We were told that it would live, then that it would die, then it was going to live again, and so on alternately for days on end until its death was finally anounced. These positive and negative signals were applied with such precision and skill that some of the British and American press and public alike became, temporarily, just as bewildered, confused and suggestible as did Pavlov's dogs in the presence of a similar barrage of their own special conditioning signals. Numerous other examples could be given of the same technique being used in recent years, and it is unlikely that these have all been just accidental happenings.

Again, before the Summit Conference, we saw the same sort of method being put into action and we have fallen for it yet again. We know perfectly well that every country uses spies of all sorts, and that there is nothing very abnormal about this. Sensibly, Mr Khrushchev again chose a particularly violent and dramatic form of positive rocket signal to fire off his present psychological cannonade, and we were afterwards also quickly informed of the dire consequences to future cooperation between East and West of this particular air spy happening. Soon, however, we were told that it need not affect in any way the approaching Summit Conference. The following day we were again being warned that nations who harbour such American spy bases would be violently attacked. Then again we were told not to worry, but almost immediately afterwards warned about atom bombs which could rain on America. And we can quite confidently expect, right through the Summit Conference and afterwards, a series of such positive and negative conditioning signals to be put out quite indiscriminately, which are simply not meant to make any sense at all to those who will vainly try to understand them.

There is one way to avoid neurotic breakdown, the inevitable disturbances of judgment, the increase in hysterical suggestibility which can result from the skilled use of these powerful physiological processes on the nervous systems of either man or animals. This is to deliberately *ignore* the signals and stop trying to make any sense of them. Pavlov could not break down dogs who took no notice at all of all the experimental flashing lights specially provided for their undoing; it was only the dog who did his best to cooperate with the experimenter and tried to sort out the signals who was so easily broken down. Unfortunately, the press of both our countries has to relay all these confusing and alternating signals, without also explaining what may really be happening, thus tending unwittingly to play the Russian propaganda game for them.

It is probably that Mr Macmillan was warned about these techniques before he last visited Russia, for he wisely ignored all the deliberately alternating attitudes adopted by Mr Khrushchev, who, during the whole of this visit, was blowing so violently hot and cold in a way that must have seemed absolutely bewildering to the Pavlovian uninitiated. But by just ignoring the whole thing, Mr Macmillan won the day. Let us hope that, with a greater understanding of what is happening, the public, the press and politicians alike will also now try to follow his example.

Yours faithfully,
WILLIAM SARGANT

The House of Commons, a Perfect Chamber

[The House of Commons chamber was destroyed by enemy action on 10 May 1941; the Commons then moved to the

House of Lords, and the Lords to Church House, Westminster]

From Mr J. Howard Whitehouse   *21 May 1941*

[Liberal MP for Mid-Lanark 1910–18; headmaster of Bembridge School 1919–65]

Sir,

Will you allow me to state a few things about the House of Commons which probably made it the most perfect debating chamber in the world?

The most important is the arrangement of its seating. As is well known, on each side of the Speaker's chair are rows of benches rising in tiers. The result is that members in any of the rows are looking at the faces of members opposite to them, with the community of interest which this means. This arrangement gave an almost unique character to the debates of the House and enabled the play of emotion and of humour to find adequate expression. Every member addressing the House spoke from the place where he was sitting, and his audience could not only see him but could hear him perfectly. If the seats had been arranged, as in so many meeting halls and churches, in long rows, one behind the other, and on the same level, life in the chamber would have been intolerable. To sit for a great part of a normal session of at least eight hours in seats which enable you to look at, but not over, the backs of the heads of those in front of you, would have been intolerable, and the arrangement would have destroued the character of the House as a debating chamber, though suitable for a meeting of the Reichstag. The seating arrangements are also perfect for the Government and their chief opponenets. Only the width of the clerk's table separates them. Both are in positions giving perfect equality and speak with the encouragement of the cheers of their supporters around them.

I have heard many of the greatest speeches made by the present Prime Minister in the House. I do not remember an instance even of comparative failure, but I have always felt that his success as an orator is greater in the House than on the platform. The arrangements of the House are the perfect setting for his superb powers, and he enjoys the opportunity of meeting opposition. There is no greater master of the art of repartee. I think, too, they greatly helped the success of orators like Augustine Birrell, Lord Hugh Cecil, Simon, Bonar Law, Balfour, and Dillon.

If I do not include Mr Lloyd George in this list it is not because I have not heard him make many great speeches in the House of Commons, but because he is the only great orator I have known who was more successful on the public platform than in the House. For his special genius he always seemed to require a large popular audience, and one which in the main was friendly. The chamber is a small one, and this is another vital factor in its success. It is the perfect size, never loses the atmosphere of a free debating assembly, or becomes a public meeting. Freedom, toleration, and equality are its controlling features. To make it larger would weaken some of these things. But it is large enough. Ordinarily there are sufficient seats. On special occasions the side galleries are used, chairs are brought in (though this has happened only once in 10 years), the steps of the gangway are used, and there is not a little standing room. I am quite sure that on these special occasions the interest and the inspiration greatly exceed that which would occur in a larger hall. No member has ever been shut out.

I discussed this matter on one occasion with John Dillon. He generally spoke from the corner seat of the fourth row below the gangway. He had attacked the Government on the Irish question (it was during the last War), and I congratulated him upon the brilliance of his speech. 'I am always helped,' he said, 'by the seating of the House. I am looking at the faces of those I am addressing, and it makes all the difference. Moreover, if I am attacking the Government I am happier in speaking from a seat above them. I am looking down upon them, hurling my defiance.'

There is this further point to be remembered about the size of the House. If it were bigger it would affect vitally the character of the speaking. There is a distinctive feature about the present method of debating, any change in which would be a great loss. Let me explain this. However great the occasion or the eminence of the speaker, our parliamentary tradition permits interruption. I am not now referring to cheers or cries of dissent, but to the fact that any member may rise and ask the member addressing the House to allow him to correct some point or put a question. The member in possession of the House invariably gives way for a moment. I think the canons of courtesy practised in this connexion greatly raise the prestige of the House and the respect – and something greater – which the members feel for it. Such a custom could not be continued in a larger hall or with a different arrangement of seating.

Complaint is made that there are no writing facilities in the chamber. Why should there be? it is a debating chamber, and it would be wholly foolish to attempt to make it at the same time a writing-room and a library. You would require a building twice the size to provide a writing desk for each member. Moreover, it is entirely unnecessary to do so. A member has only to walk through any of the doors leading into the division lobbies to find luxurious and ample writing facilities.

You, Sir, are the editor of a paper which has a great parliamentary tradition. For long decades it has reported fully the debates of the House and, if I may say so, has impartially interpreted the spirit of Parliament. May I beg you to use your influence to see that what I have described as the perfect chamber is rebuilt without substantial alteration?

Yours very truly,
J. HOWARD WHITEHOUSE

[The new Commons chamber, from the design of Sir Giles Gilbert Scott, was used for the first time on 26 October 1950]

Truly Thule

From Mr G. M. A. Harrison   *29 June 1982*

[Chief Education Officer, City of Sheffield]

Sir,
Driven to distraction by hearing BBC voices pronouncing Thule, the South Sandwich Island, to rhyme either with fool or mule, I rang the corporation's pronunciation unit to protest at a rendering that was as ugly as it was unlettered. What causes me to write to you is the awful news that it was the Foreign Office that advised the BBC on this; Thool or Thewl is the convention these days, they are alleged to say. *O tempora, o mores!* It's enough to raise Pytheas, the one to discover the Northern ultimate equivalent, from the dead.

Yours faithfully,
MICHAEL HARRISON

From Mr T. G. Wilde   *29 June 1982*

Sir,
During recent broadcasts, the BBC has frequently referred to an island in the far South, called THEWL.

90

Can this have any connection with the place mentioned by Edgar Allan Poe, in his immortal lines

> 'I have reached these lands by newly
> From that ultimate dim Thule −. . .'?

Yours,

T. G. WILDE

From Mr James Young   *7 July 1982*

Sir,

. . . or, rather earlier than Poe, by Virgil (*Georgics 1*) where the phrase 'Ultima Thule' occurs as a hecameter ending, thus putting the correct pronunciation beyond all doubt.

Yours faithfully,

JAMES YOUNG

From Mr Jonathan Varcoe   *7 July 1982*

[Director of Music, St Paul's School]

Sir,

They had no difficulty in knowing the correct pronunciation of Thule in 1600 when Thomas Weelkes published his stunning madrigal the words of which begin: 'Thule, the period of cosmographie'.

The two syllables of Thule are set to two semibreves.

Yours sincerely,

JONATHAN VARCOE

Truly More Than One

From Mr E. Murray   *2 July 1982*

Sir,

Thule, pronounced to rhyme with cool, is in Greenland, in the Arctic. Thule, to rhyme with newly, is in the Antarctic. This could matter quite a lot to anyone desirous of going to either place.

Yours,

E. MURRAY

Lessons of the Titanic

From Mr Lawrence Beesley   20 April 1912

[a former science master at Dulwich College who was a 2nd-class passenger on SS *Titanic* which, on 10 April 1912, left Southampton for New York on her maiden voyage. The following telegram was sent from the Cornell University Club, New York, on 19 April]

Sir,

As one of the few surviving Englishmen from the steamship *Titanic*, which sank in mid-Atlantic on Monday morning last, I am asking you to lay before your readers a few facts concerning the disaster in the hope that something may be done in the near future to ensure the safety of that portion of the travelling public who use the Atlantic highway for business or pleasure.

I wish to dissociate myself entirely from any report that would seek to fix the responsibility on any person or persons or body of people, and by simply calling attention to matters of fact, the authenticity of which is, I think, beyond question and can be established in any Court of Inquiry, to allow your readers to draw their own conclusions as to the responsibility for the collision.

First, that it was known to those in charge of the *Titanic* that we were in the iceberg region; that the atmospheric and temperature conditions suggested the near presence of icebergs; that a wireless message was received from a ship ahead of us warning us that they had been seen in the locality of which latitude and longitude were given.

Second, that at the time of the collision the *Titanic* was running at a high rate of speed.

Third, that the accommodation for saving passengers and crew was totally inadequate, being sufficient only for a total of about 950. This gave, with the highest possible complement of 3,400, a less than one in three chance of being saved in the case of accident.

Fourth, that the number landed in the *Carpathia*, approximately 700, is a high percentage of the possible 950, and bears excellent testimony to the courage, resource, and devotion to duty of the officers and crew of the vessel; many instances of their nobility and personal self-sacrifice are within our possession, and we know that they did all they could do with the means at their disposal.

Fifth, that the practice of running mail and passenger vessels through fog and iceberg regions at a high speed is a common one; they are timed to run almost as an express train is run, and they cannot, therefore, slow down more than a few knots in time of possible danger.

I have neither knowledge nor experience to say what remedies I consider should be applied; but perhaps the following suggestions may serve as a help:

First, that no vessel should be allowed to leave a British port without sufficient boat and other accommodation to allow each passenger and member of the crew a seat, and that at the time of booking this fact should be pointed out to a passenger, and the number of the seat in the particular boat allotted to him then.

Second, that as soon as is practicable after sailing, each passenger should go through boat drill in company with the crew assigned to his boat.

Third, that each passenger boat engaged in the Transatlantic service should be instructed to slow down to a few knots when in the iceberg region, and should be fitted with an efficient searchlight.

I am, yours faithfully,
LAWRENCE BEESLEY

[Official inquiries revealed that although there were 2,207 passengers and crew on board, lifeboats could accommodate only 1,178. A mere 703 persons were saved. The *Frankfurter Zeitung* stated that the provision of lifeboats was even more unsatisfactory on the larger ships of the *Nord-Deutscher* and *Hamburg-Amerika* lines.

Mr Beesley's superb account, *The Loss of the Titanic*, appeared in 1912]

Little-known Phrases

From Dr Claire Johnson   6 July 1985

Sir,

Miles Kington (July 2) has raised the issue of unusual foreign phrases. Might I add one that I needed last summer but which was not listed in the usual handbooks.

"Madam my son has been bitten by a mole. Has rabies reached this part of France?"

Yours faithfully,
CLAIRE JOHNSON

From Mrs Jean Buckley   *8 July 1985*

Sir,

Reading Miles Kington's brilliant column on "language essentials" brought to mind my first visit to Finland. I found an old phrase-book (this was 1961) and the ones that most impressed me were "Be quiet, and eat your porridge". "Excuse me, I hate to trouble you, but your motorcycle is standing on my foot".

Sorry, I've long since lost the book, but I remain,

Yours faithfully,
JEAN BUCKLEY

From Mrs Mary M. Hill   *24 July 1985*

Sir,

Mrs Buckley's Finnish phrase book, 1961 vintage, reminded me of my family's first visit to the same country and our 1966 "gem".

My husband, vastly amused by the euphonious-sounding translation of the sentence, "I have been stung by an insect", laced his conversations with his hostess with it at frequent intervals.

Eventually, no doubt feeling her property to be discredited with the presence of too much wild life, she replied in the same language, "poor thing". This increased his vocabulary by one word and effectively silenced him.

Yours sincerely,
MARY M. HILL

From Mr and Mrs Paul Heiney   *10 July 1985*

Sir,

It is not only in foreign tongues that the forceful and striking phrase is to be found. British codes have their share, as well.

We have been researching into ways in which the long traditions of the sea can sustain the modern plastic-boat sailor, and have come upon a fine book of *Universal Yacht Signals*, by George Holland Ackers, from the 1890s.

Hoist 5761 signifies: "Can I have . . . quarts of turtle soup?", 9852 requests the shore station for "Marmalade – orange unless specified", and 1704, followed by the hour, ensures that a vapour bath be prepared for the owner.

But the phrase which for sheer comfortable largeness and

utility beats the lot must be a hoist of flags 6419. Translated: "I can strongly recommend my washerwoman."

Yours sincerely,

E. PURVES
PAUL HEINEY

From Sir William Hayter   *13 July 1985*

Sir,

You may like to add the following to your collection of little-known phrases.

When I was appointed Ambassdor in Moscow the Foreign Office chose a tutor to help me brush up my Russian. Two of the sentences he selected for me stick in my memory, though I never found much use for them in Moscow.

One was: "Near the house there is a small, dark park." The other was "Hurrah! The Cossacks are attacking again."

Yours faithfully,

WILLIAM HAYTER

From Mr George Speaight   *30 July 1985*

Sir,

A few years ago I found myself sharing a sleeping compartment on the Moscow to Leningrad express with a commander in the Soviet Navy. Our only means of communication was my Russian phrase book. The first phrase in it was "Help! I am lost".

The book, we discovered, had been prepared by the United States Department of the Army. When I suggested that this was for the use of the parachutists, the commander's laughter, in which I unkindly joined, was enough to arouse the entire coach from its slumbers.

Yours faithfully,

GEORGE SPEAIGHT

From Baroness Twickel   *30 July 1985*

Sir,

Some 100-odd years ago an aunt of mine was unsuccessfully taught French from a lesson book which I inherited. In it was a picture of a broken-down covered wagon in a storm and underneath the phrase, *Est-il arrivé un accident au chariot?*

Years later my aunt was actually involved in a road accident in France and, seeing an opportunity for making use of her entire knowledge of the language, approached the distraught driver and did so.

His reaction may be imagined.

Yours faithfully,
ANN TWICKEL

From Mr Sidney A. Hummel   *3 August 1985*

Sir,

Baroness Twickel's aunt was more fortunate than I.

Some few years ago, a distant cousin of mine came over from Paris to pay us a visit. She was earnestly endeavouring to master a little English from a phrase book she had brought with her and came across the following piece of conversation, which I have never been able to use.

"Why do you not dance with Hélène?"

"I cannot, because she is smoking and I am wearing a celluloid 'collar'."

Yours faithfully,
SIDNEY A. HUMMEL

From Mrs Sheila Vince   *20 July 1985*

Sir,

As a student physiotherapist, I was once asked to help a seriously ill Chinese patient to get out of bed and sit in a chair. She spoke no English and her dictionary offered no practical assistance.

Of all the quaint and inappropriate phrases it contained, the two most memorable were: "I'm sorry that your concubine is sick" and "Here comes the Executioner".

Yours faithfully,
SHEILA VINCE

The Tithe Sausage

[Trouble at Demen in Mecklenburg-Schwerin, where the church claimed every year 130lb of sausage (*Mettwurst*) but where the tithepayers withheld their dues. Compelled by law to pay, they delivered (so the church insisted) an inferior article]

From Baroness Ladenburg   *10 February 1931*

Sir,

With reference to the article in your issue of yesterday entitled 'The Tithe Sausage', it may interest your readers to know that in many parishes in Mecklenburg-Schwerin it was customary for the tithepayers to deliver to their incumbent *Mettwurst* measured by the ell. The parishioners used to express their liking for their pastor in the size of the diameter of the sausage; on the other hand, if he was unpopular the unfortunate man was the recipient of the right length, but the sausage was of the smallest circumference.

I am, Sir, yours, etc.,
ASTER LADENBURG

From the Reverend Cecil Holmes   *11 February 1931*

Sir,

You speak of 130lb of sausage as being 'an idea so massive as to oppress the imagination of all but a hungry school-boy.' I do not know about that, but when I was a 'Bush-Brother' at Cunnamulla, in the West of Queensland, the horse-boy at Calwarro managed 11ft 6in of sausage for breakfast one morning. He had been out early for horses, and they had been hard to find. On his return to the homestead the Chinaman cook had just finished making his batch for the week and had retired to his hut. Into the frying-pan they all went, and Jack did not even leave one in ten for the parson.

Yours truly,
CECIL HOLMES

[In Mecklenburg-Schwerin 130lb of sausage would provide a family, children and servants with breakfasts, lunches and suppers for a whole year]

97

Station-Masters

From Mr Edwin Haward   *7 September 1956*

Sir,

When I was last in Japan – 16 years ago – the station-master, equipped with curved sword and spotless in white cotton gloves, stood to attention, facing outwards by the side of the departing engine, till the train had cleared the platform and, indeed, passed out of sight. It would be pleasant to know that this picturesque symbol of punctillious observance of railway discipline had survived. If memory serves aright the ceremony was rounded off by a deep bow.

Yours, &c.,

EDWIN HAWARD

From the Reverend H. W. R. Elsey   *11 September 1956*

Sir,

The station-master at Turnham Green station at the beginning of this century was dignified, bearded figure. He signalized the approach of a train by a stately march along the platform, announcing in an authoritative tone: 'Hammersmith, Earls Court, Victoria, Westminister, Charing Cross, Blackfriars, and Mansion House train!' This, to a boy, made the journey to the City seem at least 100 miles. When he was not available this duty was performed by a porter, who rang a bell as he peregrinated the platform. I noticed, however, that the station-master himself never condescended to the bell.

I am, Sir, yours very faithfully,

H. W. R. ELSLEY

From Sir George McRobert   *4 September 1956*

Sir,

It is not in Britain only that station-masters are special. In *Khaki and Gown* the first Lord Birdwood recorded the well known tale of Rivett-Carnac, the pompous and dignified opium agent of Ghazipur. While parading the platform of an Indian railway junction he was asked by a Bengali clerk the time and platform of departure of the next train to Calcutta. The official's furious 'How the devil should I know, why don't you ask the station-master?' earned the classic rebuke 'Sir! If you are not station-master why you thus so proudly walk?'

I am yours faithfully,

GEORGE R. MCROBERT

From an Express Train

From Mr H. C. B. Mynors   *18 October 1963*

Sir,

An article in today's (16 October) issue discusses how to send a message from an express train. Faced with this same problem on the same line, I consulted the steward in charge of the dining-car. He provided me with pencil and paper, made an incision in a large potato, and himself lobbed the potato to the feet of a porter as we ran through Peterborough, with my message wedged in it but clearly visible. The station-master did what was necessary.

The steward would not take anything: he was glad to be of service.

Yours faithfully,

H. C. B. MYNORS

From Mr H. M. Jenkins   *19 October 1963*

Sir,

Your recent article, and the letter from Mr H. C. B. Mynors, dealt with the subject of passing a message from an express train. May I suggest that they are still tackling the 'nursery slopes'? The real problem is how to get a message *on* to an express train.

On Wednesday of this week a friend of mine travelled to Plymouth on the crack Cornish Riviera Express. Unfortunately he left Hanwell too early for the morning post and was anxious to have a particular letter. By prior arrangement, therefore, I placed myself on the main down platform at Hanwell and Elthorne station. I rolled two newspapers (yours) up tightly and constructed a loop of about 1ft diameter to which I pinned the letter. The express train came through at an alarming speed and catching a glimpse of an outstretched arm, I was able to place the loop over this protrusion.

Alas, Sir, your newspapers broke into many pieces and I suffered the indignity of having to retrieve the letter from the permanent way some 100 yards down the line. More satisfactory exchange equipment is in the design stage and I hope to be able to report quite soon on the successful test of a protoype.

Yours faithfully,

H. M. JENKINS

From Mr A. R. D. Wright   *22 October 1963*

Sir,

I once had to send a message from a boat train travelling from London to Southampton. Advised by the Cunard representative to weight my plea with a half-crown, and to wrap both in a clean handkerchief, I watched him catch an erect Coldstream Guardsman in the small of the back as we passed through Woking station. Sure enough, my American visa reached me by the very last boat train.

Yours, &c.,

A. R. D. WRIGHT

From Dr W. D. McIntyre   *24 October 1963*

Sir,

Your correspondent, Mr H. M. Jenkins, who had such an unfortunate experience trying to get a letter on to the Cornish Riviera express, should have used the standard American method of the bow stick.

All that is needed is a long flexible stick with a Y-shaped end. In each of the points of the Y there should be slits, through which cotton, or light string, is looped to form a bow. In the centre of this bow the rolled-up message should be tied. Provided that the stick is held at just the right height, the passenger merely has to grab into the gap between the arms of the Y, pulling the string, and with it the message, from the stick.

At a wayside station, on the route of one of the great expresses from Chicago to the West, I have seen as many as five of these sticks, arranged fan-like in a frame, for various members of the train crew to collect their messages.

Yours faithfully,

W. D. McINTYRE

Footing the Wedding Bill

From Mr Terence Allan   *31 March 1976*

Sir,

In the days when a girl didn't go out to work, and stayed at home until an acceptable suitor could be found, her marriage was a financial as well as a social achievement for her parents − and it was the measure of a father's relief that he stumped up for the wedding.

But nowadays, when equal pay and opportunity give a girl financial independence, and changing social patterns mean that parents have little or no influence on her choice of husband, it is surely something of an anachronism that the bride's parents should still foot the bill.

As the father of three daughters of marriageable age, I admit to bias − and I do not doubt that my counterpart, with sons, would defend the practice to the pop of the last champagne cork!

Yours faithfully,
TERENCE ALLAN

From Mr Alastair Morrison   *3 April 1976*

Sir,

I am accustomed to looking at the bottom right-hand corner of your correspondence page for an insight into some of the most pressing problems of the world today. As the father of four daughters I am sure that Mr Allan's letter on the cost of paying for weddings falls into this category.

I believe that it is the practice in many countries for such costs to be shared between the two families. In default of this I can only look forward to the prospects of financial ruin, unless it is possible to arrange such expedients as enforced elopements or a multiple wedding.

There is much to be said for a system of bride price which seems to be a custom in societies with a more realistic view than ours.

Yours faithfully,
ALASTAIR C. MORRISON

Sir,

I am the father of three daughters who are not yet of marriageable age but have no prospect of being able to afford grey topper and champagne occasions when the time comes. Mr Allan could obtain some relief by insisting on a double wedding of any two from three. This would save the cost of one outing for his side of the family.

My solution is to provide a stout ladder suitable for elopement. At the moment the girls think I am joking − over the years they will become conditioned to the fact that I mean it!

Yours faithfully,

W. E. G. MANNING

From Miss Caroline Allan   7 *April 1976*

Sir,

My father who put the cat among the pigeons with his letter about wedding expenses, is quite obviously in cahoots with Mr Morrison who sugests that brides might be sold.

So be it, but if I am to be auctioned, I make the following stipulations:

1. That the price I fetch should be paid to me personally − out of which a small proportion would be set aside for wedding expenses.
2. That the balance should be nonrefundable.
3. That under no circumstances should my father get a cut.
   'Lot No 1 − Caroline Allan. . . .' May the bidding be brisk!

Yours faithfully,

CAROLINE ALLAN

From Dr Peter J. Simons   9 *April 1976*

Sir,

As it is now clear that Miss Caroline Allan is about to be sold by auction, may I inquire where and when this is to take place and whether there is a reserve price? Generally speaking of course, period pieces fetch better prices than those of rather more recent date though one hopes that this will not be the case with Miss Allan. But, most important of all, where can the article be viewed?

I am Sir, yours speculatively,

PETER J. SIMONS

From Mr Patrick Donnelly   *9 April 1976*

Sir,

Adverting to Miss Allan's letter, wherein she makes the stipulation that after deduction of wedding expenses from the auction price for herself as a bride, 'the balance should be nonrefundable.'

I am reminded that the Supply of Goods (Implied terms) Act 1973 states that goods must be substantially suitable for the purpose for which they are supplied.

May I suggest that Miss Alan or her estimable father arranges for a prospectus to be issued so that would-be bidders can make suitable assessment of the 'goods' offered. *Caveat emptor.*

Yours faithfully,

P. DONNELLY

From Mr S. Highlock   *13 April 1976*

Sir,

As an Inspector of Taxes I am taking a proper interest in the arrangements being made for Miss Allan's future. I am considering whether her case falls to be considered as a disposal of a chattel having a value in excess of £1000; in that event she will be subject to capital gains tax in her father's hands and the Inland Revenue will want to know her value on Budget Day 1965.

There is another possibility. It cannot be denied that value has been added to her in recent years and there may thus be a liability to VAT, at the luxury rate of 12½ per cent I should say.

If on the other hand Miss Allan were unchivalrously judged not to be a 'capital asset', the Inland Revenue would assess her father on any sums paid to him; they would fall to be treated as income or proceeds from a random or spare-time activity.

I hope that no one will suggest any sort of bartering

arrangements. There is a precedent, it is true, but the Revenue would certainly regard such an expedient as tax evasion.

Yours truly,
STEPHEN HIGHLOCK

[Mr Terence Allan was contacted early in 1985 for further intelligence. His eldest daughter, Caroline, was married on August 21, 1982; his youngest, Elizabeth, would be the occasion of another bill in June 1985]

A Wife's Worth

From Canon A. C. A. Smith   *1 March 1978*

Sir,

'She's worth her weight in gold!' I would say: and many of your readers sharing the sentiment would echo the saying, thinking of their own wives. But, Sir, I wonder how many of those who give their wives that worth have ever paused to work it out.

Estimating, and without sparing her blushes, my wife at, say 9 stone, gives the following interesting calculation:

9 stone = 126lb = 2,016oz.

Gold, according to your financial column, was (February 20 pm) fixed at $182.25 per oz. Converting $ to £ at a rate of 2; and oz avoirdupois to troy at an approximate rate of 16:15 gives my wife a worth of some £172,226.20 . . . and if I may say so, worth every pennyweight of it.

Yours sincerely,
A. C. A. SMITH

Names

'I name this child . . .'

[John Leaver chronicled given names as they appeared in the Births column of *The Times* from January 1948. His list of names for 1957 disappointed one correspondent]

What's Wrong with Thomas?

From Dr Thomas Bodkin   *14 January 1958*

Sir,

On reading Mr Leaver's interesting letter about the Christian names of the year. I am prompted, not for the first time, to ask: What's wrong with Thomas? He never gets a look in. Yet Thomas à Becket and Thomas More should both prove to be good patron saints, particularly for Englishmen; and Thomas the Apostle and Thomas Aquinas are surely more worthy of popularity than the Jeremys, Jonathans and the like who have high places in the annual lists.'

The name Thomas has usually been borne by some member of my own family since the Bodkins took their place among the Twelve Tribes of Galway in the twelfth century. If I am asked why I have failed to maintain this tradition I can only reply that my wife demurred to having any of our five daughters christened Thomasina, and I hoped until it was too late they might have had a brother. All five are now the mothers of sons, not one of whom is a Thomas. It seems that the name is slighted by the modern mother. 'Poor Tom's a cold.'

I am, your obedient servant,

THOMAS BODKIN

[At first Mr Leaver's researches had been tentative]

Christian Names in 1947

From Mr J. W. Leaver   *9 January 1948*

Sir,

It may be of interest to you to know that to children born in 1947 whose birth and Christian names were announced in the appropriate column of your paper the following were the most popular names given:

BOYS		GIRLS	
John	250	Ann (107) or Anne (96)	203
Michael	142	Elizabeth	158
Richard	133	Mary	148
David	117	Jane	139
Anthony	113	Susan	98
Peter	101	Margaret	97
Charles	99	Jennifer	60
James	97	Caroline	48
Christopher	95	Diana	45

Yours faithfully,

J. W. LEAVER

[It is worth noting that the lot of women has improved since the turn of the century. At first their role in replenishing the human race was somewhat anonyous:

SMYTHE – On the 10th November, in Jubbulpore, the wife of CAPTAIN HECTOR SMYTHE, 23rd Dragoon Guards, of a son. Colonial papers, please copy.

By the late 30s, things had improved:

SMITH – On Nov. 10 at The Paddock, Warmington-on-Sea, to GLADYS (nee Boggs), wife of EDWARD SMITH – a daughter.

Today it is customary for notices to include both the mother's maiden name and the chosen name, or names of the child.

After Mr Leaver's death in 1974, Mrs Margaret Brown assumed responsibility for the chronicling of births]

Christian names in 1986

From Mrs Margaret Brown   *1 January 1987*

Sir,

As in previous years, I send you my annual analysis of names given to children whose births were announced in *The Times* during the past 12 months.

James is the most popular name for boys for the 23rd year in succession. Elizabeth, as for the last 11 years, retains the lead among the girls:

James	385	(1)	Elizabeth	214	(1)
Edward	244	(5)	Louise	146	(2)
William	236	(3)	Charlotte	140	(5)
Alexander	209	(4)	Jane	107	(7)
Thomas	201	(2)	Alice	102	(7)
John	171	(7)	Mary	98	(4)
Charles	168	(6)	Lucy	89	(13)
David	145	(9)	Sarah	85	(6)
Richard	111	(11)	Emma	84	(13)
Michael	108	(15)	Emily	78	(10)
George	108	(8)			

Figures in parenthesis indicate the position held in 1985.

Richard and Michael have replaced Robert, while Lucy and Emma have supplanted Victoria and Alexandra. Names which increase in favour during 1986 are Hugh, Philip and Harriet.

The table for *first* names shows James and Charlotte once again in the lead. Robert and Christopher have overtaken Benjamin and George, while among the girls Laura has ousted Sarah (top of the list in 1984, third in 1985) altogether and Philippa, Annabel and Chloé all gained ground:

James	187	(1)	Charlotte	90	(1)
Thomas	147	(2)	Emma	68	(5 =)
Alexander	119	(3)	Laura	61	(12)
Edward	118	(4)	Emily	60	(5 =)
William	104	(6)	Alice	58	(4)
Charles	80	(5)	Lucy	55	(10)
Nicolas	72	(7)	Sophie	51	(5 =)
Oliver	66	(10)	Katherine	48	(9)
Robert	58	(13)	Alexandra	48	(2)
Christopher	56	(11)	Elizabeth	48	(8)

Five thousand, three hundred and twenty-one births were announced. Of these, 2,778 were boys and 2,538 were girls. Five births were announced without any indication of sex.

The following summary shows the distribution of names:

	Boys	Girls
None	283	283
One	436	452
Two	1,276	1,395
Three	763	401
Four	19	7
Five	–	–
Six	1	–

Sixty-seven sets of twins were recorded, of whom 31 were boys, 16 were girls and 20 were mixed. There were two sets of triplets and one set of quadruplets.

Yours faithfully,

MARGARET BROWN

[Mrs Brown's revelation that one male child was accorded six Christian names is a reminder of times more extravagant than our own. An *Army List* just prior to the First World War boasted of a Leicestershire Regiment officer:

Lieutenant Léone Sextus Denys Oswolf Fraudati-filius TOLLEMACHE-TOLLEMACHE-D'ORELLANA-PLANTAGENET- -TOLLEMACHE-TOLLEMACHE.

Doubtless his brother officers called him 'Tolly'.

The marriage of a great-great-grandson of King Carlos III of Spain must have been prolonged affair as the bishop intoned:

Alfonso Maria Isabel Francisco Eugenio Gabriel Pedro Sebastián Pelayo Fernando Francisco-de-Paul Pio Miguel Rafael Juan José Joaquin Ana Zacarias Elisabeth Simeón Tereso Pedro Pablo Tadeo Santiago Simón Lucas Juan Mateo Andrès Bartolomé Ambrosio Geronimo Agustin Bernardo Candido Gerardo Luis-Gonzaga Filomeno Camilo Cayetano Andres-Avelino Bruno Joaquin-Picolomini Felipe Luis-Rey-de-Francia Ricardo Estebán-Protomártir Genaro Nicolás Estanislao-de-Koska Lorenzo Vicente Crisostomo Cristano Dario Ignacio Francisco-Javier Francisco-de-Borja Higino Clemente Estebán-de-Hungria Ladislado Enrique Ildefonso Hermenegildo Carlos-Borromeo Eduardo Francisco-Régis Vicente-Ferrer Pascual Miguel-de-Benito José-Oriol Domingo Florencio Alfacio Benére Domingo-de-Silos Ramon Isidro Manuel Antonio Todos-los-Santos.

The bride's name was Julia]

Revolutionary Names

From Dr Nina Szamuely　　　　　　　　*30 January 1970*

[of the *Oxford Russian Dictionary*]

Sir,

I was most interested to read the note on contemporary Russian proper names in your diary (January 22). The parents of Mr Melor Sturua (whose name is a mnemonic of Marx Engels Lenin October Revolution) were by no means unique: the craze for ideologically correct, artificial "revolutionary" names was extremely widespread in the twenties and early thirties. Today there must be countless adults burdened by names such as: Marlen (Marx Lenin), Vladlen, Vladlena, Vilen, Vil' (all abbreviations or mnemonics from Vladimir Ilyich Lenin); Ninel' (Lenin read backwards).

Many girls were called simply Lenina, Stalina.

It is all very well for those whose names are connected with Lenin, but Stalin-derivatives are much trickier, let alone those unfortunates who received names like Zikatra (Zinoviev, Kamenev, Trotsky) or Lentrotzin (Lenin, Trotsky, Zinoviev). I have personally known people with the above names, as well as others encumbered by abbreviations of revolutionary concepts like Revdit (revolyutsionnoye ditya—Revolutionary Child), Mirev (mirovaya Revolyutsiya—World Revolution) or just Oktyabrina (from October).

Another fruitful source was the surnames of revolutionary heroes: the old Bolshevik Yaroslavsky, for example, called his son Frunze.

Industralization has been commemorated by names like Pyatiletka (five-year plan) or Traktor.

Finally, may I refer to Solzhenitsyn's The First Circle, where State Prosecutor Makarygin had called his daughters Dinera (Ditya novoy ery—Child of the New Era) and Dotnara (Doch' trudo-vogo naroda—Daughter of the Toiling Masses). In the English translation the names are reproduced—most faithfully—as Danera and Datoma.

　　　　　　I remain, Sir, your obedient servant.

　　　　　　　　　　　　　　　　　NINA SZAMUELY

[Diana Geddes, Paris correspondent of *The Times*, noted (12 December 1986) that in France given names have cycles of popularity before going out of fashion. Until the beginning of this century, a French child was given the name of a parent or close relatives, of the saint on whose day he was born, or of godparents. Over the past 80 years, however, the choice has been more varied.

BOYS: Jean (1913–37), Michel (1938–55), Patrick (1956–58, Philippe (1959–63 and 1966), Thierry (1964–65), Christophe (1967–68), Stéphane (1970–75), Sébastien (1976–79), Nicolas (1980–82), and Julien since 1983.

GIRLS: Maria until 1914 when Jeanne took over, Jeannine or Janine (1927–35), Monique (1936–43), Danielle (1944–47), Francoise (1948–50), Martine (1951–58), Brititte (1959), Sylvie (1960–64), Nathalie (1965–72), Sandrine (1973), Stéphanie (1975–77), Céline (1978–80), Aurelie (1981–84), and Emilie since 1985]

Name Dropping

From Mr John Cope   *28 April 1982*

Sir,
    In one single week's news items I have heard the following names preceded by the title 'Mister', and in one case 'Sir': Andy, Ben, Bert, Bill, Bob, Dick, Ed, Fred, Freddie, Geoff, Jack, Jim, Ken, Max, Mike, Pat, Ray, Rob, Ron, Sam, Sid, Stan, Steve, Terry, Tiny, Tom, Tony, Vic, Viv and Will.
    Are we to understand that at their baptisms not one of these people was given a real Christian name?

                                            Yours etc.,
                                            JOHN COPE

[On 12 October 1963 *The Times* published a letter from 'Anthony Wedgwood Benn'; a decade later, the same MP was 'Tony Benn']

Sussex Surnames

From Mr Aytoun Ellis   *17 January 1953*

Sir,
    Can any county claim more curious surnames than Sussex? Pitchfork, Slybody, Devil, Lies, Hogsflesh, Sweetname, Juglery, Hollowbone, Stillborne, Fidge, Padge, Beatup, Wildgoose, and Whiskey are a few in the county archives that would certainly

have interested Dickens. As for the names adopted during the Puritan revolution, there can surely be none so odd as those to be found in the Sussex registers. In 1632 Master Performe-thy-Vowes Seers, of Maresfield, married Thomasine Edwards; when his death was recorded his name had by then been abbreviated to Vowes Seers. A Heathfield wench was named More-fruits, and there are also on record Stand-fast-on-high Stringer, or Crowhurst; Weep-not Billing, of Lewes; Fight-the-good-fight-of-faith White, of Ewhurst; Kill-sin Pemble, of Withyam; and Fly-fornication Richardson, of Waldron.

I am, Sir, &c.,

AYTOUN ELLIS

111

In Time of Peace — 1

The Concentration Camps

[In December 1900 Miss Emily Hobhouse left England on behalf of the South African Women and Children Distress Fund. 60,000 Boer women and children were confined in British concentration camps. On 14 June 1901 Sir Henry Campbell-Bannerman spoke at a dinner in London: 'When is a war not a war? When it is carried on by methods of barbarism in South Africa.' At the time of this letter the death rate in the camps was 344 per 1,000 per annum]

From the Bishop of Hereford   *22 October 1901*

[The Rt Rev. John Percival]

Sir,

Every month brings us the dreary record of the enormous death-rate among the children in the South African concentration camps, and to-day you publish one of the worst that we have hitherto received.

According to your tabular statement there are 54,326 white children in these camps, and of these 1,964 died during the month of September. As men read these dreadful figures they cannot but ask, How long is this fearful mortality to be allowed to go on?

Meanwhile, the ladies sent out some months ago to inspect and inquire are, I presume, preparing a report. That report will doubtless testify that almost everything possible under the circumstances is being done by the officers, doctors, nurses, and other humane persons who are working in the camps.

The Government and its friends have constantly reminded us that this is so, and we all believe in their general desire that it should be so. Your Elandsfontein Correspondent, indeed, has the hardihood to assert in your columns to-day that Miss Hobhouse 'has tried her best to foster the supposition that those who have organized these camps are utterly callous as to their welfare,' and that she is thus guilty of 'fostering a base and

113

malicious untruth.' This libellous attack is itself an untruth; we will not it malicious, because he may have been misinformed, or his pen may have run away with him in South African fashion; but it is certainly mischievous, and not very manly or creditable.

The point, however, for the English public to notice is this. All of us who know the humanity of English officers, doctors, nurses feel assured that they are endeavouring to do everything that personal devotion can do under the circumstances.

This unending death-roll of children is the result. Surely, Sir, we need no other condemnation of the camp system for children.

And these recurring reports, extending over all these dreary and death-laden months, amount to a very strong condemnation of the Government for their supineness in not attempting something better long before this time.

Is no system of distribution possible? Could not all mothers with children and all children without mothers be somehow distributed among the loyalist population of Cape Colony or Natal in healthy situations?

Are we reduced to such a depth of impotence that our Government can do nothing to stop such a holocaust of childlife?

We who ask these questions ask them in no spirit of political controversy; no man would seek to make any political gain out of the sad fate of these little ones.

It is in all sadness and in the name of common human pity that we plead with our authorities here at home − the Cabinet and the responsible heads of the great departments concerned − to do something and to do it speedily.

It is a dismal and hateful thought to multitudes of English men and women, without any distinction of political party, for we are all one in our pity for these little children; and the more truly patriotic we are the more hateful is the thought that England should through the death of these children be blotting out a whole generation, to say nothing of the root of bitterness which must inevitable grow out of their graves.

We also plead for immediate action, because the good name of our country is so deeply involved.

Of all the bitter and humiliaiting legacies of this war there will be none so bitter, none so sorely felt hereafter, as the untimely death of all these unhappy children.

Moreover, when the Boer exile returns, eager to clasp in his arms the little ones he left, only to find himself a solitary or childless man, is that likely to prove the seed of his future loyalty?

It may be different if the chldren are kept alive to tell him how tenderly and with what loving kindness they were nursed by English men and English women. It is because those who are now working in these camps are doing their best to save, and yet in spite of all death laughs them in the face as he goes on reaping his ghastly harvest month after month that such camps stand utterly condemned as homes for children.

Therefore the hearts of English fathers and mothers on every side are crying to the Government to bestir themselves and make haste in this saving work, for the love of Christ to make haste.

Your obedient servant,

J. HEREFORD

[*The Oxford History of South Africa* estimates that 25,000 Boer women and children died in the British concentration camps]

South Africa and Sanctions Issue

From Professor Robert Skidelsky　　　　*24 October 1985*

[Department of International Studies, University of Warwick]

Sir,

There are two arguments against Britain, and indeed the "world community", instituting economic sanctions against South Africa.

The first is that they may not work or that most of the immediate suffering will fall on the intended beneficiaries. This seems to me to be a bad argument. The same argument applies to making war. No one can accurately predict the result of war, and anyway it is an end-state which is being aimed at.

The second argument is better. This is that South Africa has done nothing that merits having sanctions applied against it. Economic sanctions presuppose a *casus belli*. Typically, they are a measure of collective defence against an aggressor. Their logic leads to a state of war if sanctions fail. How a sovereign State treats its own subjects has not hitherto been recognized as a cause of war.

It is not enough for advocates of sanctions to show that they will help change for the better in South Africa. They must show that another sovereign State (or a group of such) is under military threat from South Africa. What are the arguments for this proposition?

It may be that advocates of sanctions are seeking to establish a new *casus belli*, namely the existence of a state of apartheid. If so, it is surely up to them to show that this is a *uniquely relevant* ground for foreign intervention in the domestic affairs of a sovereign State.

It must be remembered that our postwar system of international order rests on the principle of national sovereignty. This principle is the strongest safeguard of the independence of states. Advocates of sanctions should show convincingly why the state of affairs in South Africa uniquely requires its breach.

None of the above applies, of course, to moral suasion or private abstention from commercial or other intercourse with South Africa.

Yours faithfully,
ROBERT SKIDELSKY

An Awkward Shortage

From Dr Alec Vidler   *6 May 1976*

Sir,

I shall be grateful if you will allow me to draw public attention to the hardship that is increasingly experienced by septuagenarian men when they are away from home, and *a fortiori* by octogenarians and nonagenarians. I refer to the disappearance of the chamber pot as an article of bedroom furniture, or rather of guest room furniture. Of course some bedrooms have a bathroom directly attached to them and in that case I make no complaint. But, like many of my contemporaries, I am often invited to spend the night in a room that has no such convenience. We do not like a disturb our hosts by wandering about dark passages in quest of light switches and uncertain doors and at last by the noise of flushing.

We plead for the restoration of the traditional chamber pot to its rightful place either under the bed or in a bedside cabinet. It is true that most of them now seem to have found their way into antique shops and thence to the United States. But various sizes in plastic are obtainable and, for my part, I am ready to settle for one of those as a substitute for an elegant piece of china.

I would add that I entirely agree with the late Dick Sheppard that the recipients of such relief should always be responsible in the morning for emptying and cleansing any receptacle which they have used, and not leave that operation as a chore for their hostess or any minion of hers.

Yours faithfully,

ALEC VIDLER

From Mr A. V. Cottam   *8 May 1976*

Sir,

Dr Vidler should take his own chamber pot when visiting.

Packed in the ordinary suitcase in a neat plastic cover, it makes a useful receptacle for sponge bags, socks, collar studs, draft sermons and so on.

Yours faithfully,

A. V. COTTAM

From Mr Toby Robertson   *13 May 1976*

Sir,

Canon Vidler's problem is, by all accounts, not new. Was there not a clergyman who complained of Lambeth Palace that there were 40 bedrooms and only 39 articles?

I have the honour to be your obedient servant,

TOBY ROBERTSON

From Professor Alan Thompson   *19 May 1976*

Sir,

Those of your readers who have recently been deploring the decline in the use of the chamber pot may like to know that a personal chamber pot is still supplied by British Rail to passengers travelling by first-class sleeper between Edinburgh and London. It is a light and elegant model, and is contained in a specially designed rack under the wash-basin. It is clear that British Rail planners have given considerable thought to its provision, and a carefully worded notice gives guidance in its use. This facility is not, I understand, available for second-class passengers.

It is a disturbing thought that the chamber pot − once a classless and functional object in the days of Victorian utilitarianism − is becoming our newest status symbol.

Yours faithfully,

ALAN THOMPSON

[The professor wrongs British Rail. Second-class passengers are likewise served]

Sir,

Far from using it, well-mannered people do not even remark on it.

Yours sincerely,

JOHN HERBERT

Death from Overlaying of Children

[Christmas 1903 saw 1,600 infants put to death by overlaying, 'the slaughterer powerless under the weight of drink'. − Director, National Society for the Prevention of Cruelty to Children]

From Dr Henry Willson, JP   *3 January 1905*

Sir,

Having practised in a crowded London neighbourhood during 20 years, I can add my testimony to the truth of the statements of the Rev. Benjamin Waugh and the coroner for Nottingham.

My experience caused me to make quite different conclusions to those of the coroner for Westminster. Medical witnesses and juries have every desire to be true to their oaths, and, if any bias exists, it is generally in favour of the 'person in trouble'.

If Mr Troutbeck's opinion be correct, how is it that the great majority of these deaths are discovered on Sunday mornings? Healthy children do not as a rule die suddenly from natural causes, and delicate infants generally exhibit some signs of impending death, and do not die under the bedclothes with all the external and internal appearances of suffocation.

The term 'overlaid' may not always be absolutely correct, slow suffocation ensuing from the infant being buried under heavy be-coverings between its parents or close to one of them.

I could relate many incidents and cases which prove my statements, but their recital would scarcely suit your columns.

I agree with the coroner for Nottingham that only a proportion of these cases is due to intemperance. 'Rest to the labouring man is sweet,' and his slumber is heavy, and I have known a case where the parents were undoubtedly total abstainers, but the great majority of these deaths occur among the drunken and degraded. As long as small children sleep in bed with their parents, a proportion will be suffocated.

I conclude with a suggestion. All who have influence with the poor should recommend the use of a cheap cot which can be made by any amateur from an egg-case. A box about 36in by 18in, and 12in in depth, is fitted with two outside legs, the inside being adjusted to the side of the parents' bedstead by iron or wooden angles, or by battens inserted under the bedding. These could be made and supplied at a trifling cost. I shall be glad to confer with any individual or society that will take an interest in lessening this terrible loss of infant life, a loss we can as a nation ill-afford in view of our lessening birthrate.

Yours,
HENRY WILLSON, MD, JP

Nine-year-olds sent to war

From Mr Edward J. Mann 1 July 1982

[writing from London, Ontario]

Sir,

Each war raises the level of man's inhumanity to man one more notch. That notch has been achieved with the latest Iranian offensive in the Iraq-Iran war. Iran has seen fit to send into war thousands of infant soldiers as young as nine years of age. The atrocity is not merely the age of the infant soldiers, but the manipulation of these children by the Iranian leadership. That regime has used these children in human-wave attacks against heavily defended Iraqi positions. The children are used to clear minefields by running through them, with no protection, shouting "Allah Akbar − God is Great." Many who have not been blown up have been captured by the Iraqis.

The most innocent of recruits are selected by the Iranian military. They are usually from the poorest sections of the Iranian population. They are naive and uneducated. They are indoctrinated with a mood of religious fervour mixed with warlike excitement. They are taught to believe that they are fighting to reconquer their land in the name of their Imam and the Islamic religion.

Although Iran says that these children are volunteers; they are not volunteers. Under the pressure of adult members of the Revolutionary Guard of Iran these children are coopted into roles that no adult soldier would undertake.

They are given two weeks or a month's military training at the most. They are barely introduced to the use of a gun and often, without weapons, they are taken to the front lines, to be used as the spearhead of an attack, while adult Iranian soldiers wait in safety. They are given hand grenades and are told by their commanders, members of the fanatic Revolutionary Guard, who have assumed the role of Islamic Commissars, to throw hand grenades at Iraqi tanks in open country.

What is most appalling is Iran's refusal to take these children back after they are captured. Its actions are against the simplest rules of the great religion of Islam, which prohibits children under age from fighting in battle.

Yours truly,
EDWARD J. MANN

The White Slave Trade

From Mr John Masefield   *29 April 1910*

[succeeded Bridges as Poet Laureate in 1930; appointed to the Order of Merit 1935]

Sir,

I read with interest the leading article on the White Slave Traffic in *The Times* for 20 April.

Will you allow me to point out some of the methods by which criminals engaged in this traffic contrive to carry on their business in spite of the law?

The procureurs (the cant name is 'ponce') at work in this country are mostly foreigners. They advertise in country newspapers for good-looking housemaids. Girls living in the country answer the advertisements, send references, and perhaps photographs. The procureurs promise them positions and ask them to come to London. In some cases they send money for the ticket. When a girl arrives at the house or office of a procureur, she is told that the lady who advertised has had to go abroad, to France, Turkey, or wherever it may be; but that she has left word for the new servant to follow her as soon as possible. Money has been left for the ticket. The procureur bids the girl think well before she decides to go abroad. He recommends that she should consult her parents and obtain their written consent. When this has been done he persuades her to sign a statement that she goes abroad of her own will.

To deceive the police officials who watch the Continental

steamboats at their ports of sailing, the procureur dresses the girl in good clothes, and sends or takes her to the Continent as a first-class passenger. He can afford a lavish expenditure. A young English girl will fetch £50. On her arrival abroad the girl is taken to a brothel, and detained there as the slave of the keeper of the house. As the writer of your article shows, she is 'brought into debt to the house.' It is almost impossible for her to escape. It is said that after 12 months of existence in a brothel a girl exhibits no trace of a moral nature. in a few years she dies.

Many procureurs make their living by seducing women. Their victims are frequently deeply devoted to them. The procureurs, taking advantage of this devotion, persuade the girls to go into the streets to earn money for them. A clever procureur may have five or six woman earning money for him in different parts of the town.

Sometimes the procureur, 'dressed like a foreign nobleman,' with a display of jewellery, goes to a seaside resort in the south of England. He contrives to scrape acquaintance with some good-looking girl. He invites her to come with him to Boulogne, or to some other French port, on one of the many all-day trips. When abroad with her he contrives that she shall miss the returning steamer. As a rule the girl is without money. She is in a foreign land in the care of a ruffian. It is easy for the procureur to dispose of her as he thinks fit.

There are three methods much in favour among procureurs in this country. It is extremely difficult to obtain convictions against the criminals who employ them. All three methods are practised continually and successfully on Englishwomen. As a member of the police force said to me only a few days ago, 'They may hold a dozen conferences, but they'd do more good if they hung a dozen ponces.'

It is pitiful that the *maximum* punishment for this class of offence of procuring the swift, certain, bodily and spiritual ruin of a human being (often a girl of tender years) should be set at two years' hard labour.

I am, Sir, yours faithfully,
JOHN MASEFIELD

121

Shop Shyness

From Mr. W. Hodgson Burnet   19 May 1932

Sir,

I wonder if any of your male readers suffer as I do from what I can only describe as 'Shop-shyness'? When I go into a shop I never seem to be able to get what I want, and I certainly never want what I eventually get. Take hats. When I want a grey soft hat which I have seen in the window priced at 17s. 6d. I come out with a *brown* hat (which doesn't suit me) costing 35s. All because I have not the pluck to insist upon having what I want. I have got into the habit of saying weakly, 'Yes, I'll have that one,' just because the shop assistant assures me that it suits me, fits me, and is a far, far better article than the one I originally asked for.

It is the same with shoes. In a shoe shop I am like clay in the hands of a potter. 'I want a pair of black shoes,' I say, 'about twenty-five shillings — like those in the window.' The man kneels down, measures my foot, produces a cardboard box, shoves on a shoe, and assures me it is 'a nice fit.' I get up and walk about. 'How much are these?' I ask. 'These are fifty-two and six, Sir,' he says, 'a very superior shoe, Sir.' After that I simply *dare* not ask to see the inferior shoes at 25s., which is all I had meant to pay. 'Very well,' I say in my weak way, 'I'll take these.' And I do. I also take a bottle of cream polish, a pair of 'gent's half-hose,' and some aluminium shoe-trees which the fellow persuades me to let him pack up with the shoes. I have made a mess of my shopping as usual.

Is there any cure for 'shop-shyness'? Is there any 'Course of Shopping Lessons' during which I could as it were 'Buy while I Learned?' If so I should like to hear of it. For I have just received a price list of 'Very Attractive Gent's Spring Suitings,' and I am afraid — yes I am afraid . . . !

I am, Sir, your obedient servant,

W. HODGSON BURNET

The Case of Miss Lenton

[The saga began as farce and ended as near-tragedy. in the early hours of 20 February 1913 the tea pavilion at Kew Gardens was seen to be on fire. Before long the pavilion ceased to exist, an estimate of the damage £1,000.

Patrolling the area, but powerless to contain the conflagration, was a police constable who picked up visiting cards one of which read 'Two voteless women'. The officer next observed two women about to leave the scene. Consulting his watch, and concluding that all the women of Richmond and district should be in bed if not asleep, the constable duly arrested Lilian Lenton and Joyce Locke. Brought before the local magistrates, the Misses Lenton and Locke confused matters by insisting that their names were Ida Inkley and Olive Wharry. Declaring names to be irrelevant, the chairman refused bail to Lenton-Inkley and Locke-Wharry (or Inkley-Lenton and Wharry-Locke) and remanded both in custody. One of the defendants countered by directing a rude remark at the chairman who chanced to be mayor of Richmond. The Bench put their heads together and pondered the nature of the rude remark. 'Well!' said the chairman, emerging from communal deliberations. Miss Locke-Wharry (or Wharry-Locke) clearly did not like the tone of that 'Well!' She picked up a copy of the Richmond directory, took careful aim, and hurled it at the heads of the gentlemen before her. All ducked and so escaped injury. Before long, the accused were in Holloway Prison].

From Sir Victor Horsley and others   *18 March 1913*

Sir,

The Home Secretary recently issued a formal statement in regard to the sudden release of Miss Lenton that she 'was reported by the medical officer at Holloway Prison on Sunday, February 23, in a state of collapse and in imminent danger of death consequent upon her refusal to take food. Three courses were open: – 1. To leave her to die. 2. To attempt to feed her forcibly, which the medical officer advised would probably entail death in her exhausted condition. 3. To release her on her undertaking to surrender herself for the further hearing of her case. The Home Secretary adopted the last course.'

From these expressions employed in this letter the public were completely misled as to the true facts of the case. She was certainly 'in imminent danger of death' on that Sunday afternoon, but this was not due to her two days' fast, but to the fact that during forcible feeding executed by the prison doctors on the Sunday morning food was poured into her lungs.

The statement issued from the Home Office quoted above was not only contrary to the facts, but was also constructively misleading, in that it made no mention whatever of the prisoner having been forcibly fed.

In consequence of the real facts being generally known Mr Remnant [Conservative MP for Holborn] on March 13 asked the Home Secretary whether 'during an attempt to feed the suffragist prisoner, Miss Lenton, the tube used was introduced into the trachea, thereby causing some of the liquid food to pass into the lung; whether Miss Lenton was thereupon released from prison, it being the opinion of the medical officer in charge that her life was in danger; and whether the doctor who examined her on her release found that pleurisy was present together with lung mischief.'

To this question Mr McKenna said 'there was no foundation for this statement which has been made that the tube entered the trachea or that any food passed into the lung. Miss Lenton's collapse occurred some hours after she was fed and was due to the bad state of her health aggravated by her refusal of food.' Mr McKenna admitted that he knew her own doctor had found her to be suffering from pleurisy.

The facts of this case are as follows, and to any unprejudiced medical practitioner prove that the Home Secretary's attempted denial that Miss Lenton was nearly killed by the forcible feeding is worthless.

In the first place, Miss Lenton was seen in prison on Saturday afternoon, February 22 1913, by her solicitor, Mr Marshall, who reports that on that day he saw her officially on a matter connected with her impending trial. He found her then absolutely normal, in good spirits, and making light of her two days' fast. Yet on the following afternoon she was 'in imminent danger of death', as admitted by the Home Office, and the only cause of which could be the forcible feeding inflicted upon her that morning.

On Sunday morning, 23 February 1913, Miss Lenton was forcibly fed in Holloway Prison by Dr Forward and another doctor and seven wardresses. She was tied into a chair and her head dragged backward across the back of the chair by her hair, the usual prison method of 'restraining' these prisoners. The tube was forced through the nose twice. No food could be got through it the first time, and after the second introduction when the food was poured in it caused violent choking, the breathing became very violent and noisy, so that the doctor told her to breathe more quietly. The noise of the rattling was so loud that she actually was afraid it would alarm her fellow prisoner. Breathing was almost impossible, and she coughed violently and continuously, so though the food was poured in twice it came

124

back at once and out of the mouth. When the tube was removed she fell against the wall and continued to cough, then great pain began extending from the wait upwards and in the front of the chest and the rattling noise in breathing persisted.

Three wardresses remained in the cell, and Miss Lenton was put on a mattress and pillow laid on the floor.

The pain became intense. The doctor was fetched. He examined her chest and warned her not to sit up. He ordered hot bottles and blankets, gave her Bovril and brandy, and two hypodermic injections. He then left and returned with the governor, who said she should be released at once. The doctor then gave her another hypodermic injection (presumably for stimulation), saying it was necessary to enable her to stand the journey.

She was carried in a chair to a taxi, and the prison doctor himself with a wardress took her to the house of a friend of hers. There they gave her more 'stimulation' treatment and carried her upstairs. The prison doctor said a local doctor must be fetched at once. This was done. That night her temperature was above 102 deg., and she was gravely ill. Her own doctor found pleurisy (pleuro-pneumonia) at the base of the left lung, and slighter symptoms in the right. He certified that her condition was serious until all complications had cleared up. Under the care she has slowly recovered, and is now convalescing.

These plain facts of Miss Lenton's cas prove clearly that the food which was forcibly injected into her lung set up a pleuro-pneumonic condition which, but for her youth and good healthy physique, would have ended more seriously.

That the prison doctor and the governor recognised immediately what they had done is also obvious. They hurriedly and at further risk of injury to the patient immediately removed her from the prison, so that at least she should not die there and thus compromise the Home Office, and our horrid prison administration, of which they were the instruments.

Precisely similar maltreatment of a suffragist prisoner occurred at Winton Green Prison, Birmingham, on 24 June 1912 (see our report on Forcible Feeding, *British Medical Journal*, 31 August 1912). In that case also the food was injected into the lung and caused forthwith the same alarming symptoms and agonising pain in the chest. In that case also the patient was hurriedly thrust into a cab and sent with fever and pleurisy to a private house. Fortunately she too was young and strong, and gradually recovered after a convalescence at the seaside.

Yours faithfully,
AGNES SAVILL, MD
CHAS. MANSELL MOULLIN, FRCS
VICTOR HORSLEY, FRS

[Meanwhile the mayor of Richmond — the recipient of hundreds of congratulatory telegrams for his firmness and agility in avoiding flying directories — prepared to take on Asquith's government. 'Why had this woman been released?' The Home Secretary — Reginald McKenna — seemed vague. A High Court settlement over the Kew Gardens tea pavilion was reached in December 1913, its terms not disclosed.

Women over 30 were enfranchised in 1918, those over 21 in 1928. The first woman to be elected to the House of Commons — Countess Markiewicz (Constance Gore-Booth), a Sinn Feiner — did not take her seat; the first woman to appear in the House was the Unionist, Lady Astor, in 1919. Margaret Bondfield was the first woman to enter the cabinet, in 1929 as minister of Labour. 66 years after the act of violent at Kew Gardens, Mrs Margaret Thatcher became prime minister]

A Labourer's Weekly Budget

['Eight shillings a week!' said Mr St Lys, 'Can a labouring man with a family, perhaps of eight children, live on eight shillings a week?' — Benjamin Disraeli, *Sybil, 1845*]

From the Reverend W. Blissard   *18 April 1913*

Sir,

The question has been recently raised in your columns as to the wages of the country labourer. Can you find space to print the weekly budget for the food of a countryman, his wife, and four young children? Bread, 21 loaves, 5s 3d; tea or tea and cocoa, 1s 1½d; butter, 1lb. or margarine, 2lb, 1s; cheese, 4lb. at 8d, 2s 8d; sugar, 4lb. 8d; bacon, meat, and suet, 3s 6d; oddments, salt, pepper, matches, &c. 1½d; flour, 9d; currants, 4d; treacle or jam, 4d — total weekly cost, 15s. 9d. If each of the six persons has three meals a day this works out at 1½d per meal. This budget is given me by a countryman who has brought up a family on this scale, who knows therefore what he is talking about. No one can say that it is extravagant. Indeed life would be impossible upon it but for the vegetables which the man grows by labour outside that given in return for his wages.

Obediently yours,

W. BLISSARD

[During the next ten years the wages of country labourers increased so that by 1923 some were earning as much as £1 16s a week]

Thoughts from Roget

From Mr A. J. Woodman   *6 October 1967*

Sir,

Dr Roget included the following interesting entry in his *Thesaurus*: 'Inaction, passiveness, abstinence from action; non-interference; conservative policy.'

Can there be a moral somewhere in this?

Yours, &c.,

A. J. WOODMAN

From Mr M. F. Strachan   *7 October 1967*

Sir,

Another evocative entry in the *Thesaurus*: 'Socialism, collectivism; communism, bolshevism, syndicalism; mob law . . .'

Yours faithfully,

M. F. STRACHAN

Spectacles on Nose

From the Reverend R. J. E. Boggis   *1 February 1946*

Sir,

After your description of spectacled faces on the tomb of Henry VII in Westminster Abbey, it is interesting to note the mention of a pair about two centuries before.

Walter de Stapeldon, a good man and an eminent bishop, fell a victim to mob law in 1326, sharing the unpopularity of his master, Edward II. A full inventory of his effects has been preserved, and in his *camera* in Exeter Palace there was found a pair of spectacles (*unum spectaculum cum duplici oculo*) valued at 2s. – a considerable sum (a mirror was reckoned as worth one penny). Spectacles are said to have been invented shortly before the end of the thirteenth century, probably by Roger Bacon, so Stapeldon's must have been an early specimen. (Stapeldon's *Register*, p. 565.)

Furthermore, the benefit derived from wearing spectacles is not limited to humans, as is shown by this amusing description in the *Banner* of 13 January 1888: 'A correspondent of the *Manchester Sporting Chronicle*, thinking that his horse was shortsighted, and his eyes examined by an oculist, who certified that the house had a No. 7 eye, and required concave glasses. These were obtained and fitted on to the horse's head. At first the horse was a little surprised, but rapidly shewed signs of the keenest pleasure, and he now stands all the morning, looking over the half-door of his stable with his spectacles on, gazing around him with an air of sedate enjoyment; when driven his manner is altogether changed from his former timidity, but if pastured without his spectacles on he hangs about the gate whinnying in a plaintive minor key. If the spectacles are replaced he kicks up his heels and scampers up and down the pastures with delight.'

Yours, &c.,

R. J. E. BOGGIS

Two Sentences

From Mrs Norah Lofts   *25 January 1947*

Sir,

This is England today. A woman beats her five-year-old child until her head is swollen, her forehead protruding, and her nose injured. The mother is fined £10. Another woman is found in possession of more ration books than her family of three children entitles her to. She is sent to gaol for six months.

Comment is superfluous, but a public expression of disgust is imperative.

Yours faithfully,

NORAH LOFTS

Behind Football Violence

[On 29 May 1985, at the Heysel Stadium, Brussels, Liverpool fans charged Juventus supporters. 41 died in the crush]

From Professor Ralf Dahrendorf, hon KBE   *3 June 1985*

[Director, London School of Economics 1974–84]

Sir,

As a soccer fan (dare one still use the word?) I am deeply saddened by the events of Brussels, though, as a fan of English society, I am not entirely surprised. One day, Toxteth on the terraces was bound to happen. Your leading article (May 31) points to some of the reasons, but understates one which is worth emphasizing.

In some places soccer has turned from a working-class game into an under-class game. Elsewhere (p5) you quote Mr David Robins as saying about hooliganism that "It is part of what it is like to grow up working class in England".

Perhaps it is even more part of what it is like to grow up not working in England.

The under-class is that group which combines desolate living conditions and the lack of traditional bonds even of class with low skills and hopeless employment prospects. The result is cynicism towards the official values of a society bent on work and order.

The under-class is not a revolutionary force, but one which will make its presence felt by crime, riots, and also by forming a volatile reserve army militancy on either extreme of the political spectrum. It is an indictment of our prosperous societies, especially since a large number of those in the under-class are young.

The phenomenon exists everywhere, but more so in this country (and in the United States) than on the Continent, if only because of the unusual plight of Britain's (and America's) inner cities.

Far be it from me to blame "society" for the actions of individuals! It is entirely right and proper that ways should be sought immediately to make the recurrence of either Toxteth or Brussels less likely. But none of these immediate measures are going to have lasting success unless, at the very least, ways are found soon to make sure that every young person in the country has had some meaningful experience of training and activity by the time they reach their twenties.

Surely there cannot be greater social priorities than effective vocational training, a better system of apprenticeships, and more opportunities for community service.

If we do not succeed in including young citizens fully in our societies one must fear that there will be a frightening vacillation between situational violence and mindless law-and-order policies: a double threat which is as likely all over the free world as it is unattractive to the fan of liberty.

Yours sincerely,
RALF DAHRENDORF

[See *The Times Index* for 1985: under FOOTBALL (Association), Supporters, entries fill five columns]

Turkish Delight

From Imam S. M. Abdullah   *31 March 1948*

Sir,

Sometimes very interesting and amusing letters addressed to the doctors appear in the columns of your paper. This has tempted me to send you a copy of a letter received by me as Imam, that is, leader of the Mosque at Woking. It shows that it is not the doctors alone who have to look after all the various needs of their patients but we, the religious heads who administer spiritual food to human beings, are also required to attend to the various desires of our followers. The letter runs:

'Dear Imam, – I shall be most grateful to you if you will kindly let me know if you supply Turkish Delight, or any kind of sweet similar to it. If you do not keep any sweets, would you be so kind as to let me have the address of any other Mosque where I may obtain it? If you do keep it, will please let me know the price, &c.!'

Yours truly,
S. M. ABDULLAH, Imam

Teddy Boys

From Miss Nemone Lethbridge   *12 May 1958*

Sir,

I would wholeheartedly endorse the refusal of Miss Dickinson and Mr Paul, expressed in their letters on 8 and 9 May, to equate the problem of juvenile delinquency with that of the Teddy boy, while admitting that the two do, it a certain extent, overlap. The first problem I would not attempt to discuss here; on the second I would endeavour to make two points:

First, that in this country, for the first time since the industrial revolution, we have in these Teddy children, both boys and girls, a highly solvent, semi-articulate working-class youth with a strong sense of corporate identity, albeit in part the result of commercial exploitation and of constant attention in the Press. This group has the independence – I would almost say the arrogance – born of having money to spend; it has its own idols drawn from its own ranks, who do not for a moment attempt to repudiate their Bermondsey or Elephant and Castle origins; it has, I would submit, Sir, the beginnings of its own simple but tremendously vigorous culture. These young people do not spend their evenings watching television nor, with a few exceptions, fighting one another with bicycle chains; the ambition of the greater number of them is to play a musical instrument, even if it is only a washboard in a skiffle group.

Second, that in a time of considerable material prosperity the class war has very largely abated. Where bitterness still exists it is with the older generation of working people; certainly it is not with the Teddy children. Where the group does feel a corporate resentment it is towards the older generation as a whole; it is as if the age war had succeeded the old class struggle.

I cannot attempt, Sir, to propound a solution to the problem, but I would submit that it would be one of the tragedies of our age if this great source of energy ad potential talent were allowed to run to waste. These young people deserve a dignified and sympathetic hearing; unreasoned condemnation is as much out of place as soup-kitchen charity.

I am, Sir, your obedient servant,
NEMONE LETHBRIDGE

Dogs by Motorail

From Mr Gerald Williams   *14 July 1975*

Sir,
I am taking my wife and two dogs to Scotland and back by British Railways Motorail. My wife gets one side of a compartment to herself plus blankets and pillow. The dogs sleep on the floor, but they cost me five pence more than my wife.

Yours faithfully,
GERALD WILLIAMS

From Mr Max Lightwood   *8 August 1975*

Sir,
If Mr Williams in taking his wife and two dogs to Scotland by train gives the dogs one side of the compartment plus blankets and pillow, and puts his wife to sleep on the floor – as plainly British Rail intends and right thinking people would consider reasonable and proper – then can he not say with some satisfaction that to take his wife cost him 5p less than the dogs?

Yours faithfully,
MAX LIGHTWOOD

Coloured Soldiers

From Mr D. Davie-Distin   2 October 1942

Sir,

I am the manager of a snack bar in Oxford, and have had a rather unfortunate state of affairs, which is beginning to exist in this country, brought very forcibly to my notice. The other night a coloured United States soldier came into our establishment and very diffidently presented me with an open letter from his commanding officer explaining that 'Pte——is a soldier in the US Army, and it is necessary that he sometimes has a meal, which he has, on a occasions, found difficult to obtain. I would be grateful if you would look after him.'

Naturally, we 'looked after' him to the best of our ability, but I could not help feeling ashamed that in a country where even stray dogs are 'looked after' by special societies a citizen of the world, who is fighting the world's battle for freedom and equality, should have found it necessary to place himself in this humiliating position. Had there been the slightest objection from other customers I should not have had any hesitation in asking them all to leave.

I should like to feel that everybody shared my views, as England's reputation for hospitality is in danger of being questioned. Incidentally, the gentleman in question showed his gratitude by a donation of just twice the amount of his bill in our blind box.

Yours faithfully,
D. DAVIE-DISTIN

[Forty years later the Prince of Wales was seeking non-white faces in the Brigade of Guards]

Dr Pauling's Visit

From Lord Russell, OM, FRS   5 September 1958

Sir,

I am writing to report an incident which must bring shame to all who value the fair name of Britain. The incident concerns the dealings of the Home Office with Dr Linus Pauling, a very distinguished native-born American, Honorary Fellow of the Royal Society, recipient of honorary degrees from the

132

Universities of Oxford, Cambridge, and London, Nobel Prizeman, and well known throughout the scientific world as a man of outstanding intellect and integrity. He came to the United Kingdom on 31 August for two main purposes, to deliver an address which he has been invited to give on 15 September at the Kekulé Symposium of the Chemical Society of London and to address a meeting organized for the Campaign of Nuclear Disarmament which is to take place on 22 September.

On arrival at London Airport he was separated from the other passengers by the immigration authorities, and his son, who had come to meet him, was refused information as to whether he had arrived. He was closely questioned as to the purposes of his visit. When he mentioned the Chemical Society, he was asked whether he had any evidence that they had invited him. He replied that the evidence was in his baggage which was in the customs shed, and asked whether they accused him of lying. At the moment, they did not answer, but at a later stage they made this accusation. At first they said that he must leave the United Kingdom on 15 September. He pointed out that this made his address to the Chemical Society impossible, and they reluctantly extended her permit to the next day, 16 September. They stated as the ground of their action: 'We do not admit people to Great Britain who come principally to take part in public meetings, especially when against Government policy.'

This action by the British authorities is shocking. First, for the gross discourtesy of subjecting a man of great intellectual eminence, who has been honoured by many learned bodies in this country, to insult at the hands of ignorant officials. In the United States McCarthyism has lost its vigour, but one is compelled to believe that it is being taken up in this country.

Second, if Government policy is as stated to Dr Pauling, free speech has been abandoned and the only freedom left is that of supporting the Government.

Third, on the particular issue of nuclear weapons the Government have laid themselves open to very damaging criticism. It will be said that they know their policy to be such as no well-informed person could support. Apparently their watch-word is: 'Democracy, yes, but only ignorant democracy, for our policy is one which no well-informed democracy would tolerate.'

Yours, etc.,
BERTRAND RUSSELL

[Dr Pauling received two Nobel Prizes, for Chemistry in 1954, and for Peace in 1962]

Flight

The Problem of Flight

From Commander Wilson-Barker   *18 May 1910*

[known to snotties and boys for Elementary Seamanship which, at the time of Captain Sir David Wilson Barker's death in 1941, had reached its tenth edition]

Sir,

Being interested by Mr Gustav Lilienthal's article on 'Flying' may I add thereto a few observations of my own? That the key to the puzzle 'How to Fly' will be found ultimately, if at all, in close study of the flight of birds is certain. The true soaring birds – the albatrosses and the vultures – have distinctly different types of wings. The albatross is pre-eminently the gliding soarer of the bird kingdom; its wings are long and narrow; the body is comparatively small and short, and is thickly covered with feathers which contain a great amount of air. The wings of the vulture are broad and the body is less well provided with feather covering. Both birds have short stiff tails, massive heads, and powerful beaks. An albatross weighing 18lb. may soar from a few feet above water level to 200 or 300 feet and can glide hither and thither at will for quite a long time, without once flapping its wings. With the aid of binoculars, I have followed a ten minutes' flight of an albatross without once seeing it flap its wings. Albatrosses fly little in calm weather and then only with difficulty, but even in a calm the aid of a wing flap seems necessary only to raise the bird from the water. In a breeze – and the stronger the better – the wing is not flapped at all. The bird appears to run up a wave, patting the water with its feet, and then launches off from the wave top into a graceful glide in the air.

There is apparent, however, a movement in the primaries of the wings and in the tail which appears to serve as a rudder or steering gear. The bird's legs also move at intervals. The head is in constant motion, probably for sighting purposes. Birds are alive to their feather tips, and are extraordinarily sensitive

134

to changes of atmosphere; they feel the slightest shift of an air current before it strikes them. It should be noted also in these oceanic birds that there is a distinct though slight difference in the 'shaping' of the wings according as the bird is flying with, against, or at an angle with the direction of the wind.

Recently I took a stereoscopic photograph of flying gulls. The propeller-like action of the wings of these birds was distinctly shown on the plate owing to the shutter failing to act instantaneously, and, though at times in strong winds at great heights they may 'soar' in circles through the air, it is certain that the flap of the wings is generally necessary to propel these birds through the air.

The 'flight' of an aeroplane resembles that of flying fishes buffeted and driven along by the wind and thrown about by air waves thrown up from the sea. The flight of the great oceanic birds is entirely different. It exhibits a complete control of air and wind. The serious study of the flight of birds and a series of cinematograph photographs taken with a telephoto lens could not fail to give instructive and illuminating results of immense value to those engaged in solving the problem 'How to Fly.'

Your obedient servant,

D. WILSON-BAKER

HMS Worcester, Greenhithe.

P.S. − The area of the wings of a 10-foot albatross weighing about 18lb. is five square feet.

['A bird is an instrument working according to mathematical law, which instrument it is in the capacity of man to reproduce with all its movements but not with as much strength, though it is deficient only in power of maintaining equilibrium.' − Leonardo da Vinci, *The Flight of Birds*, 1505]

Aeroplanes and War

From Mr John Galsworthy   *7 April 1911*

[Order of Merit 1929, Nobel Prize for Literature 1932]

Sir,

Of all the varying symptoms of madness in the life of modern nations the most dreadful is this prostitution of the conquest of the air to the ends of warfare.

If ever men presented a spectacle of sheer inanity it is now – when, having at long last triumphed in their struggle to subordinate to their welfare the unconquered element, they have straightway commenced to defile that element, so heroically mastered, by filling it with engines of destruction. If ever the gods were justified of their ironic smile – by the gods, it is now! Is there any thinker alive watching this still utterly preventible calamity without horror and despair? Horror at what must come of it, if not promptly stopped stopped; despair that men can be so blind, so hopelessly and childishly the slaves of their own marvellous inventive powers. Was there ever so patent a case for scotching at birth a hideous development of the black arts of warfare; ever such an occasion for the Powers in conference to ban once and for all a new and ghastly menace?

A little reason, a grain of commonsense, a gleam of sanity before it is too late – before vested interests and the chains of a new habit have enslaved us too hopelessly. If this fresh devilry be not quenched within the next few years it will be too late. Water and earth are wide enough for men to kill each other on. For the love of the sun, and stars, and the blue sky, that have given us all our aspirations since the beginning of time, let us leave the air to innocence! Will not those who have eyes to see, good will towards men, and the power to put that good will into practice, bestir themselves while there is yet time, and save mankind from this last and worst of all its follies?

Yours truly,
JOHN GALSWORTHY

[Galsworthy died in 1933 before the names of Guernica, Warsaw, Rotterdam, Coventry and Dresden became synonymous with a new kind of horror]

Trespassing in Aeroplanes

From Mr. H. B. Devey   *27 April 1910*

Sir,

Motor-cars are bad enough, but they do not come into one's house or garden. With aeroplanes total strangers may drop in, through the roof, for a little chat at any time. I fear the law cannot protect one against such intrusion. If aviation becomes popular I shall have spikes, with long strong prongs, fixed on the chimneys of my house, and the word 'Danger' painted in large red letters on a flat part of the roof. If any flying machines come down in my garden I shall send for the police to remove the occupants, whom I shall sue afterwards for any damage to my trees or shrubs.

I am, Sir, your obedient servant,

H. B. DEVEY

From Mr Henry A. De Colyar, KC   *30 April 1910*

Sir,

According to a *dictum* of Lord Ellenborough's in 'Pickering v. Rudd' (1815, 4 Camp., at p. 221), passing over another's land in a balloon is not a trespass. This *dictum*, which is difficult to reconcile with the well-known legal maxim *cujus est solum est quoque usque ad altum*, was, however, approved of, in the Indian case of 'Bagrum v. Khettranath Karformah' (1869, 3 Bengal L. R., O.J.C., p. 43) by Mr Justice Norman, who expressed himself as follows:

'To interfere with the column of air superincumbent upon land is not a trespass. Lord Ellenborough justly ridicules the notion that travellers in a balloon could be deemed trespassers on the property of those over whose land the balloon might pass.'

I am yours faithfully,

HENRY A. DE COLYAR

[Bernard Shaw's *Misalliance* had been presented in London on 23 February 1910, Lina Szczepanowska emerging from an aeroplane which had crashed on a glass house]

The Sensation of Flying

[In July 1910, a year after Blériot had crossed the Channel, an air display was held at Bournemouth. Drexel climbed to 2,490 feet, the Belgian Christiaens flew for 2 hours and 20 minutes at 39 miles per hour; taking part in the alighting prize competition, the Hon. C. S. Rolls crashed. He was the tenth airman, and first Englishman, to die while piloting a powered machine]

From Mr Arnold White   *18 July 1910*

Sir,

In *The Times* of today your Special Correspondent at Bournemouth reports the fact that yesterday at noon Mr Grahame-White 'took up one of his mechanics for a short flight'. As I had the good fortune to be the passenger referred to, and had never seen an aeroplane before yesterday, it is possible that your readers may be interested in knowing the sensations of a sedentary sexagenarian who finds himself in the air for the first time.

The closest approach to an aeroplane in a stiff breeze is to be on the bridge of a torpedo-boat in half a gale. The switchback motion is delightful when ascending, but the downward swoop is terrifying when near the ground because nothing but the personality of the skipper is present to suggest that the machine will not strike the ground with fatal effects on captain and passenger.

When the first shock of a new environment is over the sense of a new force beats in on one's intelligence, a force that is like nothing on earth or in water, but which recalls the dream experience most people know of effortless gliding, especially when the wind is abaft the aeroplane.

As we passed over the spot where the tragedy of the previous day had occurred it seemed obvious that it was as reasonable to stop a battle when the first men fell before the enemy's shot as to stop aviation meetings because aviators are killed. The battle with the air has begun and will take its toll of human life until the air is conquered.

The combination of moral, intellectual, and physical qualificaties required for the making of a good aviator are substantially those wanted in a naval officer. Personality in the air is of the same importance as personality in sea-war. Of the brave men who are striving to win the battle with the air one can only speak with reverence and admiration, especially as, in my humble experience, the pleasantest moment was that in which the machine was induced to come safely to a standstill on the ground.

I am, Sir, your obedient servant,

ARNOLD WHITE

From Miss Money Coutts   *21 July 1910*

[writing from the Aero Club]

Sir,

I also made my first flight in the air on Saturday at Bournemouth, so I read Mr Arnold White's letter with interest and amusement.

M. Morane took me in his big two-seated Blériot to an altitude of about 400ft, the highest that a passenger was taken at Bournemouth, but 'the pleasantest moment' was certainly not 'that in which the machine was induced to come to a standstill'! Neither did I find that 'the downward swoop is terrifying when near the ground'.

I found Morane's superb *vol plané* the supreme moment of the exhilaration of flying, and the graceful way he alights, springs up, and then alights again is quite unterrifying.

The only moment of fear was the start, I thought, which Mr White does not mention. The rush and leap into the air that takes one's breath and sight away for a minute may be quite unique to Morane, however, for he rockets into the air as no one else does. As Blériot says, he is *un virtuose* in the art of flying.

This 'new force' Mr White speaks of seems to me to be most unlike the usual dream of 'effortless gliding', because I got the impression of immense, almost terrific, power, both in the aeroplane's strength, and speed and in the genius of the young pilot conquering undreamt-of difficulties beside me.

I am, however, in agreement with Mr White as to 'personality', because, unhappily perhaps for aviation at present, it seems the most important factor in flying. Take Morane as an example, who has only flown for three months, and is now perhaps the finest of them all. Blériot calls this favourite pupil his 'Benjamin' with fatherly pride.

'Oh, yes, it beats every game in the world,' I heard an

enthusiastic young flying-man say to another, and as a humble passenger I fully endorse the remark.

I remain yours faithfully,

ELEANORA MONEY COUTTS

[Less than a year later – on 12 April 1911 – a French airman, Pierre Prier, flew non-stop from London to Paris (Hendon to Issy-les-Moulineaux) at 60 miles an hour]

Shooting at Aeroplanes

[A correspondent had insisted that any good shot (possibly King George V?) should be able to hit an aeroplane. But what should he aim at?]

From Mr Percy Bono   *6 January 1915*

Sir,

The Infantry Training Manual, 1914, page 130, gives instructions for firing at hostile aircraft. It says:

'In the case of rifle fire at aeroplanes men should be instructed to aim six times the length of the machine in front, and in the case of airships at the nose of the envelope.'

Yours obediently,

PERCY BONO

[This correspondent lived in the West End of London]

Space Travel

From Mr. G. V. E. Thompson   *6 January 1956*

Sir,

I am surprised that, according to your report of 3 January, our new Astronomer Royal has stated that the prospect of interplanetary travel is 'utter bilge,' although he apparently admits both that it is technically possible and that he has no idea how much it would cost.

Surely it is unwise for him to prophesy that nobody will ever put up enough money to do such a thing, when he himself can exert little or no influence on the persons who seem most likely to have to decide whether or not to finance the first expedition − namely, the next two or three Presidents of the United States, or the corresponding wielders of power in the Kremlin? While it is obvious that the next war could not be won by the first man − or even the first regiment − getting to the moon, the cold war might well be decisively influenced. The propaganda value is obvious: a landing on the moon would unquestionably be man's greatest material achievement, and would no doubt be claimed to demonstrate its technical superiority by the nation concerned. It is hardly necessary for the expedition to be a financial success, any more than it is for the present Trans-Antarctic Expedition.

There are many fields of human endeavour which are more worthy of support − cancer research is an example which springs immediately to one's mind. Nevertheless we cannot confine our activities to one or two narrow branches of knowledge. We now seem to be approaching the stage at which we both need to colonize the other planets (where suitable), and have the means to do so. Interest in and research into space travel are not confined to this country but are world-wide. When the moment of history arrives no doubt some organisations will be prepared to play the part of Queen Isabella. Perhaps the real question facing us in this country so far as space travel is concerned is about under the spur of national rivalry or whether to press for its being undertaken under the aegis of the United Nations.

I am, Sir, &c.,
G. V. E. Thompson

['That's one small step for man but one giant leap for mankind.' − Neil Armstrong on the moon, 3.56 a.m. (BST), 21 July 1969]

Concorde

[Pan Am and TWA has cancelled their options to buy Concorde]

From Professor J. K. Galbraith　　　　　*3 February 1973*

Sir,

In telling today that the British Government wish to exercise closer control over the costs of the Concorde you say that: 'Crew seats (*sic*) developed under a contract for £45,000 were unsuitable and a consequent costs charge was first put at £216,000 and then raised to £409,000.' (Later the Government got the figure down to £325,000.)

I do not wish to comment on the high cost of furniture these days; and oen wants the men who pilot planes to be seated in the greatest comfort and security. But my chauvinist instincts were stirred by the magnitudes involved. As an American I associate this sort of thing with our aircraft industry. Are your people being imitative? Or, another thought, was the sub-contractor in question one of our experts in the design of imaginative cost over-runs? If the last is the case you should swallow national pride and, in a manly way, give us credit. These were only chairs after all.

Faithfully,
JOHN KENNETH GALBRAITH

Coach and Concorde

From Mr Philip Short   *19 January 1978*

[of the Department of Electrical and Electronic Engineering, The University, Newcastle Upon Tyne]

Sir,

How delightful it was to see your photograph of a Concorde aircraft together with an East Anglian mail coach this morning.

By consulting a recent reprint of a 1831 Newcastle guide one can see that the present postal service to London from here is about the same now as it was then. Except on Fridays the mail coach departed every night at 9.30, arriving in London at 6 a.m. on the morning after next.

How agreeable it would be if, inspired by your illustration, the Post Office were to return to the use of horses to improve the postal connection with London in these more distant regions. With improved roads, pneumatic tyres and a better class of horse, much could be done. Maybe we could then catch the night mail even if we did post after 5.30 p.m.?

Yours faithfully,
P. SHORT

In time of war

War Office and Inventors

From Dr Conan Doyle   *22 February 1900*

[knighted in 1902; an ardent cricketer, Doyle was once bowled by a ball which rose to a height of thirty feet and fell on top of the bails. This incident inspired *The Story of Spedegue's Dropper*]

Sir,

In the coming reform of the War Office there is one department which will, I trust, undergo a complete reorganization – or rather I should say organization since it does not appear to exist at present. I mean the board which inquires into military inventions. I have heard before now of the curt treatment which inventors receive at the hands of the authorities. As I have myself had a similar experience I feel that it is a public duty to record it.

The problem which I was endeavouring to solve was how to attain accuracy – or approximate accuracy – for a dropping, or high angle, rifle fire. It appears to me to be certain that the actions of the future will be fought by men who are concealed either in trenches or behind cover. In the present war it has been quite unusual for our soldiers ever to see a Boer at all. Direct fire is under these circumstances almost useless. The most of your opponent which shows is only the edge of his face, and his two hands. When he is not firing he is entirely concealed. Under these conditions except at close quarters it appears to be a mere waste of ammunition to fire at all.

There is only one side upon which the man in the trench or behind the rock is vulnerable. That side is from above. Could a rain of bullets be dropped vertically all over the enemy's position your chance shot has the whole surface of his body to strike, while the direct chance shot has only a few square inches. There is no escape from this high angle fire. No trench or shield is of any avail. Human life can be made impossible within a given area.

In this system it is not the individual at whom you shoot, but at the position, the ridge, the kopje, whatever it is that the enemy holds. If you search this thoroughly enough you will find the individuals. For example, suppose that a kopje occupied is 1,000 yards long and 100 yards deep, 100,000 bullets falling within that area gives one bullet for every square yard. But 100,000 bullets are nothing – only the contents of the magazines of 10,000 men. It can be judged then how untenable a position would be, if only fire of this sort could be made at all accurate.

But at present there is no means by which it can be regulated. If you were to say to the best marksman in the British Army 'Drop me a bullet on that kopje 500 yards off' he would be compelled to look helplessly at his rifle and confess that there was nothing to enable him to do this. He might hold his gun up at an angle and discharge it, but it would be pure guess work, and the probability is that he would be very far out, nor could he correct his error, since he would have no means of knowing where his bullet fell.

My experiments have been in the direction of affixing a small, simple, and economical apparatus to the rifle by which a man would know at what angle to hold his rifle in order to drop a bullet at any given range. It would weigh nothing, cost about a shilling, take up no space, and interfere in no way with the present sights, so that the rifle could be used either for direct or high-angle fire at the discretion of the officer. Having convinced myself that my idea was sound, I naturally wished to have it examined at once in order that, if it should be approved, the troops might have the use of it. I therefore communicated with the War Office, briefly stating what my idea was, and my letter was in due course forwarded to the Director-General of Ordnance. I have just received his reply:

'War Office, 16 February 1900
'Sir, With reference to your letter . . . concerning an appliance for adapting rifles to high-angle fire, I am directed by the Secretary of State for War to inform you that he will not trouble you in the matter.
'I am, Sir, your obedient servant,
(Signature illegible),
'Director-General of Ordnance.'

Now, Sir, my invention might be the greatest nonsense or it might be epoch-making, but I was given no opportunity either to explain or to illustrate it. It may be that the idea has been tried and failed, but, if that were so, why not inform me of it? I have shown it to practical soldiers − one of them with a Mauser bullet wound still open in his leg − and they have agreed that it is perfectly sound and practicable. And yet I can get no hearing. No wonder that we find the latest inventions in the hands of our enemies rather than of ourselves if those who try to improve our weapons meet with such encouragement as I have done.

Yours faithfully,
A. CONAN DOYLE

[Six days later Doyle sailed for South Africa as member of a hospital unit. Shortly after his return home in the summer he played for MCC against London Counties and dismissed W. G. Grace − not, alas, with a high-angle delivery but with 'one a foot off the wicket']

The War against Germany . . .

From Major H. N. Robertson   *5 October 1939*

Sir,

A correspondent asks in your columns today whether our Government are afraid to let us read neutral and even French newspapers. I crossed the Channel to France last week and returned today. On the outward journey my copy of *The Times* and other London papers and magazines which I had bought at Victoria for the journey were confiscated before I was allowed to embark. 'No printed books or newspapers may be exported or imported,' I was told. Twenty paces farther on and over the gangway the same newspapers were being freely sold on the boat! They were on sale also at the French port of disembarkation.

On my return today I threw overboard, before disembarking, my French, Dutch, and Belgian newspapers, and then, shining with conscious virtue, submitted myself to customs examination only to find that criminal tendencies are not easily suppressed even by the will to repentance. For there was discovered in my suitcase, where it had lain since I left home, an ordinary 7s 6d English novel, published in London and purchased there some weeks ago. This contraband of war was eagerly seized upon, to be forwarded, I was informed, to the Chief Censor at Liverpool, of whom any inquiries might be made.

From such blind and pompous folly of inflated functionaries not even P. G. Wodehouse, nor indeed The Book itself is exempt. Sir, will you not move to succour the shaken sanity of the censorship? By all means let them forbid to Allies and to neutrals the indiscreet or treasonable columns of *The Times*; but surely there must be on the booksellers' shelves some harmless trifles which might be exempted and even presecribed for those like myself who, endeavouring to serve their country, must undertake the long and slow and most uncomfortable journeys of wartime.

Throughout my journey I had with me a briefcase containing eight or nine pounds of typewritten documents, but these apparently are without the ban. This, I suppose, is merely an oversight on the part of officialdom.

I am, Sir, your obedient servant,

H. N. ROBERTSON

[If the Wodehouse endangered was *Uncle Fred in the Springtime*, published in London on 25 August 1939, the censorship was wise. Frederick Altamont Cornwallis Twistleton, 5th Earl of Ickenham, was notoriously a subversive influence apt to subject his nephew Pongo Twistleton to soul-testing experiences]

. . . and the New Bureaucracy

From Mr G. L. Reid   *8 December 1939*

Sir,

My father, aged 81 and confined to his room the past two years, has been picked out by the Ministry of Agriculture as a fit person to be exhorted to 'Dig for Victory'. His garden is about one-eighth of an acre. The packet delivered by post 'On his Majesty's Service 'contained 94 leaflets together with a typed slip informing him where further supplies may be obtained.

Yours faithfully,

GRAHAM L. REID

[Four days later intelligence reached Printing House Square concerning a grandmother, aged 90 and almost blind, who had been similarly approached by the department soon to become immortalized by the radio programme ITMA as the 'Min of Ag and Fish']

From Mrs H. M. Child   *11 July 1940*

Sir,

The Ministry of Aircraft Production has urgently appealed to the women of Britain to give up all their aluminium. Going this morning to buy enamel saucepans to replace the aluminium saucepans which I intend to give to the nation, I saw a woman buying a set of four large new aluminium steamers. What is the use of asking us householders to give up the aluminium we are using when the shops are full of aluminium goods which anyone can buy?

Yours &c.,
HELEN M. CHILD

[Meanwhile harsh discipline was being imposed on those who sought to be patriotic]

From Mr H. Ashton-Hopper   *9 December 1940*

Sir,

For some months the Government has been urging the public to 'Keep a Pig'. I kept a pig. In due course I arranged, subject to a permit to slaughter from the Ministry of Food, for a bacon factory to kill and cure the said pig. Having sent it to the factory with the permit to slaughter for our own consumption, I now receive from the local food office (from whom the permit was obtained) a letter in which they say that 'in no circumstances' may the bacon factory cure the pig for me and that the carcass must be collected by me the day after it is killed.

In a household of two we could not possibly eat a whole pig, and we have no knowledge of or necessary equipment for curing: we may not sell any part of the carcass, and if we were allow it to waste through being unable to eat it before it went bad, we should, I have no doubt, be liable. What does 'A' do with the pig? Is this sensible in a time of food shortage or is it crass idiocy?

Yours truly,
H. ASHTON-HOPPER

[Apparently all the writer had to do was to join, or form, a pig club. If the latter, he would appoint himself chairman and secretary. However, to form a pig club, one required a permit, and it was uncertain whether this was granted before or after acquiring a pig. But the man or woman who belonged to a pig club could legally get his/her carcass cured, before eating half and selling half to a butcher.

Sometimes, the tensions of war being what they were, one government department would disagree with another]

From Major-General R. H. Allen (retd)   *16 January 1943*

Sir,

The following extract from the files of a welfare officer in a munition factory may be of interest.

December 9 Write Welfare Officer of the Ministry of Labour asking for help to get razor blades. Point out that works are 10 miles from nearest large town and workers mostly live in villages where no blades are obtainable.

December 18 Local Welfare Officer replies he has no authority. Refers me to local Price Regulating Committee. Write this body same day.

December 28 Board of Trade replies! Refers me to H.M. Inspector Factories. Says latter has authority under Order 2149 to issue permit of razor blades.

December 29 Visit H.M. Inspector personally. He has never heard of Order 2149, but kindly rings Board of Trade. Discussion ensues on telephone. Board of Trade says order sanctions purchase of cutlery. Inspector says razor blades are not cutlery. Board of Trade says they are. Drawn battle, both sides maintain their position.

December 29 Write Board of Trade Headquarters in London asking for decision.

January 13 No reply. No decision. No razor blades.

Yours faithfully,

R. H. ALLEN

[Local Government naturally took the hint]

From Dr John Sainsbury   *9 April 1943*

Sir,

I have just received from the London County Council, Room 49, County Hall, a *questionnaire* – on the left the query, on the right my reply. It says 'I am unable to trace any record of local taxation licence duty having been paid by you this year in respect of your dog.'

It seems incredible that, when every man and woman is

wanted to carry on the war, there are still some who have time to send out these ridiculous notices. The answer, of course, is that I have never had a dog in my life. Room 49 also asks me to put a penny stamp on my reply.

Yours faithfully,
JOHN SAINSBURY

[The war with Germany was successfully concluded on 7 May 1945; that with the new bureaucracy continues]

Faith in the Führer

From Mr H. A. Smith   *6 July 1940*

Sir,

In this Gloucestershire village yesterday, a man remarked, 'Oh, well, if the Germans win, at any rate I have my pension, and they can't touch that.'

Can nothing be done by the Press, the BBC, or the Ministry of Information to bring home to people some of the implications of a German victory?

Yours obediently,
H. A. SMITH

[The above letter may have been inspired by the 'Phoney' war response of the Secretary of State for Air, Sir Kingsley Wood, when asked to set fire to German forests: 'Are you aware it is private property?']

Man-power

From Lieutenant-Colonel W. M. Campbell   *1 February 1941*

Sir,

After 17 months of war the following appeared in you yesterday's (January 29) issue: — 'Second footman or second parlourmaid required at once; four in family, 13 servants, including four in pantry . . .'

Yours faithfully,
W. M. CAMPBELL

[The address was Warfield Hall, Bracknell, Berks]

Official Advice

From the Bishop of Fulham   *3 June 1941*

[the Rt Rev. Staunton Batty]

Sir,
    A few weeks ago I was given official advice as to what action to take in a gas attack. I was recommended to put both my hands in my pockets and if I carried an umbrella to put it up.
    This morning the President of the Board of Trade told me on the wireless that if I found myself without any clothes owing to a 'blitz' I should appear before the Local Assistance Board and demand coupons. It is puzzling, but, as Mr A. P. Herbert has laid down, 'Let us be gay.'

Yours faithfully,
STAUNTON FULHAM

[Gay – adj. 1. Full of or disposed to joy and mirth. – *Shorter OED* (1952)]

Flugzeugabwehrkanone

From Dr Victor Grove   *20 September 1941*

Sir,
    'Flak' is the abbreviation of the German word-monster *Flugzeugabwehrkanone*, which consists of five parts. *Flug* is our word flight or flying. *Zeug* is stuff, implement, craft, and thus the two words together mean aircraft or flying-machine. *Ab* is our preposition off, and *Wehr* defence, a body of armed men, which makes *Abwehr* mean warding off, fighting off. *Kanone*, of course, is our cannon or gun. No wonder even the Germans, who are somewhat fond of 'word sausages', thought it avisable to reduce their word for an A.A. gun to the monosyllabic *flak*.
    Another recently adopted German word, *Panzer* (pronounced puntser), is the medieval German word for a coat of mail and now signifies armour and armoured. Thus a German *Panzerkreuzer*, e.g., is an armoured cruiser and a *Panzerauto* an armoured car.

Yours, &c.,
V. GROVE

Teutonic Brevity

From Mrs W. Murdoch   23 September 1941

Sir,
   Last time I was in Bayreuth a friend had a slight accident to
her car. The garage to which she took it for repair had painted
across the front: Kraftfahrzeugreparaturwerkstatt. To-day's
specimen of German (Flugzeugabwehrkanone) at least only
takes one line of capitals in your columns. What about mine?
                                    Yours faithfully,
                                    DOROTHEA MURDOCH

The Price of Hector

From the Bishop of Stepney   15 December 1955

   [the Rt Rev Joost de Blank]

Sir,
   On D-Day the divisional headquarters of which I had the
honour to be chaplain attended a special service in the parish
church of Wye, Kent. Hector, the indefatigible organ blower,
was at his best. A few days later I receives his request for
payment. It read: 'To blowing for the invasion . . . 7s 6d.'
                        I am, Sir, your obedient servant,
                                    * JOOST STEPNEY

Doodle-Bug

[The first flying bomb fell on London 13 June 1944]

From Mr N. E. Odell   9 October 1944

   [Geologist extraordinary and mountaineer, Professor Noel
   Ewart Odell had worked in Canada, at Harvard and at
   Cambridge]

Sir,
   There is nothing new under the sun, not even the term
'doodle-but', lately and widely applied to the flying bomb. For

the sake of historical accuracy, and before the latter barbarous instrument be haply relegated to oblivion, it may not be amiss to record that the word 'doodle-bug' has been in use in Canada and American among mining men for some 20 years.

There it has been applied to certain geophysical instruments of a magnetic, electrical, or gravitational character which are used in prospecting for minerals. Some of these instruments (the magnetic kind) have, incidentally, been in use in Sweden for the purpose of locating iron ores since the beginning of the seventeenth century, and it is even possible that a colloquial term, equivalent to the American 'doodle-bug', may have been in current usage there. In any case the flying bomb cannot have it all its own way!

I am, Sir, your obedient servant,

N. E. ODELL

Army nicknames

From Mr Reginald Bosanquet   *1 August 1977*

Sir,

Thinking about the film *A Bridge Too Far* can any of your readers explain why World War Two generals had such incredibly childish nicknames?

'Jumbo', 'Squeaker', 'Pip', 'Boy' and 'Bubbles' come to mind.

Yours faithfully,

REGINALD BOSANQUET

From Major-General Sir Alec Bishop   *3 August 1977*

Sir,

The reasons underlying the nicknames 'Jumbo', 'Squeaker' and 'Boy' referred to by Mr Reginald Bosanquet in his letter are that the first general possessed a large and impressive stature, the second a voice which would rise to a high pitch when under excitement, and the third because of his youthful appearance.

I have never understood the reasons underlying the conferment of 'Pip' and 'Bubbles' on the other two.

Yours faithfully,

ALEC BISHOP

152

Sir,

The answer to Mr Bosanquet's query is that generals of the Second World War acquired their childish nicknames, not through anything they did in that war, but through the clubby nature of regimental life at the time of their joining, which in most cases was before the Great War of 1914.

Some were purely descriptive, as in the cases of 'Jumbo' Wilson, who looked like an elephant, and 'Squeaker' Curtis, who had a high-pitched voice. Some stem from an episode, such as the emission of bubbles by Evelyn Barker on his first attempt at pipe-smoking. (Another 'Bubbles' was the infant model for the famous advertisement.)

But the most childish and most numerous nicknames are those automatically linked to a name, and these can be misleading. 'Strafer' Gott affords a good example. It occurred to me while I was writing a book on the North African campaign (recently published with title *The Plain Cook and the Great Showman*) that 'Strafer' ill described this humane and well loved general. Then I recalled the words attributed to the Kaiser, '*Gott strafe England*'. There could be no escape thereafter for any soldier with the surname of Gott from the nickname of 'Strafer'.

Yours faithfully,
GREGORY BLAXLAND

From Mrs Primrose Feuchtwanger   *3 August 1977*

Sir,

Mr Reginald Bosanquet might be interested to know that my late father, Major-General H. Essame, to whom Ronald Lewin generously referred in his review of *Corps Commander* last week, had slightly turned in feet and took shorter than normal strides. He was known to his troops as 'Twinkletoes'.

Yours faithfully,
PRIMROSE FEUCHTWANGER

From Mrs Derek Oulton   *3 August 1977*

Sir,

Mr Bosanquet refers in his letter to some unusual military nicknames. I once heard the son of one of the generals he mentions introduce himself to my husband by saying 'I'm Squeaker's boy, the Oat's godson and the Burglar's nephew'.

Yours faithfully,
THE OAT'S DAUGHTER

From Mr K. R. Simpson   *4 August 1977*

[Department of War Studies and International Affairs, RMA Sandhurst]

Sir,

Reggie Bosanquet queries why it was the British generals in World War Two had such incredibly childish nicknames as 'Jumbo', 'Squeaker' and 'Boy'. Surely this reflects nothing more than the preparatory school background of these generals. Equally childish nicknames can be found amongst the literary and artistic talent of that generation. Types of nickname have a lot to do with national characteristics.

For intance, the Germans in the Second World War preferred to give generals nicknames which were a play on words. Thus Field-Marshal Keitel was known as 'Lakeitel', a play on the German word *lakai*, meaning lackey, and Field-Marshal Hans Kluge was known as 'Kluge' Hans, a play on the German word *klug*, meaning clever. More sinister was the nickname 'Strength through Fear', derived from the Nazi leisure organization, 'Strength through Joy', given to Field-Marshal Schörner, an officer not noted for his sense of humour.

Yours truly,

K. R. SIMPSON ('Whacko' Simpson)

From Mrs Hilary Aggett   *4 August 1977*

Sir,

The incredibly childish nicknames given to World War Two generals surely derived from the fact that most of their contemporaries, both senior and junor officers, went to public schools where witty nicknames were the order of the day.

I served on the staffs of 'Monkey' Morgan, 'Dolly' de Fonblanque, 'Windy' Gale, 'Pug' Ismay, 'Jorrocks' Horrocks and, lower down the ranks, with 'Poppy' Flanders and 'Fairy' Fairhurst.

Yours faithfully,

HILARY AGGET (Captain, retired)

From Brigadier J. H. P. Curtis   *4 August 1977*

Sir,

The answer to Reginald Bosanquet's question is simple. The last war generals acquired their 'childish' nicknames at the outset of their Service careers, often while still in their 'teens.

In the early nineteen hundreds Christian names were resorted to only after a suitable period of acquaintance had elapsed. As an alternative a ready form of identification was needed amongst the junior officers who invented nicknames for each other based usually on a personal idiosyncrasy or physical feature.

By the late nineteen-thirties when I joined the Army, the invention of new nicknames had become less necessary since Christian names were used at once.

Which is why, Sir, I can but sign myself

Yours faithfully,

SQUEAKER'S BOY

[Brigadier Curtis points out that 'Squeaker's' (Major-General H. O. Curtis) nickname had nothing to do with his voice. 'Origin TOP SECRET' – see also Sir Evelyn Barker's letter, 8 August 1977]

From Mr Oliver Everett   *5 August 1977*

Sir,

Followers of the Bosanquet nicknames correspondence (admirable for August) might also like to know that the present day Indian Army has inherited the nickname habit (and much else) from their British forbears.

Examples include Major 'Pickles' Sodhi of the 61 Cavalry; Major 'Binny' and 'Mao' Sherghill of the 7th Light Cavalry and the Deccan Horse respectively, and, of course, Colonel 'Bubbles' Jaipur.

Yours faithfully,

OLIVER EVERETT

From Mr G. T. St J. Sanders   *5 August 1977*

Sir,

Were not Army nicknames immortalized after the First World War in Sapper's stories? I call to mind Spud Trevor of the Red Hussars, Dog-face (Major Chilham), Pumpkin (twice), Hatchet-face, Tiny Tim (twice), Bimbo Charteris and, of course, Captain Bulldog Drummond.

In Gilbert Frankau's *Royal Regiment* the two principal characters were 'the Hawk' (Colonel Sir Guy Wethered) and 'Rusty' (Major Thomas Rockingham).

Yours faithfully,

G. T. ST. J. SANDERS

155

From Mr Donald Wilson   *5 August 1977*

Sir,

   General Urquhart's nickname was 'Tiger' and General Sir
Ivor Thomas, who commanded respect not unmixed with
apprehension from his staff, was usually known as 'Von
Thoma'. Nothing boyish about either of those two, I do assure
you.

Yours faithfully,

DONALD WILSON

   [But was General Ritter von Thoma, who surrendered to
Montgomery on 4 November 1942, known as Ivor
Thomas?]

From Wing Commander Bentley Beauman   *5 August 1977*

Sir,

   The generals are given these strange nicknames mainly for
security reasons so that the enemy (and most other people)
cannot possibly tell who they really are.

Yours, etc.,

E. BENTLEY BEAUMAN

From Sir Alan Lascelles   *6 August 1977*

Sir,

   Army nicknames were not always affectionate. In 1915, my
divisional commander, who had been christened Richard, was
Dirty Dick to his friends, and Filthy Richard to all the rest of us.

Yours faithfully,

ALAN LASCELLES

From General Sir Evelyn Barker   *8 August 1977*

Sir,

   I have delayed my answer to Mr Bosanquet's letter just to see
what reaction it got. It has certainly produced much information
on the subject but mostly inaccurate. None of the nicknames so
far mentioned had anything to do with a private or public school
background. They all (I'm not sure about Pip Roberts) came
into being during the owner's early days in the Army and
originated from some inherent charcteristic.
   The 60th Rifles when I joined before World War I had a
number of officers with nicknames given them after they joined

such as Loony, Tripe. Oxo, Squeaker, The Oat and many others, and I know the reasons for all of them. Often on marriage their wives inherited their nicknames, and Loony's wife took exception to it. Luckily Tripe never married. As regards my own, I regret to say I have no connexion with Sir John Millais' delightful painting of his grandson (later Admial Sir William James) who naturally was called Bubbles. He died in 1974. For many years it was used as an advertisement for Pear's Soap. Nor in any case has it anything to do with pipe smoking as Mr Blaxland declared (3 August). The reason for it is Top Secret and only divulged to my closest friends. However, I will give Mr Blaxland the clue that it has some connexion with a camel and not with a pipe. Actually I only smoked a pipe during World War II.

Yours faithfully,
EVELYN H. BARKER, 'BUBBLES'

From Mr. L. G. Scales   *9 August 1977*

Sir,

To me, a ranker who served throughout the war at the sharper end of the Army, the chumminess of nicknames seems quite out of keeping with the recognized aloofness of generals. Apart from Wilson's 'Jumbo' and Montgomery's 'Monty', I never got to know what their nicknames were. Moreover, had I been able to get that close and dared to have asked them, my chances of escaping charges for insolence would have been very slender indeed.

Yours truly,
L. G. SCALES

Sartorial

A Matter of Haberdashery

From Sir Frederick Ponsonby　　　　　　*9 August 1929*

[Treasurer to King George V; later the first Baron Sysonby]

Sir,

Whether it is from a lack of imagination on the part of the college authorities, or a paucity of ideas on the part of the haberdashers, the fact remains that the Old Wykehamist tie, which to the best of my belief only sprang into existence of late years, resembles the Guards' tie so closely that expert students of haberdashery unaided by microscopes are unable to detect the difference, especially when it is somewhat faded. The Guards' tie is composed of the Royal colours, and this privilege was no doubt given to them as the Sovereign's Household troops, but it is difficult to understand what justification there is for the Old Wykehamists wearing the Royal colours in a faded condition.

Many years ago it was said that the tie of the Upper Tooting Bicycle Club was practically the same as the Guards' tie. If that club is still in existence the position must indeed be confusing, but perhaps a super-tie might be devised to denote those who, having been educated at Winchester, joined the Household Brigade and have not been subsequently black-balled for the Upper Tooting Bicycle Club.

I am, Sir, your obedient servant,

F. E. G. PONSONBY

[Sir Frederick had spent *his* school days at Eton]

Women Barristers and Wigs

[In 1922 Miss Ivy Williams was the first woman to be called to the Bar]

From Sir Herbert Stephen   *1 April 1922*

[Clerk of Assize for the Northern Circuit 1899–1927]

Sir,

I am glad to say that I do not know the name of any member of the Committee of Judges and Benchers of the Inns of Court whose recommendations concerning the forensic costume of women barristers you publish this morning 31 March. I can therefore criticize their 'wishes' without fear or favour.

I have no fault to find with what they recommend about gowns, bands, or dresses. As to wigs, I think they are hopelessly wrong. A wig is, historically and essentially, not a covering, but a substitute for natural hair. I believe the history of the forensic wig to be in substance as follows. About the period of the Restoration, some of the leaders of fashion in France, for reasons of cleanliness and health, took to shaving their heads. They accordingly wore wigs, which soon became very large and elaborate. The fashion found such favour that for something like a century all gentlemen, when fully dressed, wore wigs. During this time they either shaved their heads, or cropped their hair very close, and probably also wore nightcaps when in bed.

Then the wig gradually disappeared, and the modern method of cutting the hair short, but just long enough to make an efficient covering for the head, was gradually adopted. Judges and barristers followed this practice like other people, but found that, as long as the hair was short, the wig formed a distinctive, dignified, and convenient headdress for use in court. If women barristers are going to cut their hair short as we cut ours, our wigs will suit them well enough, but I do not believe they will do anything of the kind.

The Committee wish that their wigs 'should completely cover the conceal the hair.' Why they entertain this wish I cannot imagine. Our wigs by no means completely cover and conceal our hair. Suppose a woman barrister wears her hair 'bobbed'. Her wig, if it completely conceals her hair, will certainly not be an 'ordinary barrister's wig'. Suppose she has plenty of hair, and wears it coiled in one of the usual ways. She will then want one pattern of wig when fashion places the coils on top of her head, another when they are resting on the back of her neck, and a third when they approach the situation of the old fashioned chignon, high up on the back of the head. Each of the three will impart to the wearer a hydrocephalous, ungainly, and ludicrous appearance.

It must be apparent to every one, except the Committee, that women barristers ought to wear a distinctive, and probably dark-coloured, headdress, in approximately the form of a biretta, a turban, or a toque. I use each of these terms with very great diffidence.

I am, Sir, your obedient servant,
HERBERT STEPHEN

[In 1974 Miss Rose Heilbron, QC, became a Judge of the High Court; Sir Herbert Stephen was by then dead]

A Full Dress Parade

From Mr L. E. Jones   26 March 1931

[Sir Lawrence Evelyn Jones, Bart., was later the author of two enchanting volumes of reminiscence, *An Edwardian Youth* and *Georgian Afternoon*]

Sir,

After to-day's Levée, a brigadier, who is also A.D.C. to the King, was good enough to visit my bed of sickness. In cocked hat, scarlet tunic, and gold lace, he was, like Mrs Ewing's Lancer, 'beautiful to behold.'

Now, if a *blasé* business man of 46 can be gladdened and enlivened by the aspect of one brigadier, what might not be the happy effect if a *posse* of admirals and generals should, after leaving a levée, pass through the wards of some of our children's hospitals? Even if only one man in 10 will be unselfconscious enough to do it without a painful effort, surely the other nine, fortified by their medals, will be gallant enough to make that effort? No speeches would be expected — but they must be prepared to turn themselves round and, if required, to draw their swords. It might help to break the ice if the hospitals would take the initiative by extending an invitation.

I am, Sir, your obedient servant,
L. E. JONES

Suits for King Zog

From Major J. H. Churchyard   *15 February 1946*

Sir,

In your issue of today (February 13) you report on page 4 the departure for Egypt of King Zog from this country, with the remark that 'the King had 30 suits specially made for him in England'.

How did he get his coupons?

I am, Sir, yours, etc.,

J. H. CHURCHYARD, Major (retd.)

[On 18 February Sir Stafford Cripps, President of the Board of Trade, informed the House of Commons that since 1 June 1941 King Zog of Albania had been in receipt of 242 clothing coupons, plus a special supplementary allowance of 100 in 1942, and an extra 80 on leaving for Egypt. Total 422. The coupons needed for 30 suits depended on whether King Zog wore a waistcoat; if he did, then 780 coupons was the number, if not 630.

Members then converted King Zoe's Egyptian wardrobe into clothing coupons: one nightshirt 8, one pair of spats 3, etc. The matter was eventually cleared up by one of the King's aides; His Majesty had placed an order for suitings for himself and family to be sent to Egypt as export goods, these requiring no coupons]

New Gothic Age

From Dr Carl Bode   *2 February 1970*

[Later Professor of English in the University of Maryland]

Sir,

As the sainted McLuhan has said more than once, No fish ever defined water. So I hope I may be allowed as an American to define London, on the basis of a week's return visit, to Londoners. It is clear to me that London is in the middle of a New Gothic Age.

The clothes, especially of the young, are superbly weird; their principle is the principle of exaggeration. The mini-skirts are heaven-pointing. The maxi-skirts drag the ground. The male's

162

once sedate suit has been transformed into a thing of peaks, ridges, rough textures, and flying buttresses. I saw one young man march through Grosvenor Square in blue, belled trousers, a sleeveless lambswool jacket, a kerchief around his waist, and on his head a hat saved from some Victorian funeral. His face of course was furred.

The manners, again especially of the young, have grown Gothic also. They are elaborate in their rituals of touching, no longer as direct as when they used to clutch one another promptly. Even their speech now seems to me to have a Gothic way. Either they talk in high, astounding terms — I have heard them in Kings Road — or they speak obliquely. Then they use the passive more than the active mode. It reminds me of the speech of some of the black American militants, not the Panther type but the soul brother. Similarly: 'Turn me on', they say; 'Light my fire', they sing.

Lastly, the tone is Gothic. Once more, it is found in its extreme in the young but is manifest even in the old: note the lengthening sideburns of the City clerk. It is a tone of certainty; it is what we call in America the moral arrogance of the young. They stand convinced that their religion is the true one. They will no more listen to the pronouncements of their elders than would the medieval workman, chipping stone for a cathedral, to the seductions of the Arian.

Is London, today's London, Gothic in everything? Of course not. I do not want to force my thesis. I have only to scan, for example, the scores of new office buildings. In their bare brutality they seem even starker, even worse, then the latest skyscrapers in New York.

Anyway, I hail the New Gothic Age. May it be long and full, leaving many monuments behind it.

And I wonder what those monuments will be?

CARL BODE

Long-Haired Boys

From Sir Bernard Miles 10 February 1971

[life peer 1979]

Sir,
    Hearing on the 'Today' programme on 5 February that Mr Temple, Headmaster of Bede School, Sunderland, has banned

one of his pupils, Paul Kucharski, from future attendance until he gets his hair cut, I was reminded of the many representations of Our Lord Jesus Christ in European painting – Giotto, Piero della Francesa, Michelangelo, Leonardo, Titian, Rembrandt, the Van Eyck Bros., et alia, a First Division team if ever there was one – all of whom portray Him with shoulder-length hair.

Where does Mr Temple stand doctrinally? And where does the Local Education Authority stand?

Yours,
BERNARD MILES

PS. I believe there are also grave doubts about the Venerable Bede.

From Mr T. Y. Darling   *17 February 1971*

Sir,

If Sir Bernard Miles will refer to I Corinthians xi, 14, he will see that St. Paul asks: 'Doth not even nature itself teach you that, if a man have long hair, it is a shame unto him?'

It has always seemed to me unlikely that St Paul would have made this remark if Christ himself wore long hair. Is it not far more likely that the great painters, hundreds of years later, were quite mistaken on this point and were merely reflecting the fashion of their own times?

Yours truly,
T. Y. DARLING

Education

Stopwatch Dons

From Professor G. R. Elton   *25 November 1969*

[Professor of English Constitutional History, University
Cambridge, 1967–83; now Regius Professor fo Modern
History]

Sir,—Now and again something happens to restore one's faith
in the essential madness of bureaucratic man. Next week, some
thousands of university teachers are going to keep a daily
record, half-hour by half-hour, of all their activities from 8 a.m.
to midnight, from Monday till Sunday. For each half-hour they
have to determine their "major use of time" under seven heads,
one of them charmingly called "unallocable internal time".

With the diary comes a smug and ill-written letter to let one
that this "exercise" is to be repeated twice more this year and
hinting that it may become a regular part of academic life. The
letter is signed "Derman Christopherson, Chairman, Committee
of Vice-Chancellors and Principals", but since I cannot suppose
that any real person wrote it I take this figure to be one of the
happier inventions of some anonymous Kafka.

What are we to make of this? From one point of view, it is
a humiliating imposition on intelligent and busy men. It is
justified by some familiar jargon about a "cost attribution
exercise" apparently demanded by that near-defunct body, the
University Grants Committee, and it takes a little thought to
realise that the supposed reason for the enterprise is itself
entirely without meaning in this light, the only proper reaction,
surely, is to march upon the originators of the scheme and make
them eat their ridiculous pamphlets—the only way of ensuring
that the results of the enquiry will be properly digested.

Alternatively, this is high comedy, and one hopes that all
may join in. The thought of the fictitious Mr.Christopherson
allocking his internal time has a great deal of pleasure in it.The
boss-man should not be prevented from contributing his mite,
and I look forward to the record of Mr Edward Short's seven

days. Nor, at the other end of the scale, should the danger of leaving out the students be overlooked: if ever there was a thing in which to participate, this is it. There will be banners and slogans.

Since nothing whatsoever can make this stupidity meaningful, the game can by played in all sorts of exciting ways, by individuals or teams. For myself. I should award victory to the man who gets most ticks in the column headed "private and free time" a category which draws the covering letter's manifest disapproval. This, you will be pleased to hear, includes sleeping and eating, as well as "family contacts", being a churchwarden (truthfully!) and "non-productive travel time to and from your normal place of work". Also I suppose, writing to *The Times*.

Yours faithfully,

G. R. ELTON

From Mr P. G. Henderson   *2 December 1969*

Sir,

Dons in doubt as to how to answer their questionnaire may be helped by the reply reputed to have been given by the late Professor Dawkins, Bywater and Sotheby Professor of Byzantine and Modern Greek Language and Literature in the University of Oxford, to a former inquisition as to how he spent his time: 'I give an annual lecture – but not every year, mark you!

Yours faithfully,

P. G. HENDERSON

['Mr' Christopherson had already been knighted, Professor Elton receiving that honour in 1986. Mr Edward Short – Secretary of State for Education and Science, 1968–70 – became Baron Glenamara in 1970]

Selection Principle in Education

[Mr Reginald Prentice was a Labour MP 1957–77, Secretary of State for Education and Science 1974–5, thereafter a Conservative MP]

From Miss Iris Murdoch   *19 April 1974*

[DBE 1987]

Sir,

I hear on my radio Mr Reg Prentice, of the party which I support, saying to a gathering on education the following: 'The eleven plus must go, so must selection at twelve plus, at sixteen plus, and any other age.' What can this mean? How are universities to continue? Are we to have engineers without selection of those who understand mathematics, linguists without selection of those who understand grammar?

To many teachers such declarations of policy must seem obscure and astonishing, and to imply the adoption of some quite new philosophy of education which has not, so far as I know, been in this context discussed. It is certainly odd that the Labour Party should wish to promote a process of natural unplanned sorting which will favour the children of the rich and educated people, leaving other children at a disadvantage.

I thought socialism was concerned with the removal of unfair disadvantages. Surely what we need is a careful reconsideration of how to select, not the radical and dangerous abandonment of the principle of selection.

Yours faithfully,
IRIS MURDOCH

West Indians in School

From Mrs S.Best   *27 June 1981*

Sir,

West Indian kids fail to do well in school. First, lack of discipline all over the place; at an early age they are all taught in school that parents are too strict; they had Victorian upbringing (although Victoria died 22/1/01); parents do not understand them.

The biggest culprits are the welfare officers who leave little white babies to be battered to death but can't wait to take black kids from their home to put them with nice white aunties and uncles, where they are allowed to run wild in most cases. They can't relate to new environment, but worst of all there comes 18th birthday, no more artificial love and affection, so they are thrown in at the deep end. The few misfits glamorize their position.

So parents fail to do their duties for fear of their children being taken away from them. So the young darlings play up and blackmail parents into giving in (if not they'll tell Miss or Sir and they'll call the Welfare) or run away and lie on parents and the court will be told Topsy or Sambo needs love and affection as the blacks are too illiterate to provide same.

Leave blacks alone and children will come OK. Let them realize there is nowhere to run. They must have discipline.

As for Asians, most were not born here. Wait for the next generation before you pass judgement. Our kids have the same 4lbs of grey and white matter in the hollow of the skull so let them use it. The whites are afraid, they also look towards USA too much. A lot of the teachers do not seem to know much themselves.

Respectfully yours,

S. BEST

(West Indian parent)

Manners and Men

[On 19 May 1982 The Queen visited Winchester College on the 600th anniversary of its foundation. The next day a *Times* third leader discussed 'The Shameless Elite', and related the story of a lady entering a room which contained a Wykehamist, an Etonian and a Harrovian — the Wykehamist calls for someone to fetch a chair, the Etonian fetches one, and the Harrovian sits on it himself]

From Sir Charles Gordon   *22 May 1982*

[Clerk of the House of Commons]

Sir,

As a Wykehamist, I am happy to own a number of the soft impeachments contained in your leading article; but I cannot refrain from protesting at your shameless reconstruction of the well-known story of the chair.

It was, of course, the imperious and patrician Etonian who commanded that a chair be brought for the fainting lady; it was the unobtrusive, efficient and — dare I say it? — well-mannered Wykehamist who provided it.

Yours faithfully,

CHARLES GORDON

From Mr F. R. Salmon   *22 May 1982*

Sir,

The Wykehamist did not 'call our for somebody to fetch a chair'; he asked the lady, very politely, whether she would like one. That, surely, makes all the difference.

Yours politely,
F. R. SALMON

From Mr Thomas Morton   *25 May 1982*

Sir,

As a past inhabitant of both Harrow and New College (and therefore strictly neutral) I cannot allow the inaccurate story in the third leader today to go unchallenged).(Is your leader writer perhaps an Old Etonian?)

In the correct version an attractive girl enters a room containing an Etonian, a Wykehamist (of the junior foundation) and an Harrovian. The Etonian says, 'This lady needs a chair', the Wykehamist fetches one and the Harrovian sits down with the girl on his knee.

Yours faithfully,
TOM MORTON

From Mr T. J. Allison   *26 May 1982*

Sir,

Your editorial today has got it wrong! It is Etonians who notice that ladies have no chairs, Wykehamists who fetch them. That is why the latter make good civil servants: they assess and follow up creative thinking.

Yours very truly,
T. J. ALLISON

From Mrs Peter Spring   *26 May 1982*

Sir,

Am I, at 48, yesterday's woman? I am not surprised when any man, Wykehamist or not, opens a door for me (but then, my school motto was *In Fide Vade)*. Certainly I thank him.

Yours in courtesy,
CLARE SPRING

From Mr James Palmes   *27 May 1982*

Sir,

Some fifteen years ago I was interviewing candidates for a vacant post. One as a Wykehamist, who made a poor impression on me and my colleagues. He seemed to us obtuse and conceited. Anyway, he did not get the job.

A few days later I received a letter from the frustrated applicant, abusing me roundly for turning him down, pointing out that it was bad manners to reject Wykehamists and that I must mend my ways.

Yours faithfully,
JAMES PALMES

From Mr James Johnstone   *27 May 1982*

Sir,

The gentlemen's actions indicate that the attractive young lady can only have been a Marlburienne — anyone else would have been left standing.

Yours faithfully,
JAMES JOHNSTONE

From Professor P. V. Danckwerts, GC   *28 May 1982*

[Professor of Chemical Engineering (Shell), University of Cambridge]

Sir,

I suggest that the comparison between Wykehamists and Etonians should be extended beyond the question of manners to that of pragmatism.

During the first Atoms for Peace conference at Geneva in 1955 the Mr Big of the international energy scene was confined, raging, to his room by a cold. He instructed me and a fellow delegate to go to a pharmacy and get him some black currant syrup. My colleague (an Etonian) demanded 'courants noirs'. I (a Wykehamist) waited for the pharmacist to ask us (in English) what we required.

Yours, etc.,
PETER DANCKWERTS

. . . and Women

From Miss Imogen Clout   *29 May 1982*

Sir,

The tale of the Wykehamist and the chair calls to mind the anecdote illustrating the distinguishing chraacteristics of the five Oxford 'women's' colleges.

Five girls, one from each college, meet. Their conversation concerns a young man of their mutual acquaintance:

The girl from Lady Margaret Hall asks, 'Who are his parents?'

The girl from Somerville asks, 'What is he reading?'

The girl from St Hugh's asks, 'What sport does he play?'

The girl from St Hilda's ask, 'Who is he going out with?'

And the girl from St Anne's says 'Me'.

At least, that is the version which I was told, when I was at St Anne's.

Yours faithfully,

IMOGEN CLOUT

From Mrs Hal Wilson   *4 June 1982*

Sir,

I too remember the story of the five Oxford women undergraduates discussing the young man.

I am sorry to have to tell Miss Clout, however, that in my day at Lady Margaret Hall the young lady from St Anne's was reputed simply to have said '*Where is he?*'

Yours faithfully,

GILLIAN WILSON

From Mr Max Taylor   *31 May 1982*

Sir,

In my untypical experience, the Cheltenham girl says, 'Gosh you look pale', the Wycombe Abbey girl says, I'll get you a glass of champagne', and the Heathfield girl drinks it.

Yours faithlessly,

MAX TAYLOR

[While Mr Taylor pays?]

171

From Mr Paul Stewart   *2 June 1982*

Sir,

The story as I understood it was that a pretty girl came into a room containing three ex-public schoolboys who provided her with a chair to sit upon and then proceeded to argue amongst themselves as to which of them should receive the credit for this deed.

The girl stifled a yawn, made her excuses and left the room.

Yours faithfully,

PAUL STEWART

From Mr Nicholas Freeland   *2 June 1982*

Sir,

I seem to remember that at Charterhouse we had enough chairs for everyone to be able to sit down.

Yours faithfully,

NICHOLAS FREELAND

From Dr John Herbert   *2 June 1982*

Sir,

The young gentlemen of Harrow, Eton and Winchester may indulge themselves in idle banter about who does what with a chair, but their fathers have arranged matters so that old Lliswerrians can no longer hew the wood to make the chair.

Yours faithfully,

JOHN HERBERT

From Mrs Douce Forty   *8 June 1982*

Sir,

At St Hugh's in 1947, I was told: The young man stood outside the college.

Somerville said: 'What does he read?'

L.M.H. said: 'Who are his people?'

St Hilda's said: 'What does he play?'

St Hugh's said: 'Bring him up.'

Yours nostaligically,

DOUCE FORTY

Sir,

In the version which reached us at St Hugh's, the St Anne's girl concludes the conversation with: 'He's my husband, actually.'

Yours faithfully,
JENNIFER ORCHARD

From Mr P. A. Gascoin   *8 June 1982*

Sir,

Had the 'girl from St Hilda's' who asked 'Who is he going out with?' been a girl from University College, London, she would have asked 'With whom is he going out?'

Yours faithfully,
P. A. GASCOIN

Philistines at the classroom door

From Professor Sir Geoffrey Elton, FBA   *21 August 1986*

Sir,

It was good to see Shirley Letwin (feature, August 14) demolish the fashion which puts the blame for this country's poor economic performance on a higher education which happens to be one of the country's widely respected glories. Like so many general convictions, this is ignorant parrot talk.

To me, differences in systems seem of minimal importance, compared with differences between people. Education at schools and universities is an acquired taste, not really natural to mankind, and everywhere those who never really acquire it greatly outnumber the rest.

The misconceptions that Mrs Letwin attacked arise, I think, out of a difference in national habits. Englishmen prefer to think that everything is wrong at home and perfect abroad, while most continental Europeans tend to proclaim the opposite.

However, there are things wrong with school education in Britain, and (apart from much too early specialization) the faults arise in the main from recent 'reforms'. The introduction of the comprehensives, itself the result of dubious educational theories, destroyed not only the mind-stretching skills of the grammar schools but also the technical schools, which quite rightly provided the vocational training now so much talked of.

Nowadays our schools, often driven on by the ignorance of parents, train highly skilled examinees but educate only by accident; and the universities are, at a grave risk, to be made to follow suit.

Nor do examinations – part of the system and cocooned within it – tell us anything about the consequences of such things as pupil-centred teaching, the play theory of education, the death of Latin, or premature involvement in economies and sociology.

Ten years ago the children of visiting American scholars always had considerable difficulty in catching up with their English contemporaries at school. Nowadays, they regularly report that they are wasting their time there. How much longer before the rule of the philistine will have the same effect on our universities?

Let us train teachers as teachers and not as local council employees. This might involve ablishing unionism, but it certainly might start by ensuring that unions are led by people who have had recent personal experiences of teaching.

Let us do away with educational psychology. Let us reform curricula so as to produce trained minds rather than conditioned citizens willing to admire the comprehensive system.

Let us abolish most examinations, especially the A level as at present constructed. And let us try to create a DES which values education more highly than administration.

Yours faithfully,
GEOFFREY ELTON

This Sporting Life

Spirit of the Olympics

[Skeleton Bob N Bibbia (Italy), aggregate 5 min. 23.2 sec, – 1; J Heaton (USA), 5 min 24.6 sec, – 2; J. Crammond (GB), 5 min 25.1 sec, – 3; W Martin (USA) 5 min 28 sec, – 4; G Kaegi (Switzerland) 5 min 29.9 sec, – 5; R Bott (GB), 5 min 30.7 sec, – 6.

The Times, 6 February 1948]

From Mr John Crammond   *6 January 1956*

Sir,

In 1948, in my forty-second year, I won a bronze medal in the Winter Olympic Games. The discipline in which I had the honour to participate was a two-day event, on the first day I was placed first but, on the first and second days' results, my final position was third.

I was entirely delighted but not for long. On my return to this country three people referred to the matter. The first was a very young lady and a close relation, who, throwing her arms around my neck and bursting into tears, said: 'Only third!' The second, an eminent accountant, said: 'It is not clear to me whether we are to commiserate or congratulate you.' The third, the editor of a Sunday newspaper, asked, 'Why didn't you win?' Therefore, until this moment, I have been careful never to refer in public to 'this dark page in my career,' although I find that privately I am still entirely delighted.

I do now mention these matters because I think that the attitude revealed by your correspondents on this subject can only be damaging to our athletes' morale and obstructive to the spirit of the Games. I suggest that the importance of coming first is an obsession of professionals and the very young. Baron de Coubertin's dictum is the correct one.

There must be tens of thousands of athletes who enter and re-enter their fields of play well content in the knowledge that among the other hundreds and thousands playing they, the chosen 10,000 are likely to come in leggy last. Nor are they

175

thereby put off − on the contrary, they welcome the challenge to renew their style and bearing.

I submit, and this submission is based on the observation over a period of 30 years of many hundreds of international events on the Cresta Run, that national prestige is advanced by good style and bearing far more than by a total of points scored.If some competitors are playing hookey with the amateur status clause and ours are not, then two things can happen − our athletes can (1) enjoy the fun of beating the sponsored or (2) reinforce our national reputation of being good losers.

If your correspondents are correct we have to choose between (*a*) sponsoring our athletes or (*b*) denying the truth of (2) above. I beg to disagree. There is a third course.We can send our athletes off to the Games telling them to have fun and leave the rest to them.

I am, Sir your obedient servant,

JOHN G. CRAMMOND

A Trinity Jump

From the Master of Trinity College, Cambridge

16 March 1944

Sir,

On a recent visit to Cambridge, General Montgomery, on entering the Great Court at this college, pointed to the hall steps and said to me, 'Those were the steps my father jumped up at one bound.' The general's father, Henry Hutchinson Montgomery, afterwards Bishop, was an undergraduate at Trinity from 1866 to 1870. He came here from Dr Butler's Harrow with a great reputation as a runner and jumper.

The feat of leaping up the eight steps at a single bound has often been attempted by athletes, hurdlers, and jumpers without success. The only person to succeed of whom I know was the gigantic Whewell, when he was Master of the college; he clapped his mortar-board firmly on his head, picked up his gown with one hand, and leapt. The late Sir George Young, Bt., saw him do this, and many years later told his son Geoffrey Winthrop Young, who allows me to make this statement. I have heard that the feat was accomplished once or twice in this century: once, I was told, an American succeeded, but I have not the facts or names. It has certainly been done very seldom.

Now we have a fully authenticated case of which I had not

heard. Bishop Montgomery himself told his son the general, and the story was often told in the family. The general has asked me to send the facts to you in the hope that publication may elicit further facts.

Yours, &c.,
G. M. Trevelyan

[As William Whewell was born in may 1894, and Sir George Young went up to Trinity in 1855, Whewell was aged 61 at the time of his jump.

Correspondents seeking to champion the Cam then turned their attention to less violent activities]

In Praise of Archery

From Captain Clive Temperley   7 February 1938

Sir,

In your columns to-day you refer to the growth of popularity of archery in America, where they are said to be 1,500,000 archers. The Americans are not nit-wits and there must be a reason for this. There is! The long bow is an intriguing and temperamental weapon – far more intriguing and temperamental than any golf club in the bag. Every bow and every arrow has individual characteristics to be mastered. Part by a hairbreadth from the correct shooting style and the shot is affected: A beginner who once takes a bow in his hand is lost. He may score for his first round a few dozen points where an expert will score 500 or 600. He has a vast field ahead of him for improvement, experiment, and emulation.

And exercise? The principal archery round is the York round, in which 144 arrows are shot at distances varying from 60 yards to 100 yards. Drawing a bow is a strenuous affair, so that only three arrows are shot at a time and after each three a trip to the target is necessary. Consequently the York round takes anything up to three hours to complete – all exercise and walking, the latter some 2½ miles. The bow is drawn 144 times and each time a force corresponding to a weight of perhaps 50lb. has to be borne by the arms and shoulders and held while the aim is completed. This is roughly the same as lifting three tons is packing cases from the floor to a shelf 2ft. high.

During the summer what can a business man of the City of London do between leaving the office and sitting down to dinner? Golf courses are too far away; tennis is too strenuous. Archery provides an ideal solution. He need not change his clothes. He can start as late and stop as early as he wishes. He is in the open, in pleasant company, and taking part in a sport which is good for his health and his soul and one, moreover, which has a longer and more world-wide history than all the rest put together – a history measured not to decades nor in centuries, but in millennia.

Yours faithfully,
CLIVE TEMPERLEY

An Effeminate Game?

From Mr B. J. T. Bosanquet   *4 June 1914*

[who, after years of practice, shocked the game of cricket by bowling the 'googly' – an off-break achieved with a leg-break action. Austrialians, whose Test side Bosanquet defeated with his discovery at Sydney in 1904, still pay homage by calling the googly the 'bosie']

Sir,

The sooner it is realized that golf is merely a pleasant recreation and inducement to indolent people to take exercise the better. Golf has none of the essentials of a great game. It destroys rather than builds up character, and tends to selfishness and ill-temper. It calls for none of the essential qualities of a great game, such as pluck, endurance, physical fitness and agility, unselfishness and *esprit de corps*, or quickness of eye and judgement. Games which develop these qualities are of assitance for the more serious pursuits of life.

Golf is of the greatest value to thousands, and brings health and relief from the cares of business to many, but to contend that a game is great which is readily mastered by every youth who goes into a professional's shop as assistant (generally a scratch player within a year!) and by the majority of caddies is childish. No one is more grateful to golf for many a pleasant day's exercise than the writer, or more fully recognized the difficulties and charm of the game, but there is charm and there are difficulties in (for instance) lawn tennis and croquet.It certainly seems to the writer that no game which does not demand a certain amount of pluck and physical courage from its exponents can be called great, or can be really beneficial to boys or men.

The present tendency is undoubtedly towards the more effeminate and less exacting pastimes, but the day that sees the youth of England given up to lawn tennis and golf in preference to the old manly games (cricket, football, polo, &c.) will be of sad omen for the future of the race.

I am, yours, &c.,

B. J. T. BOSANQUET

[Golf sometimes demands physical courage from spectators, witness the occasion when Mr Spiro Agnew (once Vice-President of the United States) aimed to the north and wounded those standing to his east]

'To Caddie'

From Sir Berkeley Moynihan   *6 February 1929*

[later the first Baron Moynihan who, when not playing golf badly, was numbered among the greatest of surgeons]

Sir,

This will never do! For five days in the week we avail ourselves of *The Times* as it so competently deals with the less important affairs of life: politics, domestic or foreign; the imminence, hopes, fears of a General Election; the arrivals or departures of great people; the steady depreciation of our scanty investments; another century or two by Hobbs; or a stupendous break by Smith. But on the sixth day *The Times* is exalted in our eyes; for then your 'Gold Correspondent,' in a column of wisdom, humour, and unmatched literary charm, deals with the one real thing in life.

This week for the first time he has deeply shocked and disappointed us all. I am but a 'rabbit.' I confess to a handicap of 24 (at times) and a compassionate heart (always). I cannot bear to see a fellow creature suffer, and it is for this reason among others that I rarely find myself able to inflict upon an opponent the anguish of defeat. Today I suffer for a whole world of caddies, wounded in the house of their friend. They learn in a message almost sounding a note of disdain that the verb which signifies their full activity is 'to carry.'

By what restriction of mind can anyone suppose that this is adequate? Does not a caddy in truth take charge of our lives and

179

control all our thoughts and actions while we are in his august company? He it is who comforts us in our time of sorrow, encourages us in moments of doubt, inspires us to that little added effort which, when crowned with rare success, brings a joy that nothing else can offer. It is he who with majestic gravity and indisputable authority hands to us the club that he thinks most fitted to our meagre power, as though it were not a rude mattack but indeed a royal sceptre. It is he who counsels us in time of crisis, urging that we should 'run her up' or 'loft her,' or 'take a line a wee bit to the left, with a shade of slice.' Does he not enjoin us with magisterial right not to raise our head? Are we not most properly rebuked when our left knee sags, or our right elbow soars; or our body is too rigid while our eye goes roaming? Does he not count our strokes with remorseless and unpardonable accuracy, keeping all the while a watchful eye upon our opponent's score? Does he not speak of 'our' honour, and is not his exhortation that 'we' must win this hole? Does he not make us feel that some share of happiness, or of misery, will be his in our moment of victory or defeat? Does he not with most subtle but delicious flattery coax us to a beief that if only wehad time to play a 'bit oftener' we should reach the dignity of a single-figure handicap? Does he not hold aloft the flag as though it were indeed our standard, inspiring a reluctant ball at last to gain the hole? Does such a man do nothing but 'carry' for us? Of course, he does infinitely more. He 'caddies' for us, bless him.

Yours,
BERKELEY MOYNIHAN

[Of the three great stylists referred to, Bernard Darwin served *The Times* for forty-six years and was the most illustrious of writers on golf. The Smith in question, Willie from Darlington, later had the sad privilege (with Joe Davis) of ringing down the curtain as Thurston's before that billiards hall was knocked down in 1955 to make way for some motoring organization's offices]

Lawn Tennis Scoring

[On 25 June 1953, in the third round of the Gentlemen's Singles Championship at Wimbledon, Jaroslav Drobny (an exiled Czech now designated as Egyptian) beat Budge Patty (United States) 8–6, 16–18, 3–6, 8–6, 12–10]

Sir,

Many of those privileged to watch the historic and marathon encounter between Drobny and Patty on the Centre Court on Thursday (the writer saw brief but significant parts only) must have wondered whether our system of scoring in lawn tennis needs revision. No one who has studied the system will deny that it has great merit, but its limitations must be admitted in its lack of control of a match's duration. The writer may perhaps be pardoned a personal reminiscence, as a good many years ago he played in a county match—one of his opponents, he recalls, being our Davis Cup captain, Dr. J. C. Gregory—in which the first set of the day's play ran to 22—20, thereby disrupting the day's programme for the two teams.

The main features of lawn tennis scoring must be preserved. The rapid changes of fortune, the recovery from "set-point against," still more from "match-point against," and the emphasis on certain vital points are attractions the game cannot afford to lose. It is true that the system permits a loser to win more games, and perhaps many more points, than the winner; but that is a doubtful disadvantage. It serves to emphasize the importance of the vital points in the match on which a player must concentrate and which be must secure at all costs, by virtue of superior temperament and ability.

But it is a sad day for the game when the true rewards are denied through sheer physical exhaustion. This is in no way suggesting that this great Drobny-Patty match met this fate; but we are getting perilously near the limit when two men can be called upon to sustain the tension of a first-class singles match without remission for four and a quarter hours. There are other objections to this unknown time element, but they pale into insignificance before the serious question: Are we putting too high a premium on youth and fitness?

The remedy is not easy if we are to preserve the basic features of the system. But the writer suggests that all sets, other than the final set, be "short"—*i.e.*, terminating, if necessary, at 6—5—the final set being fought out, as at present, to a two-game lead. I must not trespass further on your space, but briefly the main effect of the proposed change, bearing in mind the emphasis to-day on service dominance, is that there must be at least one break through service for the match, whereas at present there must be at least one break through service for each set.

Yours faithfully,

A. P. MAITLAND HAWES

[*The Times* lacked space, and probably inclination, to print in full the name of Admiral Hon. Sir Reginald Aylmer Ranfurly Plunkett Ernle-Erle-Drax]

From Admiral Sir Reginald Ernle-Erle-Drax   *9 July 1953*

Sir,

Timeless Test matches proved a failure: there is even more to be said against timeless lawn tennis. Drobny recently took four and a quarter hours for 93 games, but it is not impossible, at present, for any one game to last an hour. Thus two robot men might play for 90 hours. It is well to test endurance and stamina, but this should not be overdone, as now, to the extent of crippling a player for future contests. Even heavy-weight boxers are limited to 15 rounds, with an endurance period of about an hour.

I have long played at home a local rule, "no double figures"—*i.e.*, at nine-all we play "sudden death" or best of three. This rule could equally be applied at six-all or seven-all, though any change should leave the last set to be played as at present. Aiming to achieve a reasonable time limit will ensure that there can never be comparison with the ghastly spectacle of a marathon dancing contest. Let us therefore make our tennis slightly less gladiatorial.

Yours faithfully,
R. P. Ernle-Erle-Drax

[Some statistics are called for:

1 Cricket's timeless Test matches were not a failure; of 60 such games played in Australia, 1900–1937, only seven extended beyond the 30 hours now made available.

2 The Drobny-Patty marathon of 1953 was beaten by the first round match in 1969 when two Americans, Richard Gonzales and Charles Pasarell, battled for 112 games – the score to Gonzales 22–24, 1–6, 16–14, 6–3, 11–9.

3 Wimbledon adopted Admiral Ernle-Erle-Drax's tie-break in 1971 (at 8 games-all), amended to 6 games-all in 1979]

The Test Match of 1882

[When, at the Oval on 29 August, England lost to Australia by 7 runs – her first defeat at home. The famous 'Ashes' obituary then appeared in the *Sporting Times*]

From Mr N. L. Jackson   *30 July 1931*

['Pa' Jackson, founder of the Corinthians FC]

Sir,

As a member of the Surrey Club, I was present at the famous Test match at the Oval when the English team had its first defeat. I had a chat with C. T. Studd in the dressing room shortly before he went in, when wickets were falling remarkably fast, and 'C. T.', like most of the other late players, was horribly nervous. I remember remarking at the time that most of them were out before they went in. With 'C. T.', however, it is probable that he would have quickly recovered after a few balls and would have averted defeat. He was a fine fellow, mentally and physically. He called on me only two days before he left on his first missionary journey to China and gave me advice, which I much regret I did not follow.

In my long connexion with sport I do not remember anything so extraordinary as the finish of that match. I was in the secretary's office at the Oval when the last English wicket fell. I saw Bonnor throw his 'pork-pie' cap (as were then worn) higher into the air than I thought was possible. On turning round I saw Charlie Alcock (the Surrey Club secretary) sitting inside the iron safe with his head in his hands and apparently oblivious of everything, while one of the committee, Dr Blades, was so overcome that he almost collapsed. Only during the Great War have I ever seen a company so absolutely miserable as that assembled in the secretary's office on that occasion.

To my mind 'Monkey' Hornby lost that match by calling 'W. G.' for a short run, thus getting him run out, when these two looked like getting all the runs required to win. Hornby was an adept at these short runs, but 'W. G.' was a heavy man and could not get into his stride as quickly as the smaller man could.

Yours truly,

N. LANE JACKSON

[W. G. Grace was not run out but caught, long after Hornby's dismissal. And why were Studd and others horribly nervous? Because at the close of Australia's second innings one George Eber Spendlove had suffered a haemorrhage, Dr Grace taking charge: 'Take him to the room above the pavilion.' There the dead man lay as England strove to make 85. Studd asked to be sent in late; he was, at No 10, and did not receive a ball.

F. R. Spofforth, wishing to change ends, bowled both the 15th and 16th overs *legitimately* in England's second innings. LAW VIII (amended in 1889) – 'No bowler shall bowl more than two overs in succession']

'Body-Line Bowling'

[D. G. Bradman was the cause; in 26 innings for Australia prior to 1932–33 he had averaged 112. England's captain, D. R. Jardine, ordered Larwood and Voce to direct their very fast and often short-pitched deliveries in a line with the batsman's body.

'Leg-theory' bowling – used by such players as C. F. Root – consisted of in-swingers which produced snicks or glances to a battery of short-legs. This made for dull, though hardly dangerous cricket]

From Mr Leonard Crawley   *27 January 1933*

[who played for Cambridge University, Essex and the Gentlemen]

Sir,

May I trespass on your valuable space to discuss the article which appeared in your pages on 19 January with regard to the protest recently received by the MCC from the Australian Board of Control against the employment of a 'leg-theory' in cricket?

In the first place, though Macdonald and Gregory did undoubtedly send down an occasional ball at the batsman's body, they cannot be said, anyway while playing for Australia, to have employed a 'leg-theory,' in that such balls were exceptional and were bowled to a field with only two men on the leg-side. It is surely unfair to compare these tactics with the policy of delivering six such balls per over to a field so set as to penalize a batsman who is defending not his wicket, but his head.

Your correspondent further suggests that 'so long as a "shock" bowler is not deliberately bumping down short-pitched balls or purposely aiming at the batsman, his bowling is perfectly fair.' Granted: but when six such balls are bowled in each over, either the action is a deliberate one, or else, if the bowler is continuously doing it accidentally, he is a rank bad bowler. You cannot have it both ways. The last thing I wish to do is to bring a charge of malice-aforethought towards the batsman against either our captain or the bowlers he employs. But that our 'shock' bowlers bowl deliberately at the batsman's body cannot honestly be denied.

The real objection of the Australians, your correspondent alleges, is to the 'array of leg-fielders.' I submit that it is to this, in conjunction with body-line bowling, that the Australians, very rightly, in my view, take exception. As long as these tactics are allowed, the batsman will be frightened into giving up his wicket, and if Bradman cannot survive them, I am satisfied that not one of the great players of the past could have fared any better.

It would obviously be impossible for even so august a body as the MCC to dictate to a captain as to how he should place his field. But a short-pitched ball is a bad ball, and one which, without the remotest chance of striking the wicket, stands a considerable chance of doing the batsman bodily harm. And it seems to me that the very least that can be done in the best interests of the game is to empower the umpire to 'no-ball' a bowler for pitching his deliveries short. But to my mind the whole question demands consideration from an entirely different angle. Your correspondent urges the point that 'Cricket is not played with a soft ball, and that a fast ball which hits a batsman on the body is bound to hurt.' Rugby football is also considered by some a fair training ground for manly and courageous virtues. And yet in the event of a player wilfully hacking, tripping, or striking another player, instead of going for the ball, the referee is required by the Laws of Rugby Football to order the offender off the field on the second offence. It seems to me that the analogy between this and the policy of deliberately bowling at a portion of the batsman's body which is not obscuring the wicket is a fairly close one; and the penalty is as well deserved in the one case as the other. In either game enough knocks are given and received in the ordinary course of events to satisfy the most bloodthirsty fire-eater among the spectators. But I would like to see some of the most eloquent supporters of the 'leg-theory' step into the arena against a bowler of Larwood's pace and face it for themselves.

Yours, &c.,

LEONARD CRAWLEY

[England won the series, during which no one was killed, Bradman averaging only 56. Eventually intimidatory bowling was prohibited under Law 46. The side led by Jardine, an Old Wykehamist, included a third and highly successful fast bowler, G. O. Allen, who refused to employ 'body-line'. Allen was an Old Etonian. After playing a further 46 innings for Australia with an average of 100, Bradman was knighted]

Meredith at Melbourne

From Mr Charles Morgan   *8 January 1947*

[Novelist, drama critic of *The Times* 1926–39; his review of *The Old Ladies* (4 April 1935) was acclaimed by James Agate as the finest piece of dramatic criticism since C. E. Montague]

Sir,
    May a faithful reader of cricket reports be allowed to thank you and your Special Correspondent at Melbourne for the best he has read these 40 years? Who shall dare to say now George Meredith is forgotten?

'Naturally the English players were now men uplifted: mercury bubbled in the blood. . . The issue was here a very ache of intensity; the arms of the deities above were stretching far beyond their reach as Miller went out of his ground to Wright. . .'

And might not this be a fitting end to *The Tragic Comedians*: 'A great match, even if much greater than the players in it'?
                    Your obedient servant,
                                        CHARLES MORGAN

[The stylist in Melbourne – for whose services *The Times* paid £500 to the *Manchester Guardian* – was, of course, Neville Cardus. Four years later *The Times* Special Correspondent in Australia was R. C. Robertson-Glasgow]

The English language

The Purity of English

From Professor J. Churton Collins   *29 March 1906*

[Professor of English Literature in the University of Birmingham 1904–8, once described by Alfred, Lord Tennyson as 'a louse on the locks of literature']

Sir,

As since its foundation *The Times* has always been distinguished among English journals by its regard for the purity of our language, and as therefore we feel that we have a sort of right to appeal to you on such a subject, may I venture in your columns to enter a protest against the latest hideous importation from American journalism? The monstrous word 'electrocute,' for kill by electricity, is now of regular occurence, and bids fair to become part of our language. When we have the legitimately formed word 'electrocide' at our service why should it not be adopted and so detestable a solecism as the word referred to be repudiated?

I am, Sir, your obedient servant,
J. CHURTON COLLINS

['To *electrocute* appeared inevitably in the first public discussion of capital punishment by electricity.' – H. L. Mencken, *The American Language*, New York, 1919]

Betrothed or Fiancé?

From Sir Robert Edgcumbe   *26 April 1922*

Sir,

I do not know whether your literary page, now a daily and welcome addition to *The Times*, is intended to admit of correspondence, but, if so be such is the case, I should like to enter a protest against the continual use by various writers of the words *fiancé* and *fiancée*, words distinctly unEnglish. In the Press we continually read that so-and-so was present with his *fiancée*, and in almost every novel one takes up these same words occur again and again.

Our kinsfolk across the ocean, with good judgment, have coined as an noun 'uplift' from the verb 'to uplift'. Why cannot we coin as a noun the word 'betrothed' from the verb 'to betroth'? We already have in use the beautiful word 'betrothal', and how much better it would sound that so-and-so was present with his (or her) betrothed. Such a word is badly wanted, and all the while it is at hand, ready for use. If *The Times* would in future announcements substitute 'betrothed' for *fiancé* or *fiancée*, this much needed word would soon be established in our language.

Yours faithfully,
ROBERT EDGCUMBE

[The discovery that Shakespeare has used 'betrothed' ended the argument. However one correspondent did suggest another reason for avoiding *fiancé* – very few Englishmen could pronounce it correctly]

'Evacuees'

From the Reverend F. H. J. Newton   14 October 1939

Sir,

If ordinary English usage counts for anything, an evacuee is a person who has been evacuated, whatever that may be, as a trustee is one who has been trusted; for 'evacuee' cannot be thought of as a feminine French form, as 'employee' is by some.

Where are we going to stop if 'evacuee' is accepted as good English? Is a terrible time coming in which a woman, much dominated by her husband, will be called a dominee? Will she often be made a humiliee by his rough behaviour and sometimes prostree with grief after an unsought quarrel?

Must sensitive people suffer the mutilation of their language until they die and are ready to become cremees?

I am, Sir, your obedient servant,
F. H. J. NEWTON

BBC Pronunciation

[The BBC Advisory Committee on Spoken English was formed in 1926 with Robert Bridges as its chairman. In 1934 its members included Lady Cynthia Asquith, Rose Macaulay, Sir Johnston Forbes-Robertson, Lord David Cecil, Kenneth Clark, Edward Marsh, Logan Pearsall Smith and Professor I. A. Richards. In a letter to Bridges – 4 February 1910– Shaw had acclaimed Forbes-Robertson as 'the finest speaker on the English stage']

From Mr Bernard Shaw   *2 January 1934*

Sir,

As chairman of the committee which in the discharge of its frightful responsibility for advising the BBC on the subject of spoken English has incurred your censure as it has incurred everyone else's, may I mention a few circumstances which will help towards the formation of a reasonable judgment of our proceedings?

1. All the members of the committee speak presentably: that is, they are all eligible, as far as their speech is concerned, for the judicial bench, the cathedral pulpit, or the throne.

2. No two of them pronounce the same word in the English language alike.

3. They are quite frequently obliged to decide unanimously in favour of a pronunciation which they would rather die than use themselves in their private lives.

4. As they work with all the leading dictionaries before them they are free from the illusion that these works are either unanimous or up-to-date in a world of rapidly changing usage.

5. They are sufficiently familiar with the works of Chaucer to feel sincerely sorry that the lovely quadrisyllable Christemasse, the trisyllable neighebore, and the disyllable freendes should have decayed into krussmus, naybr, and frens. We should like to vary the hackneyed set of rhymes to forever by the Shakespearian persever; and we would all, if we dared, slay any actress who, as Cleopatra, would dare degrade a noble line by calling her country's high pyramides pirramids. But if we recommended these pronunciations to the announcers they would, in the unusual event of their paying attention to our notions, gravely mislead the millions of listeners who take them as models of current speech usage.

6. We are not a cockney committee. We are quite aware that that Conduit Street is known in the West End as Cundit Street.

189

Elsewhere such a pronunciation is as unintelligible as it is incorrect. We have to dictate a pronunciation that cannot be mistaken, and abide the resultant cockney raillery as best we can.

7. Wireless and the telephone have created a necessity for a fully and clearly articulated spoken English quite different from the lazy vernacular that is called modd'ninglish. We have to get rid not only of imperfect pronunciations but of ambiguous ones. Ambiguity is largely caused by our English habit of attacking the first syllable and sacrificing the second, with the result that many words beginning with prefixes such as ex or dis sound too much alike. This usage claims to be correct; but common sense and euphony are often against it; and it is questionable whether in such cases it is general enough to be accepted as authentic usage. Superior persons stress the first syllable in dissputable, labratory, ecksmplary, desspicable, &c.; and we, being superior persons, talk like that; but as many ordinary and quite respectable people say disputable, laborratory, exemmplary, and despickable, we are by no means bound to come down on the side of the pretentious pronunciation if the popular alternative is less likely to be confused with other words by the new human species called listeners-in.

We have to consider sonority also. The short i is much less effective then the long one; and the disturbance I created in the United States last April by broadcasting privvacy instead of pryvacy was justified. Issolate is a highly superior pronunciation; and wind (rhyming to tinned) is considered more elegant in some quarters than wynd; so that we get the common blunders of trist (rhyming to fist) for tryst and Rozzalind for Rosalynde; but we recommend the long i to the announcers for the sake of sonority.

Some common pronunciations have to be rejected as unbearably ugly. An announcer who pronounced decadent and sonorous as dekkadent and sonnerus would provoke Providence to strike him dumb.

The worst obstacle to our popularity as a committe is the general English conviction that to correct a man's pronunciation is to imply that he is no gentleman. Let me explain therefore that we do not correct anyone's pronunciation unless it is positively criminal. When we recommend an announcer to pronounce disputable with the stress on the second syllable we are neither inciting him to an ungentlemanly action nor insinuating that those who put the stress on the first ought to be ashamed of themselves. We are simply expressing our decision that for the purpose and under the circumstances of the new art of broadcasting the second syllable stress is the more effective.

Yours truly,

G. BERNARD SHAW

[Ten years previously 'issolate' had been the subject of a lively correspondence between Shaw and A. B. Walkley, drama critic of *The Times*, who objected when an actress used this pronunciation in a production of *Back to Methusalah*]

BBC Refinement

From Mr C. A. C. Hendriks   *24 September 1937*

Sir,

As an example of the 'naiceness' of the BBC's mind may I quote from a *cri de coeur* − an SOS on Saturday night last − when instead of a 'wet nurse', or 'foster mother', 'a source of of human milk for new-born twins' was called for.

Could 'refainement' move further along the path to the lunatic asylum without actually enforcing an entrance?

Yours etc.,

CECIL A. C. HENDRIKS

Value of the Third Programme

[The BBC had launched its Third Programme on 29 September 1946 with 'How to Listen' by Stephen Potter and Joyce Grenfell, Bach's Goldberg Variations, talks by Field-Marshal Smuts and Sir William Haley (the Corporation's Director-General), orchestral music, and a recording of Sir Max Beerbohm's 1935 'London Revisited.' Inevitably there was an Epilogue − from St Mark's, North Audley Street]

From Mr T. G. Miller   *16 February 1957*

Sir,

We must be indebted to the distinguished American critic, Mr R. P. Blackmur, for pointing, a few years ago, to the rise, side by side with the spread of general education, of a sinister, blind, and powerful force in the world — the 'new illiteracy.'

Mr Blackmur saw a steadily increasing proportion of the world's steadily increasing population learning to read, without knowing, and of course without wanting or needing to know, what to read. In fact, not knowing that there might *be* anything to read, with profit, beyond the advertisement, the paycheck, and the 'comic.'

More ominous still, Mr Blackmur demonstrated the invasion of the world of learning itself by the 'new illiteracy,' as that world falls more and more under the domination of the scientists and the technologists and the humanist occupiers of the more narrowly gated ivory towers. An unwillingness — an inability — to become in any intelligently human way committed to humanity spreads and multiplies its devastating tentacles. In this process the possibility of the disappearance of the BBC's Third Programme is the latest appalling symptom.

One does not need to be a slavish and uncritical admirer of the Third Programme to fear the prospect of its foundering. Its simple existence is a strong-point in the struggle to maintain our standards against the spread of the 'new illiteracy.' Whatever one's private views on coteries and cliques and charmed circles there has come now the time to close the ranks and to declare that all who value our ancient heritage and who are able to fight for it must straightly do so. Moreover, it is not just the poets, the musicians, and the political economists who must fight this action, but all who feel themselves involved and concerned to keep the values and standards and aims of a cultivated society, whether physicists, engineers, historians, dramatists, biologists, linguists, chemists, or whatever.

If we allow the Third Programme to be sapped away in an atmosphere of self-centred apathy then we in our turn deserve to be submerged by the flood of the dull, the rootless, the vulgar, the second- or third- or tenth-rate — ultimately and completely the valueless. The full and strong expression of opinion in this situation cannot be anything but academically respectable.

I am, Sir, your obedient servant,

T. G. MILLER

Plain English

From Mr G. H. Palmer   *2 August 1939*

Sir,

At the foot of the menu in use in the restaurant cars of our most up-to-date railway we read that: 'A supplementary portion of any dish will be served on request.' I suppose the first six words mean 'second helpings.' Why not say so?
I am, &c.,

G. H. PALMER

From Mr A. P. Herbert, MP   *3 August 1939*

[Independent Member for Oxford University; knighted 1945; Companion of Honour 1970]

Sir,

Your correspondent Mr G. H. Palmer should read *Punch*, in which (on March 8, 1939) the official answer to his question was recorded.

A lady wrote to the manager of a railway refreshment department asking as he does, 'Why not second helping?' The manager made this disarming answer: –

'I . . . have great respect for the English language but, knowing the public so well, I feel sure, for the few who do not understand the meaning of "supplementary" there would be many who would accuse us of uneducated crudity if we quoted the phrase in such plain verbiage as you suggest.

I fully agree we should all be the better for expressing ourselves in simple terms, but in official printed documents it is "not done," and I will confess I fear to make myself look odd by being different from others.'

It is for the same sweet reason, no doubt, that almost all politicians and papers now say 'anticipate' when they mean no more than 'expect,' 'as to whether' instead of 'whether,' 'following' instead of 'after,' and 'emergency' when they mean 'war.' One might also mention such recent recoils from 'plain verbiage' as 'deratization,' 'redecontamination,' and 'self-evacuating persons.'

It is almost unfair to blame a refreshment department when Government Departments set such an example. And, alas, the strong silent Services have been corrupted, too. If Nelson had to repeat his famous signal today it would probably run thus: –

England anticipates that as regards the current emergency personnel will face up to the issues and exercise appropriately the functions allocated to their respective occupation-groups.

I am, Sir, your obedient servant,
A. P. HERBERT

Economic Evidence

From Mr William Waldegrave   12 December 1977

[Conservative Member for Bristol West since 1979]

Sir,

Mr David Lea, of the TUC Economic Department, said in his oral evidence to the Wilson Committee: 'I do not think we can say it is a black or white situation but in the 1980s what we are emphasizing is that we are in a whole new ball game when we hope we will have a growth scenario when we believe that profitability in a secular as well as in a cyclical sense will be important.' (Wilson Committee Evidence, Vol. 2, HMSO, p. 93).

Mr Lea is, I believe, Mr Len Murray's key adviser on economic and industrial matters at a time when the TUC is expanding its ambitions towards an ever greater role in economic policy. Some even say that there is a chance that he may be Mr Murray's successor.

I have read the sentence quoted above a good many times. I don't get any nearer to understanding it. It is not untypical of Mr Lea's evidence. Perhaps other will be better than I am at extracting meaning from it. But surely it must be a matter of some concern that people as powerful as Mr Murray and his TUC colleagues draw their ideas from thinking which appears as incoherent as this?

Yours faithfully,
WILLIAM WALDEGRAVE

Leading Roll

From Mr Nick Alexander   7 *June 1986*

Sir,

The morning menu on British Airways' Super Shuttle from Edinburgh offers "*Selected* breakfast roll" – which surely takes the biscuit as the year's most meaningless adjective.

Or are they serious? Is there a mountain of rejected rolls sold off cheap to the Russians? Are there sandwich courses for school-leavers, starting with the basic craft of roll-modelling and culminating in a degree as Master of the Rolls?

Yours sincerely,
NICK ALEXANDER

Degree of Doubt

From Mr M. T. Phillips   7 *August 1986*

Sir,

According to your correspondent (report, July 297 "British Rail has a number of crossings in the pipeline . . . but these will now be put on ice".

Though contrasting in degrees Celsius, this reminds one of the beleaguered football manager who, when asked last season what he intended to do about his team's plight, replied that he had several irons in the fire, but that he was keeping them close to his chest.

Yours faithfully,
M. T. PHILLIPS

Without Letters

From Mr Richard Hughes   10 *February 1971*

Sir,

We have now tasted a total absence of postal services without finding it half so unpalatable as we had expected. Letter-writing is no longer our only or even principal means of communication beyond shouting-distance. We have already outgrown the Railway Age: are we now outgrowing the Postal Age too?

In the past, state letter-carrying has served many purposes. Queen Elizabeth first made it a royal monopoly to facilitate postal censorship. In the 17th century its monopoly profits were the attraction, for pensioning royal mistresses; and in the 18th, for financing French wars. Not till the 19th was it envisaged as primarily a service to the community (while still paying its way). If in the 20th it can no longer even pay reasonable wages out of reasonable charges, how can we avoid a suspicion that it is beginning to outgrow its usefulness?

Were letter-post suddenly abolished the inconvenience to business, the social injustices and hardships are obvious. No letters in hospital, no letters from boarding-school – and of course, no bills. The poor would suffer worse than the rich. But it may well be that we shall have to adopt in the future a deliberately discouraging policy of rundown (as with the railways) till only a minimal, essential skeleton-service remains. If we want to keep our friendly village postman we must pay him properly – or else do without him, collecting our own letters or setting our mail-boxes on the nearest mail-route (as in America) to be filled from passing vans.

The one thing that will not be affected is the *art* of letter-writing: for that is stone-dead already.

> I am, Sir, &c.,
> RICHARD HUGHES

From Mr John J. Smith   *22 March 1971*

Sir,
   I have just been told by the manager of the local sorting office to collect today's mail by hand. The reason is that our postman is sitting as a J.P. *Tempora mutantur.*

> Yours faithfully,
> JOHN J. SMITH

Personally Speaking

From the Public Orator, Oxford Univeristy   *5 April 1975*

Sir,
   Our legislators are regrettably no longer distinguished for verbal felicity, but since far-reaching powers are, it seems, to be vested in the Equal Opportunities Commission, the once-great British Public must exercise its inalienable right, before it

relinquishes the last shreds of personal freedom left to it, to be consulted by the new-fangled device of a referendum on the choice of words it will be allowed to use. The suggested—*person* suffixes to replace the unacceptable termination in—*man* produce some curious additions to the dictionary, so that the claims of rivals, such as—*body* (eg *pigbody, cowbody, and ploughbody*, which have an attractively agricultural ring) should be seriously considered.

Unfortunately our legislators' proposals show that they have not the vision to finish the job off. They have failed to consult vested interests: the crossword industry will have strong views. Here *signalperson* will commend itself since it is made up of *sign + Alp + Norse* (anag) whence ready-made clues suggest themselves: signalbody lacks this virtue.

Song-writers are vitally affected: 'My old person's a dustperson' makes a casualty of a catchy tune. The Church is not exempt: the Rt Rev the Bishop of Sodor and Man must submit either to embodiment or impersonation. Geographers in particular are in serious legal jeopardy: the Tasman Sea must in future be the Tasbody (or Tasperson) Sea, while Manchester must resign itself to becoming Personchester or Bodychester, with grievous consequences for the postcodes of the surrounding countryside, while the residents of Godmanchester deserve special sympathy.

Further afield the Sultanate of Oman must recognize itself as Operson or Obody. Academe too is threatened: holders of degrees in social anthropology will be suspected, to say the least, but will justly complain if they have to enter the employment market with a DPhil (PhD) in social gynandrology, with its unsavoury ambiguity.

For my part I shall cheerfully go to the stake or the concentration camp for my contumacious determination to admire and even worship women for their charm, skill in housewifery and other distinctive virtues, while turning my blind masculine eye to any countervailing characteristics which, as one of the few survivors of the nearly extinct breed of gentlepersons (gentlebodies), I have, like the ancient Greek historian, 'forgotten on purpose'.

Believe me to be, Sir, in deadly earnest,

Your obedient servant,

JOHN G. GRIFFITH

197

Elision Course

From Mr Leslie Fielding   *3 April 1986*

Sir,
   The elided English of some of today's newsreaders takes a lot
of swallowing. The Pry-Mister, the Chance-a-Chequer and the
British-Gum surely deserve fuller mention. Is Co-stree the coal
industry or the Coldstream Guards?
   If normal diction is not rapidly restored, we shall be even less
unstood by our Ewer-peer partners. (I write as what might be
called a Loyal sizn of the Nye-King of Gray-Brit-Nor-Nisle.)
                                        Yours seer-ly,
                                        LESLIE FIELDING

   [A female newsreader on Radio 4 refers to members of the
   army as 'sojers'; many BBC women pronounce 'soon' as
   something like 'see-une']

From the Director of the Royal School for the Blind
                                        23 December 1986

Sir,
   Radio 4 this morning (December 15) introduced the verb
'anonymise'. May I therefore letterise you that such verbising
terribilises the English langue and should not be radioised by
the BBC.

                                        Yours sincerely,
                                        BERNARD COOTE

'Literally Speaking'

From Mr B. W. M. Young   *18 April 1949*

Sir,
   Your recent report that a rackets player 'literally blasted his
opponents out of the court' suggests that gamesmanship is
becoming less subtle. Is not the use of dynamite as out of place
in a first-class match as, for instance, the word 'literally' in a
metaphor?
                                        Yours truly,
                                        B. W. M. YOUNG

From Mr E. W. Fordham   *20 April 1949*

Sir,

Perhaps the most picturesque use of 'literally' was that of a writer who asserted that 'for five years Mr Gladstone was literally glued to the Treasury Bench.'

Yours faithfully,

E. W. FORDHAM

From Mr G. Millington   *22 April 1949*

Sir,

The story recalled by Mr E. W. Fordham about Mr Gladstone being literally glued to the Treasury Bench is incomplete without the comment that appeared in *Punch*: 'That's torn it,' said the grand old man as he literally wrenched himself away to dinner.

Yours faithfully,

G. MILLINGTON

From Mr Gerald Barry   *22 April 1949*

[Director-General Festival of Britain, and knighted 1951]

Sir,

My own favourite for the 'Literal Stakes' is the biographer who wrote of his subject that 'he literally died in harness.'

Yours faithfully,

GERALD BARRY

From Mr Philip Jordan   *22 April 1949*

Sir,

My small collection of 'literallys' was bombed in the war; but two I recall. Writing of a horse, it was, Sir, your own Racing Correspondent who said that it 'literally ran away with the Two Thousand Guineas.' My second appeared in the gossip column of an evening paper, which wrote of a naval officer that he 'literally won his spurs at the Battle of Jutland.' It was, I recall as I write, that same paper which said that 'Clemenceau literally exploded' during an argument.

Yours faithfully,

PHILIP JORDAN

From Lady Eileen Orde   *23 April 1949*

Sir,
    Last summer a BBC commentator describing as easy victory
in the ladies' singles at Wimbledon, said: 'Miss so and so
literally wiped the court with her opponent.'
                              Yours faithfully,
                                             EILEEN ORDE

From Mr Edward Evans, MP   23 April 1949

[Labour member for Lowestoft]

Sir,
    I submit the following, long and lovingly remembered from
my 'penny dreadful' days: 'Dick, hotly pursued by the scalp-
hunter, turned in his saddle, fired, and literally decimated the
Indian.'
                              Yours faithfully,
                                             EDWARD EVANS

From Miss I. Davison   *25 April 1949*

Sir,
    When I was assistant editor of the *Saturday Review* in the
early 1920s, during a temporary absence of the editor I allowed
a reviewer to declare in those august pages that his heart was
literally in his boots.
                              Yours faithfully,
                                             IVY DAVISON

From Mr F. J. B. Watson   *25 April 1949*

Sir,
    A widely-read pre-war guide to Greece used to describe the
inhabitants of that country as so interested in politics as to be
visible daily 'in cafés and restaurants literally devouring their
newspapers.'
                              Yours faithfully,
                                             F. J. B. WATSON

From Miss E. M. Bullock   *26 April 1949*

Sir,
    The over-large vicarage of a Westmorland parish was

described at a local meeting as 'literally a white elephant round the neck of the incumbent.'

Yours faithfully,

E. M. BULLOCK

From Mr L. A. Impey   *29 April 1949*

Sir,

The author of Printers' Imp is correct. The phrase 'literally devouring a book' should be removed from the index of square adverbs in round holes. An Eton tutor once wrote of a boy who nibbled the edges of his Virgil while construing that 'he devoured the classics without digesting them.'

Yours, etc.,

L. A. IMPEY

From Mr Compton Mackenzie   *2 May 1949*

[Knighted 1952]

Sir,

For over 20 years Lord Samuel and I have been exchanging 'literallys' for our respective collections. We have between us most of those recorded by your correspondents, but that decimated Indian is a new gem. Here are a few more chosen at random. From a book about Isadora Duncan: 'Our eyes were literally pinned to the curtain till it went up.' From a newspaper report of Highland Games: 'Literally yards of a brawny beef and red hair assembled to toss cabers.' From a speech in the House of Commons in 1932: 'Our industries will be literally poleaxed.'

Your obedient servant,

COMPTON MACKENZIE

[For the correct use of 'literally', see letter on p. 51–2]

From the horse's mouth

From What a Depth Proceed Thy Honours

From Lord Rosebery   *16 February 1927*

[who became Prime Minister of Britain and won the Derby in the same year, 1894]

Sir,

Will you assist an embarrassed old fogey to understand the present position, for he hears that in the newspapers it is reported that negotiations are going on with regard to a certain electoral fund, in the possession of Mr Lloyd George, which appears to be a main asset in the business.

Now the question, which is never asked, but which must occur to us all, is: What is this sum, how was it obtained, and what is its source? Certainly it is not from Mr Lloyd Geroge's private means; it comes from some other direction. What is this! It surely cannot be the sale of the Royal Honours. If that were so, there would be nothing in the worst times of Charles II or Sir Robert Walpole to equal it. But what amazes me is this: no one seems to think that there would be anything unusual in such a sale. If so, all the worse, for it would be the prostitution of the Royal Prerogative, and so the ruin of the British Constitution.

On such a matter there should be no possibility of doubt. Scores, nay hundreds, of 'Honours' have been distributed. Have any been sold and helped to produce the sum in question? An authoritative statement should be furnished as to the source of this fund.

I am, Sir, yours respectfully,

ROSEBERY

[Some Honours had been sold, the proceeds going to Lloyd George's £2m secret fund. Perhaps because the Honours (Prevention of Abuses) Act had become law in August 1925, the British Constitution survived]

202

The Wooster Chin

From Mr P. G. Wodehouse   *30 November 1937*

[from 1939 Dr Wodehouse; briefly, in 1975, Sir Pelham]

Sir,

Your correspondent Mr John Hayward is to a great extent right in his statement that Bertie Wooster has a receding chin.

A fishlike face has always been hereditary in the Wooster family. Froissart, speaking of the Sieur de Wooster who did so well in the Crusades — his record of 11 Paynim with 12 whacks of the battleaxe still stands, I believe — mentions that, if he had not had the forethought to conceal himself behind a beard like a burst horsehair sofa, more than one of King Richard's men — who, like all of us, were fond of a good laugh — would have offered him an ant's egg.

On the other hand, everything is relative. Compared with Sir Roderick Glossop, Tuppy Glossop, old Pop Stoker, Mr Blumenfeld, and even Jeeves, Bertie is undoubtedly opisthognathous. But go to the Drones and observe him in the company of Freddie Widgeon, Catsmeat Potter-Pirbright, and — particularly — of Augustus Fink-Nottle, and his chin will seem to stick out like the ram of a battleship.

Your obedient servant,

P. G. WODEHOUSE

In Place of Tobacco

From Sir Stephen Tallents   *1 September 1941*

Sir,

Pipe tobacco is none too plentiful nowadays and briars themselves are in short supply. Can I persuade your readers to pool any experience they may have of home-grown substitutes for either?

Coltsfoot, as the old botany books show, is the countryman's traditional substitute for tobacco. The French, I read, are being advised to smoke the leaves of lime, ash, or nut trees. I have lately come across memories of a clergyman who always smoked watercress and of a Scotsman who preferred lavender – whether flowers, stalks, or leaves is not clear. I have experimented with these last two herbs and with a few others primitively dried. My results so far are instructive rather than alluring either to the smoker or those about him; but I have hopes of devising before winter some more tolerable blend.

Of pipes I can write more confidently. I have lately made, out of both pear and medlar wood, pipes which, if they do not as yet colour or polish so handsomely, taste just as well as briar and better than cherry. But here, too, your readers may have wisdom to contribute.

Yours faithfully,
STEPHEN TALLENTS

From Dr J. A. Stewart   *3 September 1941*
Sir,
    I have been smoking home-made pipes for over a year. Pipes made of *padauk* (Pterocarpus macrocarpus, Kurz), holly, and yew all give a satisfying smoke. I have recently tried Burma teak, which promises to be equally good.

Yours faithfully,
J. A. STEWART

From Mr J. M. Symns   *3 September 1941*
Sir,
    The other day in one of our local almshouses an old man assured me that he always smoked the sun-dried leaves of the chrysanthemum; I tried it, but found it rather over-scented. I have since found that mixed in equal proportions with tobacco it makes a good smoke and reduces one's tobacco bill by 50 per cent.

Yours faithfully,
J. M. SYMNS

From Canon R. G. F. Wyatt   *3 September 1941*
Sir,
    I wonder if Sir Stephen Tallents has tried a mixture of raspberry leaves with his tobacco. One can get them from the chemist at about 4d per oz., and I have used them in the proportion of one to two of tobacco. They are not bad. My gardener always has a supply of coltsfoot drying off, and mixed with equal quantities of tobacco it smells very good.

Yours faithfully,
R. G. F. WYATT

From Miss Eleanor Adlard   *3 September 1941*

Sir,

Why not grow our own tobacco on ground already proved suitable? For over 100 years tobacco growing was a flourishing industry in Gloucestershire in spite of fines and high taxes against the growers. Armed forces of the Crown destroyed no less than nine plantations of it near Bristol in 1692, the idea being to encourage the Virginian trade. A reversal of this policy now seems indicated.

Yours truly,
ELEANOR ADLARD

From Mr G. A. Tomlin   *5 September 1941*

Sir,

No correspondent has yet, so far as I can perceive, mentioned smoking for medicinal purposes, such as *Datura Stramonium* in asthma cigarettes. Coltsfoot (*Tussilago Farfara*), mentioned by a correspondent, forms the basis of a herbal smoking mixture. I have also seen lavender smoked in a hookah.

Your obedient servant,
G. A. TOMLIN

From Mr A. G. Philipson   *5 September 1941*

Sir,

Why not follow the example of Sherlock Holmes and save all the 'dottles' for future smoking?

Yours faithfully,
A. G. PHILIPSON

From Mr R. E. D. Cunningham   *6 September 1941*

Sir,

As good a substitute for tobacco as any of those yet suggested, and one which should easily be procurable by many of your correspondents, is the stuffing from an old hassock. Nice smokers will prefer it in a churchwarden's pipe, if the church-warden has no objection.

Yours faithfully,
R. E. D. CUNNINGHAM

English as she is wrote

[Mr Norman Fowler, Secretary of State for Social Services, had sent the draft of a new government funded advertising campaign warning of the dangers of acquired immune deficiency syndrome (Aids), the killer disease which particularly affects homosexuals.

Lord Hailsham, the Lord High Chancellor of Great Britain, reacted in a letter to Lord Whitelaw, Leader of the House of Lords and deputy Prime Minister. This letter appeared on the front page of *The Times* on 10 July 1986]

Dear Willie,

I have read Norman Fowler's letter of 24 June 1986 and the draft he envisages.

Whilst I share his view that a future round of national advertising should be much on the lines of the last round, but with shorter text and simpler language, I am convinced there must be some limit to vulgarity!*

Could they not use literate 'sexual intercourse'? If that is thought to be too narrow, then why not 'sexual relations' or 'physical practices', but not 'sex' or, worse, 'having sex'!!!

I am copying this letter to the Prime Minister, Norman Fowler and other members of the committee, the members of the inter-departmental ministerial group on Aids and Sir Robert Armstrong.

Yours,

QUINTIN

* And illiteracy. 'Sex' means you are either male or female. It does not mean the same as sexual practices. Nor does 'having sex' mean anything at all.

[Mr Norman Fowler was on the staff of *The Times* 1961–70]

Information — 2

Staircase Ties

[A Fourth Leader was read at Peterhouse, Cambridge]

From Professor D. W. Brogan   *14 May 1951*

Sir,
   The author of the erudite article on school and other ties in today's issue of *The Times* may be interested to learn that in a college in this university (not Peterhouse) there are not only college ties and club ties, but staircase ties.

Yours, &c.,
D. W. BROGAN

[The Master of Trinity supposes such ties would have been private affairs made for the occupants of a particular staircase. Ryder & Amies, University Outfitters, echo the Master: 'because of the small numbers involved, the ties were most probably hand embroidered privately.' Can any Cantab of 1950 vintage enlighten the Cuckoo?]

Nowhere

From Mr C. E. C. Dickens   *17 June 1978*

Sir,
   It is not only dates that make nice patterns of numbers. Some years ago I was bringing a Destroyer home from the Far East and was required to report my position twice a day.
   One evening, I saw that we would be passing close to where the Greenwich Meridian cuts the Equator so arranged to arrive there dead on midnight. Once there I altered course to due North and stopped engines so my position signal read:
   At 0000 my position Latitude 00°00′N, Longitude 00°00′E. Course 000°. Speed 0.

I had considered saying I was Nowhere but thought (probably correctly) that Their Lordships would not be amused.

Yours faithfully,

CLAUD DICKENS

['Speed 0' – Their Lordships, dismissing the idea of Commander Dickens's crew being on strike, would surely have despatched a tug]

From the Reverend J. H. Powell　　　　　*6 December 1929*
　　　　[Vicar of Christ Church, Nailsea, Somerset]

Sir,

This parish can lay claim to 'Nowhere', a name given to a small group of old cottages and to be found on the relevant Ordnance Survey Sheet. The only postal address of an occupant of one of the cottages is, therefore, Mr X, Nowhere, Nailsea, Somerset.

Yours faithfully,

J. H. POWELL

[Mr Powell's signal probably read: At all times my position Latitude 51° 42'N, Longitude 2° 14'W. Course Heavenward. Speed In Thy Hands]

The Pig in Legend

From Mr Edwin Brough　　　　　　　　*7 June 1923*

Sir,

'Tantony' is a new name to me for the small one of a litter of pigs or dogs. Some years ago I made the following collection of names all in use in various parts of the country:

Nisgil (Midlands), Nisledrige and Nestletripe (Devon), Darling, Daniel, Dolly and Harry (Hants), Underling, Rickling, Reckling, Little David (Kent), Dillin, Dilling (Stratford-on-Avon), Cad, Gramper, Nestletribe, Nestledrag, Nestelbird, Dab-Chick, Wastrill, Weed, Dandlin, Anthony, Runt, Parson's Pig (the least valuable to be devoted to tithe purposes), Nest Squab, Putman, Ratling, Dorneedy (Scottish), The Tit-man (Vermont), Nestledraft, Pigot, Rutland, Luchan, Piggy-Widden.

Yours faithfully,

EDWIN BROUGH

Luminous Owls

From Sir Digby Pigott   *9 January 1908*

[Controller of HM Stationery Office 1877 – 1905]

Sir,

The appearance of a luminous night-bird in North Norfolk, which you were good enough to allow me to chronicle in *The Times*, has attracted so much attention and given rise to so many questionings that, if you can, before finally dismissing the matter, find space to allow me to add a few words to what I have already written, I shall be much indebted to you.

I have this afternoon returned from a two days' visit to the gentleman on whose property the birds (there are two) have made themselves at home. Though not fortunate enough, as I had hoped, to see them myself, I have personally interviewed ten trustworthy witnesses of the many who have been more favoured, including, among others, the wife, daughter, and son of my host, the last an officer who served in the South African war, his bailiff, a policeman, the village schoolmaster, and the clerk and porter at the railway station.

I cannot expect you to spare room for the details of the stories they have to tell, interesting though they would be to every one who cares for natural history, and will only say that, unless evidence, one-half of which would be considered by any Court of law sufficient to hang a man, is to be entirely ignored, there can be no doubt that a pair of birds carrying a yellowish light, so strong as to have been when first noticed mistaken by two men at different places for bicycle lamps, have during the last few weeks been seen by some one (often by many people at once) almost every night hawking, like barn owls, along the hedge rows on brook side, resting for five or ten minutes at a time on a gate or trees, and every now and then swooping on to the ground.

A swoop a few nights ago, was, the schoolmaster told me, in his hearing followed immediately by what he believed to be the squeal of a young rat.

Perhaps the most interesting story of all was that told by the farm bailiff, who assured me that when one of the birds, which he had been watching for some time as it hunted round a wheat stack on a very dark night, flew off and lit on a tree, which he pointed out to me, on the other side of the field, the light it gave out was so strong that he could see distinctly the outlines of the branches round it.

I confine myself to a repetition of the facts as told to me, and do not attempt to offer any explanation. But to no one who has puzzled over the phosphorescent trail of such small creatures as centipedes on a damp autumn evening, or read in the reports of the Challenger expedition or elsehwere of the wonderful light-carrying contrivances of many deep sea fishes, will the phenomenon appear either impossible or unnatural.

If the use or purpose is asked, none who as boys have caught sparrows with a bull's eye lantern or watched the startled amazement which for a moment paralyses a dormouse if a match is struck suddenly and held to the cage, will have any difficulty in finding a possible answer.

If, as your correspondent 'A Shropshire Teacher' believes, the light is brightest when the bird is in a poor condition, one might be tempted to fancy that nature, red in tooth and claw, may have her softer moments and be ready at times to step down from the iron pedestal from which she watches with impartial eye the struggle for existence, to lend a hand to help the lame dog over the stile.

From stories which have reached me since 'luminous owls' became the talk of the neighbourhood I am inclined to think lights of the kind may be less rare than has been supposed, and that, but for the fear of ridicule, we might oftener hear of them.

I should like to repeat some of the strange tales told me, but have already, I am afraid, put a dangerous strain on your patience.

Your obedient servant,
T. DIGBY PIGOTT

Indexes

From Mr Evelyn Waugh   *13 October 1961*

Sir,

You say in your leading article today, 'No one has ever suggested that novels should have indexes'.

I possess a translation of Tolstoy's *Resurrection*, published by Messrs Grosset and Dunlap of New York and 'illustrated from the photoplay produced by Inspiration pictures Inc', which has a particularly felicitous index. The first entry is: 'Adultery, 13, 53, 68, 70'; the last is 'Why do people punish? 358'. Between them occur such items as: Cannibalism, Dogs, Good breeding, Justification of one's position, Seduction, Smoking, Spies, and Vegetarianism.

I am, Sir, your obedient servant,
EVELYN WAUGH

King Tutankhamen

From the Bishop of Chelmsford   *3 February 1923*

[the Rt Rev John Edwin Watts-Ditchfield]

Sir,

I wonder how many of us, born and brought up in the Victorian era, would like to think that in the year, say, 5923, the tomb of Queen Victoria would be invaded by a party of foreigners who rifled it of its contents, took the body of the great Queen from the mausoleum in which it had been placed amid the grief of the whole people, and exhibited it to all and sundry who might wish to see it?

The question arises whether such treatment as we should count unseemly in the case of the great English Queen is not equally unseemly in the case of King Tutankhamen. I am not unmindful of the great historical value which may accrue from the examination of the collection of jewelry, furniture, and, above all, of papyri discovered within the tomb, and I realize that wide interests may justify their thorough investigation and even, in special cases, their temporary removal. But, in any case, I protest strongly against the removal of the body of the King from the place where it has rested for thousands of years. Such a removal borders on indecency, and traverses all Christian sentiment concerning the sacredness of the burial places of the dead.

J. E. CHELMSFORD

[Queen Victoria once told Lord Melbourne (*Journal*, 2 January 1840), 'I should like to be burnt after I died']

Intellectuals

From Mr John Moore   *15 April 1966*

Sir,

Ten years ago, at a luncheon in honour of Shaw's centenary, I sat next to the Russian Chargé d'Affaires. He was a taciturn fellow. After our initial exchange of pleasantries a silence fell. He seemed lost in thought. Five or 10 minutes went by. Then he said to me suddenly:

'You are an intellectual?'

Like any Englishman worthy of the name, I hotly denied the distasteful accusation.

Another silence fell. The saddle of lamb came and went. The Russian brooded darkly. I could see he was deeply troubled. At last he turned to me and demanded:

'If you are *not* an intellectual, why are you here?'

I had no answer.

I am, Sir, your obedient servant,

JOHN MOORE

Farewell to the Farthing

From Mr W. McG. Eager   *13 January 1961*

As the farthing becomes no more than a numismatist's specimen you may care to put on record one use of it contained in an account of his childhood given me a few days ago by a friend who was a member of a boys' club in Bermondsey at the time of the First World War. His father, a decorator in more or less regular work, earned 6½d an hour, and every Saturday gave his wife 'a golden sovereign' to pay the rent (which was 7s 6d a week) and to buy food and clothing for parents and four little but growing boys. The baker at the end of the street changed the sovereign, deducted the amount of the mother's weekly bill for bread, and added to the change one penny, which he obliged her by changing into four farthings. Each child was given one farthing as pocket money and invariably spent it on sweets. Whether the weekly indulgence in sweets or general dietetic deficiency had more to do with the children's bad teeth could be a nice question.

I am, Sir, yours, &c.,

M. McG. EAGAR

[It may be necessary to remind younger readers that whereas the present ½p coin is worth £1/200th, the farthing (¼d) was worth £1/960th]

Where the Prince Died

From Dame Rebecca West   *18 December 1961*

Sir,

The article on 'Where the Prince Consort died' in your issue of 13 December raises a mystery over which I had often brooded. I have never been able to understand why Mr Lytton

Strachey or Dr Randall Davidson [appointed Dean of Windsor in 1883; later Archbishop of Canterbury], much less two of the Queen's pages, should have regarded it as singular of Queen Victoria to preserve the Prince Consort's bedroom after his death in the same state as it had been during his lifetime.

The writer of that article gives an instance of a similar memorial action at the Court of Hanover; but surely the custom was followed not only by royalty but by all sorts of people who had such large houses that they could afford to sacrifice a room.

I have been told half a dozen times in my life of families who had observed this custom; and the last instance was recent. Only about four years ago the father of an American friend of mine died in the state of Kentucky, aged 92; his wife had died 20 years before him, and until his death her bedroom was kept exactly as it had been when she was alive. Her clothes hung in the wardrobe, her brushes and hand-mirrors were on her dressing-table, and the bed was turned down every night. The old gentleman was of German origin.

Yours faithfully,

REBECCA WEST

'Not for Joe'

From Mr D. B. Hague *19 October 1960*

[of the Royal Commission on Ancient Monuments in Wales and Monmouthshire]

Sir,

One of the unstratified finds encountered this summer during the excavation of a medieval monastery on a tiny Welsh island was a stem of a nineteenth-century clay pipe. On it was stamped the inscription 'Not for Joe'. I am mildly curious about Joe and would appreciate any enlightenment.

Yours faithfully,

D. B. HAGUE

From Mr J. C. Trewin *21 October 1960*

Sir,

I imagine that the inscription, to which he refers in his letter today, on Mr D. B. Hague's excavated clay pipe stem derives from a comic song written, composed, and sung by Arthur Lloyd in the 1860s. Its chorus ran:

213

Not for Joe! Not for Joe!
Not for Joseph, if he knows it!
No, no, no! Not for Joe!
Not for Joseph, oh dear, no!

Apparently Joseph Baxter was a London bus-driver whose favourite catch-phrase was 'Not for Joe!' The song, triumphant on the halls, had a very large sale.

Yours faithfully,

J. C. TREWIN

From Mr M. M. Chisholm   *22 October 1960*

Sir,

My father's (born 1857) favourite joke was about a little church which had a kind of barrel-organ for a limited number of hymn tunes.

One day it had to be carried out playing 'Not for Joe', having come to the end of the sacred music. That pipe must have been engraved with the song title.

Yours faithfully,

M. M. CHISHOLM

The Name of Britain

From Professor D. W. Brogan   *3 January 1949*

[more generally concerned with French or American affairs, Sir Denis Brogan was Professor of Political Science at Cambridge 1939 – 67]

Sir,

In a world in danger of death because of pathological nationalistic nonsense, it is perhaps being unduly severe to comment on the letter addressed to you by the representatives of the St Andrew's and St George's Societies. Yet their protest against the use of 'Britain' for 'Great Britain' is surely a symptom of the disease, if in a very mild form. It is also, I think, mistaken, even from a nationalist point of view. Britain has been the name of our island since the beginning of recorded history. Great Britain is a new term, useful in law but not in any other department of life. I was told more than once by that deeply patriotic Scot, the late Sir Robert Rait (Historiographer Royal for Scotland) that the term was invented by one of his predecessors as head of Glasgow University, John Major (or Mair), as a punning title for his history of Britain (*Historia Majoris Britanniae*).

When James the Sixth was graciously pleased to become James the First of England, he invented the term Great Britain, ostensibly to distinguish it from Brittany. It was as if his colleague, Henri IV of France and Navarre, had called his kingdoms Transalpine Gaul. To insist now that, in ordinary speech or writing, we should use 'Great Britain' is like telling the inhabitants of York that they must write 'Old York'. In France, it is true that in writing it is necessary to use 'la Grande Bretagne' to avoid confusion with 'la Bretagne'. In speech, of course, in spite of 'the auld alliance', the French always say 'l'Angleterre', unless they specifically mean Scotland. Let our island keep the name it has had.

'Since Britain first at heaven's command, Arose from out the azure main.'

Yours faithfully,
D. W. BROGAN

The Forsytes

From Mr Henry Williamson   *25 March 1966*

Sir,

I wonder if the producer of the proposed serial on television would consider the pronunciation of the name *Jolyon* as Galsworthy once told me it should be pronounced: the name being a variant (in spelling) of *Julian*.

Yours faithfully,
HENRY WILLIAMSON

From Mr Donald Wilson   *28 March 1966*
   [then Senior producer, BBC Television Centre]

Sir,

I am indebted to Mr Henry Williamson for giving us Galsworthy's own pronunciation for Jolyon.

I have never been quite sure, myself, particularly in view of the abbreviations, Jo, Jolly, and Jon, given to Old Jolyon's son and two grandsons respectively. Perhaps something midway between Joelyon and Julian would be appropriate in dialogue.

Could Mr Williamson now please confirm for me Galsworthy's pronunciation of the surname? I incline towards emphasis on the first syllable, but should it perhaps be on the second?

Yours faithfully,
DONALD WILSON

From Mr Rex Roberts   *31 March 1966*

Sir,

While we are finding out how to pronounce their name could we decide how to pronounce their author's name?

The late Horace Vachell told me that when he knew John Galsworthy the first syllable rhymed with pals. Now most people think it rhymes with palls. Can we have a ruling, please?

Yours faithfully,
REX ROBERTS

From Mr Henry Williamson   *4 April 1966*

Sir,

John Galsworthy said to me: 'The Galsworthys come from Galsworthy moor near Torrington in North Devon. When one left and became a builder in London, and went up in the world, he prounounced his name Galsworthy' – to rhyme with pals. 'I, in reaction, reverted to the original Devon pronunciation' – Galls-worthy.

Now, Sir, I understand, the greater uplift from having a famous author (and OM) in the family has restored the *status quo*.

Yours faithfully,
HENRY WILLIAMSON

The Earwig's Better Nature

From Mr Malcolm Burr   *17 August 1936*

Sir,

Your correspondent can be reassured that the earwigs which annoy her are not more than a minor nuisance. They are really inoffensive creatures; they smell not, neither do they sting. They are, in fact, deserving of our admiration, for they are unique among insects in their personal sense of maternal duty. After the honeymoon in early winter in a gallery dug under a big stone the mother earwigs, when their time draws night, expel the fathers from the home, lest they devour their own offspring.

Then they lay their eggs, from January to March, which they cherish and keep clean till the babes come out, and even then do not relax their care. Often one may disturb a nest of young earwigs in the spring, and if the mites are scattered the dam will gather them together again under her capacious abdomen like an old fowl. Meanwhile the fathers lead a bachelor existence until the early summer, when all the parents die off, leaving the youngsters to carry on the species. These come of age about the beginning of August, and rejoicing in their newly found strength and the hardened integument of puberty fare forth into the world to carve out their careers.

> I am, Sir, your obedient servant,
> MALCOLM BURR

The Singing Mouse . . .

From Miss Alison Holmes   *26 April 1937*

Sir,

In *The Times* of 22 April it was stated that a singing mouse had been found in Wales and that it is to broadcast on 8 May.

It may interest your readers to know that, according to Red Indian mythology, 'Mish-a-boh-quas', the singing mouse, always comes to tell of war.

It may sing at other times, but not to the same extent.

I read of this in Ernest Thompson's wonderful book *Rolf in the Woods*.

> I am your obedient servant,
> ALISON HOLMES

. . . and a Coal-heaving Mouse

From Mr Dudley Illingworth   *28 April 1937*

Sir,

While two men were working in an outhouse here last week they saw a large mouse carrying pieces of coal, held by the mouth and a front paw, over a wood partition and dropping them into a near-by empty corn bin. The coal is of the size sold as 'nuts', measuring about 4in. by 1in. by 1in. The nuts were so transported with almost incredible rapidity. Unfortunately, before the completion of the mysterious task the owner of the coal disturbed the pilferer, but not before some 30 pieces had been dropped on the corn. He is, however, convinced that the mouse was building for itself a ladder of coal from the corn bin, as two mice had been trapped in it the previous day. I wonder if anyone has ever observed a similar operation to its explanatory conclusion?

Yours faithfully,
D. H. ILLINGWORTH

Dukes and Dustmen

[Mr P. Whitlock of the Transport and General Workers' Union had denounced the Duke of Bedford for remarks made at Dunstable Grammar School: 'I told my four sons, "If you don't study you will probably end up as dustmen".' Mr Whitlock insisted that dustmen should be referred to as 'refuse collectors']

From Mr J. A. Fendley   *16 October 1956*

Sir,
Cannot the difference between the Duke of Bedford and Mr Whitlock be ascribed to a simple misunderstanding? For surely the schoolboys of Dunstable can by diligent application to their studies avoid the prospect of finding themselves mere dustmen, and aspire to the dignity of refuse collectors, whose scholarship and courtesy Mr Whitlock so rightly upholds.

I remain, Sir, your obedient servant,
J. A. FENDLEY

From Miss Margaret Stewart Roberts   *16 October 1956*

Sir,
The Duke of Bedford has upset Mr Whitlock by calling dustmen 'dustmen'. Dustmen are dustmen and rat-catchers are rat-catchers. If Mr Whitlock has the time, in these busy days, to call dustmen 'refuse-collectors' and rat-catchers 'rodent-extermination officers,' let him do so – but most people will

prefer the shorter, old-fashioned names which can give as much dignity to reliable and hard-working dustmen and rat-catchers.

Yours faithfully,

MARGARET STEWART ROBERTS

[Oddly, no one saw fit to mention the most famous of all dustmen/refuse collectors, Alfred Doolittle. However, a voice of reason was heard from Trinity College, Cambridge]

From Mr D. F. Lawson   *18 October 1956*

Sir,

Surely all your readers have not misunderstood the Duke of Bedford's clear statement of the purpose of education? The schoolboys of Dunstable should aspire, as all schoolboys and undergraduates should, not to be dukes and dustmen, but 'enlightened' dukes and 'enlightened' dustmen. Surely Mr Whitlock cannot quarrel with this vision of dustmen with degrees? More and more penurious undergraduates spend their vacations in such occupations, and some, no doubt, finally hear the call to be dustmen. I feel sure that Mr Whitlock is one of these for it is they who insist on their proper recognition by 'unenlightened' dustmen and call themselves refuse collectors.

Yours faithfully,

D. F. LAWSON

[It is good to know that *The Times* took readily to the new age of euphemism. Reviewing a Young Vic production of *Romeo and Juliet* on 13 February 1986, a critic wrote of Juliet that she had 'emerged from the Central School of Speech and Drama with the kind of "classless" south-eastern accent that nudges "woe" closer to "wow".' Perhaps the critic meant Juliet sounded cockney]

Thinking in Octals

[The United Kingdom was the last major country in the world to adopt a decimal currency — on 15 February 1971]

From Professor Fred Hoyle   *28 December 1961*

[Plumian Professor of Astronomy and Experimental Philosophy at Cambridge 1958 – 73, Sir Fred Hoyle is now Research Professor, Manchester University]

Sir,

If we are being forced by economic reasons into a decimalization of our coinage, and of other units, then plainly we must go ahead. But if, as one suspects, much of the impulse towards decimalization comes from the wish not to appear impossibly archaic in the eyes of the world, then this is the moment to reflect on whether the decimal system is likely to survive into the future as the operative form of practical arithmetic.

It appears safe to say that the electronic digital computer, using binary arithmetic, will become steadily more important to technology. It is likely that 50 years hence the computer will play an indispensable part in human society, much as electricity itself does today. And just as the increasing importance of electricity has modified our educational curricula — nowadays schoolchildern are introduced to ideas that were considered esoteric 50 years ago — so we can expect a modification to meet the needs of a population employing computers as normal articles of everyday life. One emphatic need will be an easy interchange between ordinary numbers and binary numbers.

Conversion from decimal to binary is at best an awkward process, even to most professional mathematicians. Conversion from octal to binary, on the other hand, is simple and quick — for example, an hour's practrice is sufficient to enable most non-mathematicians to convert a six digit octal number to binary in a matter of seconds. During the next few decades the octal system is certain, for this reason, to come into widespread use. (Octal is based on eight, so that 100 in octal is 64 in decimal.)

It is often said that scientists are ardent decimalizers. While this may have been the case 20 years ago, it has no force as an argument today. Today, the calculations of greatest scientific complexity are made in binary — with its close relation to octal. It is true that, having carried through our calculations, we still prefer to convert our answers to decimal, but the fault lies in us not in the octal system. We have not yet learnt to think naturally in octal.

Although adults reared on decimal find octal thinking strange, this would not be so for children. A new generation could learn to think naturally in octal. Indeed, octal could be learned more easily since multiplication tables would only be about half the burden they are in decimal. Perhaps as much as a year's mathematical education could be gained by the average pupil, a 10-year-old being the equal in octal of an 11-year-old in decimal.

One notices, with a sense of irony, that our present monetary reckoning from an octal point of view is superior to decimal coinage, since eight half-crowns make up the pound. Sir, there is the very real danger that in attempting to get ourselves up to date we may find ourselves falling behind the times.

F. HOYLE

A 'Clowder' of Cats

[A Fourth Leader had begun 'There is no noun of assembly for cats.' Ignoring later sentiments such as 'the only perfect cat is a kitten', correspondents corrected the writer]

From His Honour Judge Blagden   *11 May 1951*

Sir,

You have, I believe, for once fallen into error in your leading article. Cats, I have always understood, assemble, on the rare occasions when they do, in a 'clowder', and kittens in a 'kendle'. While I regret that I cannot, off-hand, quote chapter and verse for these words, perhaps some of your more erudite readers can; and they are, I believe, words of more respectable antiquity than (for example) a 'pomposity of judges.'

I am, Sir, yours faithfully,
J. BASIL BLAGDEN

From Mr Peter G. Masefield   *14 May 1951*

Sir,

Judge Blagden is certainly right. Some years ago I copied out, from an eighteenth century book on the 'Lore of the Chase', 88 collective terms for various birds and beasts, among them, on the domestic side, a 'kindle of kittens' and a 'clowder of cats', in addition to some antagonistic collections as a 'cowardice of curs', a 'kennel of raches', and a 'litter of whelps'. The 'haras of horses' allied to a 'stud of mares' or with a 'pace of asses' would produce either a 'barren of mules' or a 'rag of colts'. Among the wilder beasts one could take not only the well known 'pride of lions' but also a 'lepe of leopards', coming down to a mere 'nest of rabbits' and a 'down of hares', hotly pursued by a 'skulk of foxes'.

By far the widest selection is to be found among the birds. The 'gaggle of geese' is well known (on the land or water) but they change into a 'skein' when they are on the wing and are associated with the more common or garden 'baddling of ducks' followed by a 'fleet of ducklings'. At this time of year what could be more delightful than an 'exaltation of larks' with a 'charm of goldfinch', a 'watch of nightingales', or a 'murmuration of starlings'? But, though the names are recorded, I personally have little knowledge of a 'rush of dunbirds', a 'fling of oxbirds', or a 'trip of dottrel'. All these ancient collections are, of course, brought up to date with some modern examples as a 'flush of wing commanders', while in my university days I remember hearing of an 'obfuscation of dons'.

Yours faithfully,
PETER G. MASEFIELD

From Mr H. H. Brown   *16 May 1951*

Sir,

The *Boke of St Albans*, first printed in 1486, provides an authoritative list in its 'Companys of Beestys and Fowlys'. This supports your contention, for cats are not included. Judge Blagden appears to be approximately correct about kittens, for a 'Kyndyll of yong cattis' is mentioned; but he is wrong about judges, where the correct term is 'A sentence of Juges'.

I am, Sir, your obedient servant,
H. H. BROWN

The correspondence ended with these lines

'An Explosion of Canons' – what term could be apter
   For use in describing a turbulent Chapter?
Though some have been known, with indecent jocosity,
   To call the Episcopal bench 'a Pomposity',
I venture to urge that with greater propriety
   A party of Prelates be known as 'a Piety'.

C.A.A.

[Those cherished initials were those of Dr C. A. Alington, a former headmaster of Shrewsbury (where he briefly employed Neville Cardus as his secretary) and Eton, and later Dean of Durham. A son-in-law was the future prime minister, Sir Alec Douglas-Home, now Lord Home of the Hirsel]

Fate of the Leading Nazis

From Mr A. J. P. Taylor   *17 September 1968*

[Fellow of Magdalen College, Oxford]

Sir,

The other evening Baldur von Schirach appeared on London Weekend Television. This man was Gauleiter of Vienna when the Jews were being despatched to the gas chamber. Though he professed to have no knowledge of this, the Nuremberg Tribunal sentenced him to 20 years' imprisonment, which he has served.

Rudolf Hess left Germany before the extermination of the Jews began. There is no evidence that he knew anything of Hitler's plans for this or for war. The Nuremburg Tribunal opined that, as Deputy Führer, 'he must have known'. His real crime was to have sought peace between Great Britain and Germany, so that Germany could turn against Russia. This policy, however misguided, was supported by some prominent Englishman and by Senator Harry S. Truman.

For the sole crime of being a premature advocate of NATO, Hess was sentenced to imprisonment for life. He is now alone in Spandau.

Yours faithfully,

A. J. P. TAYLOR

[Baldur von Schirach had an American mother; his great-grandfather, a Union officer, had lost a leg at Bull Run; two forebears had signed the Declaration of Independence. – William L.Shirer, *The Rise and Fall of the Third Reich*]

Drawing the gladius

From Mr James Wykes   *20 August 1982*

Sir,

With reference to your Archaeology Correspondent's article (August 17) on the problems of drawing a Roman *gladius*, memories of a school production of Shaw's *Caesar and Cleopatra* many years ago may perhaps shed a little light. In Act II Caesar is required to draw his sword (in this case about 18 inches long, as supplied by Clarksons), not with any aggressive intent, one hastens to add, but merely to test its edge.

The unsheathing problem was referred, naturally, to the omniscient head of the classical department, who decreed that the sword should be slung from from the left shoulder, and worn on the right side, *à la* Astérix. Drawing it was effected by gripping the hilt as one would a tennis racket, pushing down firmly to tighten the sling, turning the sword though a 90-degree arc so that it pointed to the front and then extracting it with a sharp jerk towards the rear. This routine worked like a charm and there were no nasty accidents.

I think, therefore, that Astérix is probably right, although I am sorry to learn that he has apparently changed sides and joined the Roman army (Sendervictorius, Appianglorius *et al*). A pretty useful recruit, though, by all accounts.

Yours faithfully,

JAMES WYKES

From Dr T. Healey   *23 August 1982*

Sir,

The difficulties in your account of investigations into Roman sword harnesses may be more apparent than real. There might be no necessity to change the grip as apparently awkward grips and withdrawals can rapidly be mastered with practice. A comparable example was to be found in those gunmen of the American West who drew, right-handed, a gun which was slung on to their right hip with grip pointing forwards.

An example of the extreme rapidity at which the expert could draw and fire a gun from this position was shown on television last month in *Revenge at El Paso*. It should be remembered that the Roman soldier had no occasion to make a 'lightning draw', and suffered no handicap from a relatively clumsy unsheathing of his sword.

Yours,

T. HEALEY

The Clock Tower Light

[The Second World War in Europe was approaching its end, a fact duly noted by the Mother of Parliaments]

From Mr A. J. Waterfield   *24 April 1945*

Sir,
You have told us that the lantern at the top of the famous Clock Tower is to be switched on again, starting on Tuesday, April 24. It was at the suggestion of the late George Jacob Holyoake, made in 1866 to Lord John Manners, First Commissioner of Works, that the limelight was placed over the clock tower at Westminster at night to denote that Parliament was sitting (see Dictionary of National Biography).

Yours, &c.,

A. J. WATERFIELD

[The House of Commons was sitting in committee on the Budget when the Speaker (Colonel D. Clifton-Brown, later Lord Ruffside) entered at 9.11 p.m.

'In peace-time it has always been the custom that the lantern light upon Big Ben shone out after sunset [Britain was on Double Summer Time] to show the House of Commons was at work. For five years, seven months and 23 days this light has now been extinguished, and when I press this switch our lantern light will go on again. In doing so I pray that with God's blessing this light may shine not only as an outward and visible sign that the Parliament of a free people is assembled in free debate, but also as a beacon of fresh hope in a sadly torn and distracted world. I now turn on our lantern light.']

From Mr Herbert F. Betts   *28 April 1945*

Sir,
It is right that Mr Speaker's eloquent words should be recorded, but the origin of the clock tower light was very prosaic. In the sixties most members dined at home or had social engagements and it constantly happened that they returned only to find that the House had risen. The purpose of the light was to save them a useless journey.

Yours, &c.,

HERBERT F. BETTS

Professional Pedigrees

From Dr Guy Kinneir   *19 April 1945*

Sir,

Recently, while examining documents which included my family pedigree, I noticed that there has been an unbroken line of doctors commencing from Walter Kinneir, born 1671, and terminating so far with myself. Walter Kinneir practised at High Worth, North Wiltshire, and was buried in that church.

There has therefore been an unbroken line of medical men from father to son for 274 years. It would be of interest to know if this constitutes something of unique record or could other families equal or even surpass it.

Yours faithfully,

GUY KINNEIR

From Lieutenant-Colonel P. R. Whalley   *24 April 1945*

Sir,

With reference to Dr Guy Kinneir's letter, my own pedigree (set forth in full in Sergeantson's 'History of the Church of St Giles, Northampton') shows an unbroken clerical descent from 1634 to 1895.

This, however, is unimpressive compared with that of the Southcomb family, who have held the rectory of Rose Ash, near Barnstaple, continuously from 1675 to the present day, a record, according to Kelly's *Devon*, believed to be unique in the history of the English Church.

Yours truly,

P. R. WHALLEY

From the Reverend H. Copinger-Hill   *28 April 1945*

Sir,

With reference to letters and pedigrees from Dr Kinneir and Colonel Whalley, the following is perhaps the record.

The family of Copinger, whose heiress married a Hill, have supplied the rectors for this parish of Buxhall since 1564 without a break except for two 'pot-Warmers' who filled a few months' gap. A Copinger was rector in 1411 and the estate was in their hands from about 200 years before that date.

Yours truly,

H. COPINGER-HILL

Curious Hat-Rights

[The death had been announced, at the age of 83, of the Reverend Henry Copinger-Hill, for 47 years Rector of Buxhall, Suffolk. His ancestors enjoyed a special association with kings of England in that they were permitted to wear their hats when in the presence of the reigning sovereign. A 'parchment' relating to the privilege was apparently in the British Museum]

From Mr B. Scholfield   *2 January 1949*

[Department of Manuscripts, British Museum]

Sir,

The 'parchment' of Henry VIII, granting to Walter Copynger in 1512 the privilege of wearing his hat in the royal presence was deposited in the British Museum by the Rev. H. Copinger-Hill in 1929. The text of the document is as follows:—

'Henry, by the grace of god king of England and of Fraunce and lord of Irland, To almaner our subiectes, aswell of the spirituell preemynens and dignities as of the temporall auctorite, these our lettres hering or seing, and to euery of them, greting; Where as we bee credible enfourmed that our trusty and welbiloued subject Walter Copynger is so diseased in his hede that without his grete daugner he cannot be convenyently discouered of the same; In consideracion whereof We haue by these presentes licenced hym to vse and were his bonet vpon his said hed, aswell in or presence aselles where at his libertie; Wherfore we woll and commaunde you and euery of you to permite and suffre hym so to doo, Withoute any your chalange disturbance or interupcion to the contrary; as ye and euery of you tendre our pleasur. 3euen vnder our signet at our Manour of Grenewiche, the xxiiii Day of Octobre, the fourthe yere of our Reigne.'

Yours faithfully,

B. SCHOFIELD

[The Reverend Henry Copinger Hill's son − the Reverend Arthur Percival Hill − had been killed in a motor accident in Nairobi in 1927]

A Rolls in Russia

[A strange object had been noted in the Soviet Union]

From Mr John Fisher Evans   *3 June 1985*

Sir,
   Anachronistic as may have been the Rolls-Royce in Russia, so must have been the early Rover bicycle, equally distinguishable in its own genre, whose precedent presence in Lhasa, leaning unattended against a wall, astonished Sir Francis Younghusband's exalted expedition on its entry into the Forbidden City in 1904.
Yours truly,
JOHN FISHER EVANS

From Mr John Williamson   *5 June 1985*

   [writing from Canterbury]

Sir,
   Some years ago, when President Brezhnev was in power, our firm supplied upholstery leather for the top official cars in Russia and one of the sections of the contract stated that "the quality of the leather had to be up to the standard of that supplied to Rolls-Royce, or better".
Yours faithfully,
JOHN WILLIAMSON

From Sir Thomas Armstrong   *11 June 1985*

Sir,
   Some years ago in a Moscow museum I saw a fine old English bicycle, a BSA or Raleigh of vintage character — a veritable Rolls-Royce among bicycles. It was said to have been presented to Tolstoy by the makers, or by a group of English admirers. Was it in Tolstoy's house, and is it still there?
Yours sincerely,
THOMAS ARMSTRONG

From Miss Helen Edmondson   *14 June 1985*

Sir,
   I can confirm that the bicycle seen by Sir Thomas Armstrong in Moscow is on view in Tolstoy's house along with a Singer

sewing machine and English biscuit tins. It was still there when I last visited it in 1976.

There is, in fact, another Rolls-Royce in Moscow, that of the British Ambassador.

Yours sincerely,
HELEN EDMONDSON

The Blackthorn Winter

From Sir Napier Shaw   *25 April 1931*

[Director of the Meteorological Office 1905 – 20]

Sir,

In your issue of Wednesday 22 April, Mr H. St Barbe, asking for an explanation of a 'blackthorn winter', raises a meteorological question of a more general character than those which form the subjects of official reports. It may be connected with a line of thought concerning the movement of air over the surface of the globe which came into a talk of the BBC in the holiday season last summer; the association is perhaps of sufficient general interest to justify my asking for space to indicate it.

Let us bear in mind that in ordinary circumstances a square foot of surface at sea-level carries about a ton of air, and the movement of air is wind. Next, in the middle of January, the total stock of air on the surface of the northern hemisphere is five billion tons above par, and in the middle of July about the same amount below par. So between January and July 10 billion tons of air are transferred from the northern hemisphere to the southern and brought back again within the year. The process of transfer of those tons of air may have something to do with the question. It is of course merely by-play on the atmospheric stage in which the sun takes the 'star part', and common experience tells us it never repeats itself exactly year after year.

The winter stock of air is kept in cold storage on the great land-areas and the ice-covered polar regions. Not merely the opposite hemisphere, but also the very oceans of their own are preyed upon by the ares which are greedy for cold air. There is a mechanism well known to meteorologists which prevents the store leaking away across its boundary, but with the turn of the sun the mechanism begins to fail, and with January the delivery to the southern hemisphere begins. The blackthorn winter and

St Luke's summer, each a month after the equinoxes, when the distribution of pressure over the hemisphere is comparatively speaking featureless, are in the middle of the busiest traffic. Between March and May 3·3 billion tons of air have to be got across the equator, and between September and November 4·2 billion tons have to find their way back.

It may be allowed that the escaping air starts cold and will hug the surface. It would be interesting and it may perhaps be possible to make out its track — certain it is that it cannot get over the backbone of the Eurasian continent; it has to find an easier way than that. The supply may come from different parts of the depôt at different times; northern Asia may come first, north polar regions next, and the commencement of the midnight sun in the north may be the preliminary signal for evacuating the area to the north of us. For us air from the north (if it misses the North Sea) is dry, and air from the south carries moisture; so the scheme fits, for March is our driest month and October our rainiest.

Moreover, we know that the north-east trade winds carrying northern air to the equator are strongest, and the doldrum line, where north and south meet, is farthest south in April — and the south-east trades carrying the air northwards are strongest in September, when the doldrum line is farthest north and the season of West Indian hurricanes at its height.

Let us say, then, that the 'blackthorn winter' arises from the transfer southward of the surplus air of the polar regions, cold when it passes us; and St Luke's summer is part of the process of stocking the northern hemisphere with air for the winter supplied from the southern hemisphere, warm when it passes our islands but chilled on its arrival at the depôt.

This, of course, is outline; some day the filling in will make an interesting scene in the drama of the atmosphere.

I am, etc.,

NAPIER SHAW

'Esquire'

From Mr L. Pendred   14 November 1941

Sir,

Among the minor reforms that are coming would not the suppression of 'Esquire' in general and businesss correspondence be welcomed? It is a relic of mid-Victorian snobbery, and has little or nothing to commend it. I believe the United Kingdom is the only part of the Empire that uses it.

Yours truly,
LOUGHLAN PENDRED

From Sir Max Beerbohm   *17 November 1941*

Sir,

How right Mr Loughlan Pendred is in denouncing the use of this word as 'a relic of mid-Victorian snobbery' and in demanding its 'suppression'! But why does he not go further? Is not our all too infrequent utterance or inscription of the word 'Mr' an equally gross survival from an era which men of good will can hardly mention without embarrassment and shame? I do hope Pendred *will* go further.

Your obedient servant,
MAX BEERBOHM

From Mr Osbert Sitwell   *21 November 1941*

Sir,

Beerbohm's suggestion that the prefix 'Mr' should be abolished does not go far enough. We are still left with our surnames, and this is undemocratic. I demand that we should all be called by the same name, as plain a one as possible. If this should render difficult the filling up of forms, a number could be attached to each − or rather the same − name.

Yours faithfully,
OSBERT SITWELL

Cocking a Snook

From Sir Carleton Allen, QC   *5 December 1961*

[Warden of Rhodes House, Oxford, 1931 − 2]

Sir,

The Lord Chief Justice is shocked, not surprisingly, because a boy who had just been fined five shillings for his third offence submitted to the majesty of the law by cocking a snook at the court. Very rude, very 'deviant', very 'anti-social'; but what, my lord, was the court to do? Give him 'a good dressing-down'? He would have cocked another snook, probably a double one this time.

231

Contempt? Juvenile Courts, and indeed all courts of summary jurisdiction, have no powers in contempt. Insulting behaviour? That would mean issuing a fresh summons and taking a steam-hammer to crack the nut of going through the whole business again and perhaps fining him as much as *ten* shillings. Order him a dozen of the best? Illegal! Barbarous! What would Mr Butler's Advisory Committee and the Howard League say ? A well-directed cuff by a policeman? An assault, which would probably cause some champion of liberty to press for a Tribunal of Inquiry, costing some thousands of pounds.

No, this poor boy is a subject of pity rather than of indignation. He is obviously 'maladjusted'. Some secret sorrow is gnawing at him, and cocking snooks is his only way of expressing his personality. And if the Ingleby Report becomes law, and if he is under 12, he will not be a *bad* boy at all, but simply in need of 'discipline' or of 'care and protection'. A little care and protection for the public and for courts of justice would not come amiss.

Yours faithfully,

C. K. ALLEN

Vicarial Bounds

From Mr D. I. Carter   *23 January 1978*

Sir,

I see from *The Times* of 14 January that the appointment has been announced of the new Vicar of Upton Snodsbury with Broughton Hackett and Naunton Beauchamp and Grafton Flyford with North Piddle and Flyford Flavell.

Is this, Sir, a record?

Yours faithfully,

D. I. CARTER

From the Reverend Reginald Lee   *25 January 1978*

Sir,

If in using the word 'record', Mr D. I. Carter means the record number of churches in the charge of one incumbent, then the answer to his question is in the negative.

As a contender for such a record, the Tarrant Valley Benefice here in Dorset should merit serious consideration. This benefice contains the churches of Tarrant Grenvile, Tarrant Hinton,

Tarrant Monkton, Tarrant Rushton, Tarrant Keynston and Tarrant Crawford and runs throughout the length of this beautiful valley.

Yours faithfully,
REGINALD LEE

History of the Cinematograph

From Mr W. Friese-Greene   *6 April 1904*

Sir,

My attention has recently been called to the article on the cinematograph in the 'Encyclopædia Britannica,' volume 27, page 95. Certain statements in this article are likley to give a wrong impression to those not familiar with the facts; and therefore I request you as a matter of justice, which I am sure you would be the first to recognize, to allow me to state in brief the history of this invention.

I have been working on this invention for over 20 years – that is to say, over ten years prior to the time that it was brought out commercially in 1894. In 1885, at a meeting of the Photographic Society, Pall-mall, I showed an apparatus for taking pictures by merely turning a handle. This camera was made for glass plates, but I specifically mentioned that it would be used for films in the future. At that time no suitable film was obtainable, although they were being experimented with. (See report of the journal of the Photographic Society, December 1885.) From that date until 1889 I continued experimenting and perfecting my invention, and in 1889 brought out my first patent for a camera for taking pictures on a celluloid film at the rate of 600 per minute. This was made possible at that time by reason of the fact that celluloid films were then made for the first time in long lengths. One of these films which I took in 1889, a scene in Hyde Park, is now in possession of the Bath Photographic Society.

This camera and films were exhibited before various photographic societies in Great Britain in 1890, and also before a Friday meeting of the Royal Institution in 1892.

On 29 November 1893 I took out a further patent giving the improvements made up to that date, which patent not only covered the apparatus for taking the pictures, but also the apparatus for the projecting of the same upon a screen. This, in connexion with my patent of 1889, is the master patent on the cinematograph.

Yours respectfully,
W. FRIESE-GREEN

[At the time of his patent in 1889 Friese-Greene also had the idea of synchronizing motion pictures with Edison's phonograph, so anticipating the 'talkies' by almost forty years. He later worked on stereoscopic and colour fims. He died in 1921, penniless]

Don't Blame the Toad

From Mrs M. E. Parsons   *17 March 1978*

Sir,

I must protest at the untrue remarks (copied from a disgraceful article in the *Daily Mirror* last year?) concerning the behaviour of toads towards gold fish which you have printed today (15 March). This is how myths are propagated and for such a paper as yours to persist in this fallacy to the detriment of the much maligned and ill treated toad is disgraceful.

I have many gold fish in two ponds. For years each spring hundreds of toads visit these little ponds engaging in eager song and dance in competition for the more rare female toads that chance their way. Frequently in warmer weather they form the extraordinary Knot of Toads which can become so heavy that it sinks to the bottom of the pond and writhes there for a time.

Never, in the closest watch upon these amazing activities of these enchanting little creatures, have I ever seen one reach out to a goldfish who stand about rather nonplussed during these goings on, or keep to a lower level of water.

Toads may clutch at other male toads in their games among the weeds, but almost immediately let go again − sensing their error of course. Should any deranged toad clutch in a most unlikely incident at a fleeting goldfish (I do not believe this tale) he would obviously let go again as he does with other male toads. If goldfish die in consequence of the invasion of toads to the ponds, let the owners consider the oxygen content of the water, and ask if it is not *that* which causes goldfish to die and give up this ridiculous motion that the fish are 'strangled'.

Please will you correct this wrong information.

Yours sincerely,

M. E. PARSONS

A Matter of Address

[Mr Edward Bernays, an adviser to presidents and governments, offered $5,000 for the best ideas to improve transatlantic understanding]

From Mr Robert Graves   *24 April 1967*

Sir,

I am not angling for Mr Edward Bernays' $5,000 prize (18 April) when I suggest that one of the principal causes of Anglo-American misunderstanding, and one simple enough to remove by wide publicity, is a current American habit (in all except business correspondence) of putting the letter-writer's address on the back of the envelope only and not at the head of the letter. It has been explained to me that this is a national rule of epistolary etiquette, as taught in schools and colleges.

Few of us English, however, keep the envelopes in which letters reach us, nor do we as a rule answer our friends in the States until at least three or four days have elapsed, by which time the contents of our wastepaper baskets or refuse-bins are likely to have been collected by the municipal authorities for incineration. On finally getting down to the job and writing two or three affectionate pages to dear Bob, Hank, Chuck, Lambie, or Kiki, we can seldom find his or her address – even at the close of the letter where, I admit, it does sometimes half-apologetically appear. We are left only with our correspondent's boldly printed name at the head of the letter, unsupplied even by a telephone number.

(United States papers, please copy!)

On the other hand, we English have such faith in the infallibility of all post offices that we seldom put our addresses on the backs of our envelopes: so that if a letter goes astray we cannot hope to get it back, and are left without any means of knowing whether or not it has reached Bob, Hank, Chuck, Lambie, or Kiki.

(English papers, please copy!)

Yours faithfully,
ROBERT GRAVES

Definition of Pakistan

[The *Concise Oxford Dictionary* had been banned in Pakistan on account of its definition of that country's name]

From Mr J. M. Wyllie   15 September 1959

Sir,

The definition of Pakistan in the *Concise Oxford Dictionary* should read, 'Until 1947, a proposed separate Moslem State in India, Moslem autonomy; after 1947, the independent Moslem Dominion in the Indian sub-continent.' The mistakes in the fourth edition of *COD* are due to the fact that for this edition the definition in the 1944 Addenda to the third edition was touched up instead of being entirely rewritten.

I say 'mistakes' because the etymology is also faulty, and was given more correctly by *The Times* Own Correspondent in Pakistan in a special article in *The Times* of 26 February 1948, on 'The Rise of Pakistan,' in these words: 'Pakistan means "Land of the Pure." It was often incorrectly said that its first three letters were chosen from the initials of Punjab, Assam and Kashmir . . .' Ire ported this to the Clarendon Press on 21 April 1951, concluding my letter with these words: '*The Times* Correspondent in Pakistan should have been in a position to ascertain the truth – which as you know is what etymology means.'

A fuller investigation which I made into this interesting word, with the help of my friend Dr C. C. Davies, Lecturer in Indian History in the University of Oxford, showed that it had been coined in 1933 by the late Sir C. Rhamat Ali, and a further letter to the Clarendon Press is relevant not only to this question of etymology, but also to the problem of dealing with the action which the Pakistan Government has now seen fit to take. I give this letter in full. The quotation is from the third edition of *Pakistan* (1947).

'4895/Corm/D.M.D., New Bodleian, Oxford, 27 April, 1951.
'Dear Davin. – Here is the extract from Sir C. Rhamat Ali's book *Pakistan*.

'''Pakistan' is both a Persian and an Urdu word. It is composed of letters taken from the names of all our homelands – 'Indian' and 'Asian.' That is, *P*anjab, *A*fghania (North-West Frontier Province), *K*ashmir, *I*ran, *S*indh (including Kachch and Kathiawar), *T*ukharistan, *A*fghanistan and Balochista*n*. It means the land of the Paks – the spiritually pure and clean. It symbolizes the religious beliefs and the ethnical stocks of our original Fatherland. It has no other origin and no other meaning; and it does not admit of any other interpretation. Those writers who have tried to interpret it in more than one way have done so either through love of casuistry, or through ignorance of its inspiration, origin and composition.''

'As Sir Rhamat Ali was responsible both for the idea of Pakistan and the word itself, this statement of his should be regarded not only as the last word on the question but (literally) as the last letter. All subsequent disclaimers emanating from official circles in the Pakistan Government ought to be discounted. Even the gods cannot change the past.

Yours sincerely,
(signed) J. M. WYLLIE
(Editor of the *Oxford Latin Dictionary*.)'

It must be a rare occurence for a professional lexicographer to be able to say that the etymology of a word given by the coiner of it is erroneous; and it would be more accurate to call this confusion than error in the case of Sir C. Rhamat Ali. But what can definitely be said is that the *Concise Oxford Dictionary* is wrong and *The Times* Own Correspondent right.

Yours faithfully,
J M. WYLLIE

An 'Inverted Rainbow'

From Mr M. G. Micholls   *28 April 1941*

Sir,
At about 6.30 on the evening of 21 April I saw an inverted rainbow north-west of Wentworth. The arc was quite small.

Perhaps one of your readers who also saw it may be able to give some explanation of this phenomenon.

Yours, etc.'

M. G. MICHOLLS

[In 1882 Charles Ashley Carus-Wilson, later Professor of Electrical Engineering at McGill University, had been sent to Bucharest to fit the King of Roumania's palace with electric light. Approaching — or perhaps approached by — *The Times*, he dealt with the 'inverted rainbow'.

'This appearance was part of a magnificent phenomenon called the Parhelia, and is caused by a the sun shining through an atmosphere filled with minute crystals of ice. The sun is surrounded by two rings and flanked on each side by two cross-shaped masses of golden light.

'Above the inner ring is an inverted arc, crystal white, and above the outer ring another inverted arc brilliantly coloured like a rainbow. The whole is seldom seen in this country, but parts of it may sometimes be seen. Some years ago I saw it completely in Canada, and was able to identify it with the vision of Ezekiel, who gives a very accurate description of the whole phenomenon.']

The Arts

Daphnis et Chloë

From M Maurice Ravel   *9 June 1914*

Sir,

My most important work, *Daphnis et Chloë*, is to be produced at the Drury Lane Theatre on 9 June. I was overjoyed, and, fully appreciating the great honour done to me, considered the event as one of the weightiest in my artistic career.

Now I learn that what will be produced before the London public is not my work in its original form, but a makeshift arrangement which I had agreed to write at M. Diaghilew's special request in order to facilitate production in certain minor centres. M. Diaghilew probably considers London as one of those 'minor centres', since he is about to produce at Dury Lane, in spite of his positive word, the new version without chorus.

I am deeply surprised and grieved; and I consider the proceeding is disrespectful towards the London public as well as towards the composer. I shall, therefore, be extremely thankful to you if you will kindly print this letter.

Offering you thanks in appreciation, I remain,
dear Sir, faithfully yours,
MAURICE RAVEL

[Notwithstanding, 9 June 1914 was a memorable evening. Thomas Beecham conducted Balakirev's *Thamar* for Karsavina and Boln, Pierre Monteux *Daphnis et Chloë* for Karsavina and Fokine]

An Opera Broadcast

[*Fidelio* (Lotte Lehmann the Leonora, Erna Berger Marzelline, Alexander Kipnis Rocco and Herbert Jansen Don Fernando) had opened the Covent Garden season on 30 April. Part of a fashionable audience arrived late, then talked with animation until loudly cursed by Sir Thomas Beecham]

From Sir Charles Strachey   *26 May 1934*

Sir,

The other day Sir Thomas Beecham, by the interjection of a few timely and well-chosen words, defended his audience from stupid and vulgar interruptions. Listeners to the opera on the wireless have, unfortunately, no such powerful protector.

Last night, just as Sir Thomas had launched his chorus into the serene glory of 'Wach' Auf' – Wagner's most magnificent choral composition – the music was switched off, and 'an announcer' blandly informed us (without apology) that the transmission of *Die Meistersinger* would be suspended in favour of a weather forecast from Daventry. When the opera was resumed that noble hymn was coming to end, and we had been robbed of one of the most lovely things in the whole range of operatic music. Surely the weather forecast could have been postponed for half an hour or so – when the opera ended. Nobody could possibly prefer a weather forecast, however optimistic, to 'Wach' Auf'. One wonders what words Sir Thomas would have used had he known of this outrage – perpetrated, of course, without his knowledge.

Your obedient servant,
CHARLES STRACHEY

[Sir Thomas always insisted that the BBC once faded him out during the closing pages of the 'Jupiter' symphony in order to broadcast a talk on 'The Sex Life of the Ant']

A Matter of Tempo

[Two London concerts by the Berlin Philharmonic Orchestra in January 1955 were cancelled on the death of Wilhelm Furtwängler. However, Sir Thomas Beecham agreed to conduct the Royal Philharmonic Orchestra in the same programmes as a tribute to his old friend. The work referred to in the letter below was the third Brandenburg concerto; Sir Thomas's affable tone was doubtless due to the rave notice accorded his performances of Strauss's *Don Juan* and Brahms's C minor syphony. What he did with the *Eroica* symphony and *Till Eulenspiegel* in the second concert seems to have been even more remarkable]

From Sir Thomas Beecham, CH   *25 January 1955*

Sir,

I believe it that it is generally well known that I have much respect for and sympathy with those brave fellows who attempt the hazardous task of musical criticism. More particularly does this partiality of mine apply to *The Times*, which alone among London journals of the present day devotes adequate space to the consideration of music in its various aspects. For these good reasons I refrain from uttering a word of reproach when I read something that strikes me as being unusually inexplicable.

But last Tuesday, 18 January, I played with my orchestra at Festival Hall a minor work of Johann Sebastian Bach, by no means representative either of his greatness or of his period. The following morning I was positively dazzled to read in one of your esteemed columns that my performance of this trifle was a positive travesty, and that the nature of the crime was to be discovered in the headlong speed adopted by me; comparable, according to the genial writer of the critique, with the famous ride of John Gilpin or it might have been Richard Turpin, Esq.

Now, Sir, I hope that you will agree with me that 'travesty' is a mighty word to use when belabouring an executive artist in respect of some alleged offence. I therefore am emboldened to enter a modest defence against such a grave charge. What is the truth of the matter? It is that my tempi on this occasion differed in no way from those adopted by 19 out of 20 conductors throughout the world during the past 50 years. All my concert programmes are tape recorded and each one is played to me on the day after the event. On this occasion I was able to verify that the respective tempi employed by me in the two movements of this concerto were – in metronomic language – 92 and 80.

241

Since then I have obtained the gramophone records of four other orchestras playing under their regular conductors the same piece, and what do I find? (Incidentally these other records were played in the presence of four skilled and grimly independent witnesses.) They are:

1	Boston Symphony Orchestra	92 and 76
2	Danish Orchestra	92 and 76
3	Boyd Neel Orchestra	92 and 84
4	Stuttgart Chamber Orchestra	88 and 80

From this it will be seen that four of us adopted exactly the same tempo in the first of the two movements, three likewise in the second movement, and where there was any difference it did not exceed one point of metronomic indication. (In the metronomic calculation there is nothing between 76 and 80, this slight difference being hardly distinguishable.) I think then, if I am to be convicted of the misdemeanour of 'travesty', there must stand in the dock beside me the vast majority of my colleagues and their orchestras over the long period of time to which I have referred.

What is the explanation of this apparent mystification? I think, if I may so suggest, that it lies in the comparative inability of nearly all listeners to distinguish correctly between the three separate entities of speed, rhythm and accent. I freely admit that I play this particular piece with a great deal more vigour and emphasis than any of my distinguished colleagues, and it is possible that there are those that do not care for this treatment of it. But their complaint, if they make it, cannot be directed against me on the ground of excessive speed. Long ago I commented in a book of mine upon the tendency of so many persons to imagine that I was an apostle of rapid tempi, although I was able through the evidence of gramophone records to establish that the majority of my interpretations might have erred in the contrary direction.

I trust that both you and the writer of the notice in question will look upon this little remonstrance of mine as having been uttered in a spirit of friendliness and respect.

I am your obedient servant,

THOMAS BEECHAM

Toscanini and Elgar

From Sir Landon Ronald   3 June 1935

Sir,

I have been constantly told that Elgar's music is so English in character and feeling that it could only be really understood and interpreted by one of his own countrymen. I have always strenuously denied this.

Last Monday's magnificent performance of the 'Enigma' Variations by Toscanini has, I lay claim, proved me to be correct. This great conductor rendered the work exactly as Elgar intended, and the composer's idiom obviously has no secret for Toscanini. Some of the best performances I have ever heard were from the composer himself, but this one on Monday night last excelled, because Toscanini has a genius for conducting and Elgar had not.

Elgar knew exactly how he wished his music interpreted, and the result was often magnificent. However, this was due, in my opinion, not so much to his powers as a conductor, as to the love and respect he inspired in the orchestra, both as a great musician and a lovable man.

We had the 'Variations' from Toscanini exactly as Elgar wished them played, plus the genius of a great master of the orchestra. I maintain that Elgar did not write English music – whatever that may be; he wrote great music. On Monday last a great foreign conductor proved this.

Your faithfully,
LANDON RONALD

[Sir Landon was the dedicatee of Elgar's *Falstaff*. 'Never could make head or tail of the piece, my dear boy,' he said to the young John Barbirolli]

What Mahler Ordered

From Sir John Barbirolli   29 November 1955

Sir,

In his generous notice of the Hallé performance of Mahler's First Symphony which appeared in your issue of November 23 your Music Critic includes the following: 'and it was not really necessary for Sir John Barbirolli to ask his horn players to stand up, like jazz musicians, when playing the triumphant chorale at the end.'

Might I be allowed gently to point out to him that the standing up of the horn players for the triumphant final statement of the chorale at the end of the symphony, far from being an unwarranted act of vulgarity on my part, arose simply from what is by now, I hope, my well-known passion for precise detail, and fidelity to the composer's intentions. If your writer will kindly refer to a full score of the Mahler First, he will find quite elaborate instructions for the precise moment at which the horn players are to stand. My knowledge of German being to say the least, rather sketchy, I took the precaution of asking an eminent Viennese colleague to translate the pertinent paragraph for me.

Yours, &c.,
JOHN BARBIROLLI

[Bar before cue 56: '*Alle hornisten stehen auf . . .*'
A supreme Mahler interpreter, Sir John was aged 54 when he first conducted a complete symphony by the composer]

A Record Disclaimed

From Sir Malcolm Sargent   *12 January 1950*

[Chief conductor of the BBC Symphony Orchestra 1950 – 57]

Sir,

Your Music Critic claims for me 'a record-breaking performance of the Meistersinger Overture . . . passing the last crotchet two minutes ahead of time.' In all modesty I must disclaim this honour. He continues: 'We know this because we had to wait two minutes before the next item.' On behalf of the BBC I must explain that the programme was arranged to allow ample time for this two-minute break in the music. Our broadcast began at 7.30 Overseas, but the announcers in the Home Service broadcast could not begin until 7.45. Hence the delay in the concert hall.

With regard to the tempo of the Meistersinger Overture, it is interesting to compare the following official timings from Broadcasting House and gramophone recordings. The slowest is

Sir Adrian Boult, 10 minutes. Mr Cameron has three times taken 9½ minutes; Sir Thomas Beecham takes 9 min. 5 sec. Knappersbusch takes 9 min. I have three times taken 9 min., as I did on Monday. De Browen takes 8 min. 54 sec., and it is interesting to note that Bruno Walter, a traditional Wagnerite, takes 8 min. 43 sec. From the above it would seem that the two-minute record that I have been given is slightly exaggerated. Walter and Boult are the winners, according to which end you favour. I am a mere third – unless the slowest wins.

Yours faithfully,
MALCOLM SARGENT

[What is a 'traditional Wagnerite'? More recently, Böhm was timed at 9 mins. 58 secs. True to reputation, Klemperer took 10½ mins.]

The Interrupted Symphony

From Mr Clifford Curzon   *11 September 1947*

[Knighted 1977]

Sir,

Last evening the Home Service broadcast a concert from the Edinburgh International Festival given by the Vienna Philharmonic Orchestra, reunited for the first time since the war with its former conductor Bruno Walter. The fact that the programme was announced in three languages indicated that the BBC considered this a special event, intended also for listeners abroad. As the orchestra reached the last page but one of Beethoven's Pastoral Symphony (one of the most superb performances England has heard for some time), it was suddenly 'faded out' and we were told in silken tones that we would now 'leave the Edinburgh Festival,' but that the entertainment woiuld continue with . . . 'Twenty Questions: a New Kind of Parlour Game'!

We go to the trouble of promoting an International Festival which arouses world-wide interest and then behave with a Philistinism that must surely dissipate any prestige the venture has brought us. Apart from this, can nothing be done to stop an institution which officially represents the nation from insulting distinguished guests in this way by cutting off the sublime to make way for the ridiculous? Are even English manners to

succumb to the general decline, and must we become as fit a
subject for caricature in the cultural world as we are fast
becoming in several others?

Yours faithfully,
CLIFFORD CURZON

[A broadcast on the Third Programme would have solved
the problem; unfortunately, very few parts of Britain could
receive the new wavelength]

Sweet Harmony

From Mr Ernest Bradbury   *19 June 1962*

[music critic, *The Yorkshire Post*]

Sir,

I write to you at 3 am, my sleep having been broken beyond
the possibility of recovery by a group of what you aptly call
transistor louts (actually, in this instance, university students)
doing the twist outside my front gate, which is on a main road.
An appeal to them to take their music elsewhere met with the
response that this is a free county. Your timely leader on 12 June
will also be supported, I am sure, by many fellow-musicians
who, by instinct as well as training, are unhappily compelled to
attend to sounds that are impinged on their hearing, from
whatever source.

On three successive Saturday journeys to London transistor
louts caused annoyance and unhappiness to railway passengers.
On the first occasion an elderly traveller called in the inspector
at Wakefield. A brusque 'Turn that thing off: it's illegal on here'
surprisingly met with obedience − mutinous, but obedience
none the less. On the two later occasions, there being no official
at all in attendance, passengers' requests for similar peace met
only with hostility, ridicule and abuse.

The remedy on railway and other public vehicles seems
simple: warning notices should be carried drawing attention to
the by-law and the penalties for infringement, and these should
be rigidly enforced. One feels that if, long ago, similar stringent
methods had been employed, there would be no need, in 1962,
for anti-litter campaigns.

Yours sincerely,
ERNEST BRADBURY

Sir,

All thrushes (not only those in this neck of the Glyndebourne woods) sooner or later sing the tune of the first subject of Mozart's G minor Symphony (K.550) – and, what's more, phrase it a sight better than most conductors. The tempo is always dead right and there is no suggestion of an unauthorized accent on the ninth note of the phrase.

Yours, &c.,

SPIKE HUGHES

Concert Hall Acoustics

[In June 1957 Stokowski conducted the LSO in two concerts at the Royal Festival Hall – one devoted to Berlioz, Ravel, Debussy, Prokofiev and Stravinsky, the other to an unusual programme: Schubert's *Rosamunde* overture, the second symphony of Schumann and the eighth of Vaughan Williams]

From Mr Leopold Stokowski   *13 July 1957*

Sir,

After conducting recently the splendid London Symphony Orchestra in the Royal Festival Hall, which in so many ways is well planned, I have the impression that it is a pity that the children and adolescents now growing up in London, and who are interested in the compositions of the great masters and also in contemporary music, often hear these either with too much reverberation, as in the Albert Hall, or with little, as in the Royal Festival Hall.

Such conditions are far from ideal for the future of English music, both for the listeners and for the English contemporary composers when they hear their music performed for the first time in either of these halls. Because of the great amount of absorption in the Royal Festival Hall the high tones sound thin and metallic and the low tones of the cellos and basses are correspondingly weak, so that the music is distorted and the tonal balance intended by the composer is not achieved.

The great violin-makers, such as Amati, Stradivari, and Guarneri, have clearly shown the ideal resonant and reflectant qualities of wood. If the walls and ceiling at the stage end of the

247

hall were sheathed with good, simple wood at reflective angles so as to diffuse equally the sounds from the stage, and if the end of the hall farthest from the stage remained as absorbent as it is at present, thereby still avoiding echo but lengthening the reverberation, this hall could be greatly improved so that the acoustics could be of the same high quality as its other well-planned characteristics.

I write this letter not in a spirit of criticism but in the hope of being constructive, and with the thought in mind of composers, listeners, performers, and the art of Music.

Sincerely,
LEOPOLD STOKOWSKI

The Musical Glasses

[While I'd gladly waft a *Vale*
To the fife and ukulele,
And the saxophone to me is simply chronic — Ah!
   Words would fail to paint my passion
   If this nightmare proved the fashion,

Viz.,
The
Hydrolaktulopsychicharmonica
— Punch, 20 January 1932]

From Mr W. McG. Eager   *31 January*

Sir,

Some neat verses in *Punch* have now raised to notoriety the lady of Twyford who recently figured in the news as entertaining a Women's Institute with a performance on the 'Hydro-dactulopsychicharmonica.' Thus was the portentous instrument spelt in the daily papers, and thus in *Punch*. Can it be, Sir, that a misprint even in dog-Greek can now pass undetected, and that the strolling players who in late Victorian times awed villages with the Hydrodactulopsychicharmonica can no longer protest that their little Greek is strictly descriptive? Have the Rural Community Councils and the cinemas, making fashionable topics everywhere of 'pictures, taste, and Shakespeare,' destroyed the very memory of 'the musical glasses?'

For fear that this is so will you, Sir, record in your imperishable pages one memory of a Cornish village in the nineties? My brother and I, being of less than preparatory school age and still innocent of the classics, reported home to the vicarage that a Professor and his Talented Family were going to give a refined music entertainment in the school. There were bills posted up all over the place, on the door of Mr Tripp's shop, on gate-posts, and even on the churchyard gate, promising that the entertainment would include the Hydrodaktulopsychichar-monica. I remember that the name ran right across the bill, and that we pronounced the 'ps' as in Topsy and the 'ch' as in cheese. Surviving the shock the vicar first gave us a brief lesson in the pronunciation of Greek, and then went to find the bold invader of his local monopoly of the learned languages. Happily the Profession stood fire. His interpretation 'music of the soul drawn out by fingers dipped in water' made the vicar wince, but it passed and, sitting in the front row that evening, we heard strange harmonies produced from batteries of wine-glasses, red, blue, and green. We thought it very beautiful and the Talented Family, supping at the vicarage after the show, not only demonstrated their skill on our poor stock of wine-glasses, but taught us boys how to strike a note. . . . May the lady of Twyford continue for many years to delight women's institutes, but for the sake of the humour which lies in little pedantries let her not corrupt the 'Professor's' unsophisticated Greek.

I am, Sir, yours, &c.,
W. McG. EAGAR

Organ Symphony

From the Reverend D. G. Richards   *1 May 1982*

Sir,

In 1973 there was a concert and organ recital in the church of SS Peter and Paul, Neath. Next the church was the fire station. During the playing of a piece by Bach the fire siren sounded; with great presence of mind and skill the organist changed key with the siren and earned spontaneous applause. Not true Bach but great fun.

Yours faithfully,
DEREK RICHARDS

From Mr P. A. Gascoin   5 *May 1982*

Sir,
    Against the possibility that concerts or organ recitals at SS
Peter and Paul, Neath, may again coincide with alarms at the
adjacent fire station, would not Mr Richards's organist friend be
well advised to practise a rapid substitution of Parry's 'Blest
Pair of Sirens' for whatever is on the programme (again with
appropriate tranposition of key?)
                                                Yours faithfully,
                                                P. A. GASCOIN

From Mr George E. Hill   8 *May 1982*

Sir,
    I am the organist at a local crematorium, and at a recent
ceremony I was asked to play Bach's 'Sheep may safely graze'.
I dutifully did so.
    I discovered, later, that the lamented deceased had been a
New Zealand lamb importer!
                                                Yours faithfully,
                                                GEORGE E. HILL

Musical Dogs

From Sir John Squire   11 *January 1936*

Sir,
    All dog-lovers must be interested in Lieutenant-Commander
Elwell-Sutton's account of his white whippet which insists on
singing to the accompaniment of his (or, may I hope, his young
son's?) accordion − presumably one of those gigantic new
instruments, invented, I think, in Italy, which make noises as
loud as those made by cinema organs and rather like them. This
dog's taste is low; but a musical ear is a musical ear.
    Some of your readers may think the gallant officer's story a
tall one; so do not I. Of course I have known dogs who simply
could not stand music, dogs who have bayed the moon when
one's nearest and dearest were singing, dogs who have crept
miserably under the chintz valances of sofas and armchairs when
the wireless was turned on. But I have known at least one dog
which had a passion for music no less ardent than that of the
accordion-fan whippet (as some of your contemporaries would

                            250

put it), although he was too modest to essay his voice in public – whether he practised, like so many of us, in private I do no know.

A good many years ago I was staying with the late Mr Thomas Hardy at Max Gate. He possessed then, and for long, a delightful fox terrier who nonchalantly supported the name of Wessex. His owner said of him that he bit bad poets and nuzzled good ones; I was let off, so naturally was flattered. During dinner Mr Hardy, a man of free mind who was willing to admit any fact if it was demonstrably a fact, remarked casually that the dog had a passion for the wireless. 'He won't,' he said, 'let us leave this room (the wireless, as Dr Watson might deduce, was in the dining room) until he's had a few minutes of it. He insists on it, even when we don't want it ourselves.' I listened, not incredulous, for Mr Hardy had one of the most accurate minds that ever I encountered. The ladies left the room, and I and that gentlest and most modest of great old poets were left alone with our (or, at that date, it may have been my) port. We talked a little about Chesil Bank, Dead Man's Bay, geology, and the Cerne Abbas giant (the dog meanwhile couched comfortably beneath the silent loudspeaker), and then, as manners bade, but forgetfully, we rose to go and I was graciously ushered towards the door.

Not a bit of it! Wessex's ears were pricked. He would no more go without his Sir (or was it then Mr? – historians must be exact about these things) John Reith than he would go without his breakfast. As Mr Hardy was about to pass out of the room the dog sprang at him, and gave him a fierce nip in the trouser-leg. Mr Hardy turned with that smile that wrinkled all his country face, and said: 'Well, well, Wessex, we forgot you, didn't we?' He closed the door and switched on what was then, I suppose, Daventry; and we resumed our seats. Melodiously forth came – well, I won't say a Bach Fugue, for I do not remember asking Mr Hardy whether his dog's Bach was worse than his bite. We watched the dog with affectionate and solicitous eyes, while the dog, squatting on his haunches with his jaws wide and his tongue hanging out, intently watched the 'set.' After five minutes he had had his ration, and he made no complaint when he was asked to join the general company in another room.

Sir, I am not saying or suggesting that all dogs' tastes in music are the same. One dog's Bartok is another dog's poison. Even among humans there are the tone-deaf: we remember the classic Victorian instance of the man who confessed that he could not tell 'Pop goes the Queen' from 'God save the Weasel.' But is there not a scientific field for investigation here? What percentage of dogs like music? Do particular breeds like particular kinds of music? What variations are there within the breeds themselves? Which kinds of dogs sing best? A hundred such problems await the attentions of research – and we must have many thousands of proved instances before we can draw the most provisional of deductions.

Mr Wodehouse's Ukridge, in the course of his many optimistic efforts to turn some kind of a penny, started a farm in Kent where dogs, which their owners thought had developable intelligences, could have their intelligences developed – probably on Montessori lines. Could not some scientist, or body of scientists, more competent and better endowed than Mr Ukridge attack a more limited sphere in a more practical manner, collect a large number of dogs of various kinds, experiment on them with music of various kinds, and assist dogowners who wish to have the sort of dogs who like the sort of music that they like themselves?

I forgot to add that when Mr Hardy was describing his terrier's passion to me he added (with a poet's exactitude): 'Mind you, he doesn't like the talks.'

I replied: 'I can't tell you how I agree with him!' I had just delivered some myself.

Yours faithfully,
J. C. Squire

Academy of Ancient Instruments

From Mr G. D. Dew   *10 August 1985*

Sir,

Sooner or later there was bound to be a revolt against baroque instruments but this is really going too far. During the last few months your "musical instruments" column has carried "for sale" notices for the following items: (a) a 4ft. boa constrictor; (b) a black labrador and (c) a spaniel pup.

Are we soon to hear the Appassionata arranged for Bactrian camel (4 hands) or a Mozart concerto for solo baboon? My mind continues to boggle.

Yours in total disbelief,
Gordon Dew

[Brahms spoke of Bruckner's 'symphonic boa-constrictors'. . .]

Art Forgeries

From Mr Bernhard Berenson   *4 April 1903*

[who in 1903 brought out his *Drawings of the Florentine Masters*. This immediately became a standard reference book and established Berenson as a major authority on Italian Renaissance painting. He died in 1959 aged 94]

Sir,

Whether the famous Tiara of Saitapharnes turns out to be a forgery or not the discussion will have done much good in bringing before the public the general question of forgeries. That there is nothing impossible in the Louvre authorities falling victims to fraud is proved by at least one of their recent purchases. The body that could buy the obviously cinquecent copy of Desiderio's famous Putto at San Lorenzo, believing this statue of forms at once mincing and puffy to be Desiderio's own handiwork, would seem to be the natural prey of the clever forger.

And if a responsible committee, living under the continuous menace of public reproach, is thus liable to error, how much more the irresponsible private buyer! Last spring at Christie's there was exposed for sale, and in fact actually sold for a relatively large price, a picture by a now well-known Sienese forger, a picture that several of us had seen brand-new on the painter's easel, before it underwent the process of staining and cracking and 'worm-boiling.' To draw 'un po' di mistero' – a little mystery – over the face of a picture is a process well known in Italy; and even for those who live there and keep their eyes open the veil of mystery is not always easy to lift. For the Italians, from the Quattrocento on, have always been clever forgers, and the technical skill of the race that produced the greatest European school of painting is by no means dead. Taste is dead and honesty has not yet come to take its place; but extreme dexterity remains. And this dexterity is now more and more turned to account to satisfy the constantly increasing demand for old masters. Their facility enables these forgers, as soon as the public begins to get on the track of a certain kind of falsification, to change to another style so different that only the eye trained to know a painter's work as the expert knows handwriting, almost by the pulse-beat vibrating in the stroke, can follow the Protean metamorphoses. My Italian friends addicted to this practice are constantly bringing me fresh specimens of their skill, hoping to wring from me the confession

253

that this time, at last, I could not, left to myself, have followed their doublings.

It is by no means an unknown case in literature that a writer may possess great talent as a forger, while being incapable of doing even mediocre work on his own account. And so it is with these imitators in paint and bronze and marble. When left to themselves, without a classical model, they can produce nothing but vulgar and flashy specimens of the 'Art Nouveau,' which in his heart, the average Italian greatly prefers to anything in his *patrimonio artistico* he is so eloquent about. But as imitators they are admirable, betraying their native bad taste only in the most subtle ways that may well escape even the best educated *dilettante*. There are, indeed, amateurs who take the ground that, if the work of art is beautiful, it makes no difference whether it is a modern forgery or a genuine production. These people forget that a large part of our enjoyment of art depends upon the good will which we bring to its contemplation. No considerable work of art but has its defects; but we forgive them, we even do not see them, if we are well disposed to the object as a whole. But the moment the fatal word 'forgery' is pronounced these defects start into prominence, and little by little our loss of associative pleasure reacts upon our vision, and we actually see the object as less and less beautiful.

The curious thing is that these Italian forgers, unless they chance to be dealers as well, which is often the case in Italy, make very little money by this work. A few hundred francs will satisfy their happy-go-lucky natures, for the adventurous, dare-devil spirit of the Renaissance is still alive in them. And for all born forgers (the born forger is scarcely less common than the born artist) forging is its own reward. A volume would scarcely suffice to develop this theme – and what a fascinating volume, by the way, it could be, if one did not confine oneself to art alone, but included literature and even scholarship! But to return to our subject – it is the dealers who make the enormous profits out of the credulous amateurs and ignorant gallery directors. A dealer who is also a forger has an undoubted advantage; and in this connexion I feel that the public ought to be especially warned against some of the cleverest dealer-forgers whose centre of operations is Florence. These 'artists' get hold of old ruined panels with just enough patches of the original paint left on them to enable them, if suspicion is aroused, to experiment on these carefully-chosen parts with solvents that would destroy modern work, and to point triumphantly to their resistance as a 'scientific proof' of the picture's genuineness. The rest of the panel they fill in, with undeniable skill, in the style of Filippino Lippi, Ghirlandajo, Raphael – whom you will, according as they think they can spare their purchaser. The productions are rarely to be found in such a vulgar place as a shop; they are 'discovered' in old palaces and castles, sometimes in the most out-of-the-way villages of Tuscany, and they boast an undisputed pedigree, sworn to by some spendthrift scamp bearing an historic name. What wonder if the unsuspecting American or English buyer is taken in, especially if the dealer has the cleverness to hypnotize them by dangling the picture before their eyes as an unheard-of bargain!

If my remarks have been followed to this point it may pertinently be asked how the well-meaning collector is to escape the forger? Escape absolutely he never can. Even the expert buys his experience at the cost of his purse and his vanity. He can only hope to avoid being too grossly deceived if, having a definite passion as well as talent for the subject, he devotes himself seriously to training his eye to distinguish quality. Let him not imagine that a practical acquaintance with last year's forgeries will prevent his falling victim to this year's crop. Moreover, let him not pay the slightest attention to supposed pedigree of provenance, nor to the various papers and documents and alleged traditions that purport to guarantee the genuineness of a work of art, for these are much more easily forged than the work of art itself, nor is there anything to prevent a picture being painted or a marble carved to correspond with a description in a perfectly authentic document. Nothing but a fine sense of quality and a practised judgment can avail against the forger's skill. Technical, documentary, stylistic standards may all be satisfied, but the one thing the forger cannot do is to satisfy the standard of a specially trained taste, and to avoid betraying himself by some mannerism of his own which the experienced eye can learn to detect.

I am, Sir, your obedient servant,
BERNHARD BERENSON

[The Tiara of Saitapharnes, purchased by the Louvre in 1896 as a work of the third century BC, was made by Israel Rouchomowsky of Odessa (born 1860).

The marble taberbacle of Desiderio da Settignano (died 1464) is in S. Lorenzo at Florence. It is topped by a figure of the Christ Child which was considerably copied, perhaps because it was removed to the sacristy in the sixteenth century and was shown on the high altar only at Christmas. There are several sixteenth-century copies of the figure and that (of marble) in the Louvre is now usually recognized as such. It is so recorded and reproduced in L. Planiscig, *Desiderio da Settignano*, Vienna, 1942]

A Tale of Two Pictures

[To mark the occasion of Sir Winston Churchill's eightieth birthday in 1954, Parliament presented him with his portait by Graham Sutherland. Both Churchill and his wife disliked the painting, and it was on Lady Spencer-Churchill's initiative that the portrait was destroyed before Sir Winston's death]

From Mr G. S. Whittet   *17 January 1978*

[former Editor, *The Studio* and *Studio International*]

Sir,

Soon after the presentation I was invited to view the portrait by Sutherland at Churchill's home in Hyde Park Gate. There in the garden drawing-room, fortified by a glass of sherry, I examined the picture alone for some time. Now looking up the number of the magazine I find I described it as 'an unconventional work of an unconventional sitter'. Its chief defect was that it looked unfinished in as much as his feet were concealed in a carpet that seemed to have sprouted a dun-coloured grass − the artist had obviously been unhappy about them and they had been painted over since it would have been impossible to 'cut off' his legs below the knees without radically altering the proportions and placing of the picture on the canvas.

One has to remember that the portrait was a gift to Churchill by colleagues past and present in Parliament as a token of their affection for him as a man of long service in that institution. It was not a state or official portrait but a personal symbol of good will and respect of which there was little evidence in the painting; I wrote the 'mood and the manner of the study do not awaken sympathy or warmth' as anyone looking at the colour repduction acompanyine my critical comments may confirm. Also, Churchill had a keen sense of history and his own place in it; lacking a present-day Holbein, he and his wife were not going to risk being preserved for posterity in a painting that they felt did neither him nor the artist full justice.

As footnote to the above, soon after I had viewed the portrait

I visited Arthur Jeffress, the art dealer, who told me that a portrait of him by Sutherland had actually been begun and 'laid in' on the canvas the artist then used for Churchill — not that it mattered, for that initial sketch was undetectable. Jeffress asked me not to mention this in print and I didn't until some six years later after he had died. As I said then it would have been another reason for the Old Man to have disliked the portrait though by that time apparently it did not exist.

Yours, etc.,
G. S. WHITTET

[In February 1974 Vermeer's *The Guitar Player* was stolen from Kenwood House.

Later a letter announced that the picture would be destroyed on St Patrick's Day unless the Price sisters, Dolours and Marian, on hunger strike in Brixton prison after being convicted of taking part in London bombings, were returned to Northern Ireland to complete their sentences]

From Mr R. G. T. Lindkvist   *15 March 1974*

Sir,

Mr Murray Mindlin (14 March) gives voice to the anguish one feels over the fate threatening the Vermeer painting, and he quite correctly spots an ideology and a logic at work. But is that logic impregnable? I think it right to argue that the thieves, were they to set fire to the Vermeer, would simultaneously see their own framework of logical thought perish in the flames.

Take the very act of stealing the painting. As it was not an act perpetrated for criminal gain as commonly understood, I assume it to fall within the category of creative protest which, some will argue, is an art form. Well, and I am not joking, this places the thieves and the painter Vermeer in the same group where members have the same rights of expression. Therefore, whatever damage they do to the painting they also do to their own action and to any right they may argue they had or have to take that or any consequential action. I take the thieves seriously. Do they?

This is quite apart from another argument militating against them: by hitching any success of their venture to a star priced at £1,000,000 they have, of course, *de facto* accepted the values of the capitalist society they profess to be fighting.

Yours faithfully,
T. LINDKVIST

[On May 1974 the Vermeer was discovered in the graveyard of St Bartholomew's Church, Smithfield — damp and with a slight cut but otherwise undamaged]

Called to Mind

From the President of Trinity College, Oxford 1 October 1964

[Sir Arthur Norrington]

Sir,

Mr Sylvester, in his article on Joan Miró on 22 September, suggests that the theme of 'Blue II' is interval and proportion.

'The series of blobs . . . call to mind a medieval musical score . . . painting is *seen* to aspire towards the condition of music.' They also call to mind, in fact they are almost indistinguishable from, the break-up of a thread of liquid issuing from the tip of a vibrating hypodermic needle, a phenomenon illustrated in an article by Professor B. J. Mason in the September number of

Endeavour on 'The collision, coalescence and disruption of drops'. I enclose the two illustrations for comparison.

Could anything be more encouraging than this collision and coaslescence of two cultures? 'Painting is *seen* to aspire to the condition of physics.'

Yours faithfully,

A. L. P. Norrington

258

The Artist and His Levels

From Mr John Bratby, RA   *22 April 1974*

Sir,

For some time to obtain entry to an art school a student has needed O and A levels − the equivalent of five O levels. As a result many embryo artists, with real dynamic creative powers and talent, do not go to art school, and will not develop. How can this misunderstanding of the nature of an artist exist? The ability to obtain O levels and A levels, and artistic ability, are different things.

Other educational establishments are concerned with students assimiliating information, like blotting paper, but art schools are concerned with the development of creative abilities, the finding of an identity that is so important to an artist − nothing to do with O and A level abilities.

An artist can be a totally unintelligent person in the sense that he cannot pass examinations, but he has the creative personality.

Students of definite artistic talent and learning ability wishing to go to art school, who, for example, obtain four O levels, have to remain at school to obtain the requisite passes to qualify them for art school.

The Leonardo da Vinci type of artist, highly intellectual, is not what an artist is oftentimes. Painting does not spring only from the intellect, but primarily from spring sources of creative drives. Picasso, for example, like Soutine and van Gogh, was a creative animal, driven to make pictures compulsively. Like Leonardo he had ideas, the result of the creative personality.

The receptive personality, who can pass examinations, O and A levels, is another kind of human being, a robot fed with knowledge.

Yours sincerely,
JOHN BRATBY

VIPs at the Academy

[Mr Jeremy Thorpe was leader of the Liberal Party 1967 – 76]

From Ms Duffy Ayers   *28 February 1975*

Sir,

Early today thousands of people were queueing outside the Turner exhibition at the Royal Academy, now in its last week. At ˙9.30 a.m. before the doors were opened to us all and the queue was turning back on itself like a great snake, a black car drew up and parked quickly – a keeper approached and out leapt Jeremy Thorpe, glanced embarrassedly at us all, ran up the steps as fast as he could and dived inside. Presumably to see this great show in peace and quiet, undisturbed by the common people (not so common really as most were reading *The Times* or *Guardian*). Surely the VIPs, especially politicians, could slip into these exhibitions at some other time and not be seen to be so privileged. Even our greatest *living* artist, Henry Moore, joined the queue like an ordinary mortal. Is an MP more important than an OM?

Yours sincerely,
DUFFY AYERS

From Mr Kenneth Gregory   *3 March 1975*

Sir,

Moore queues, Thorpe does not: Ms Ayers asks if an MP is more important than an OM. Of course, dear lady, there are twice as many OMs as Liberal MPs.

Yours faithfully,
KENNETH GREGORY

Art and the Film

From Mr Nicolas Bentley   *9 March 1943*

Sir,

Your critic, commenting on *The Magnificent Ambersons*, is hopeful that 'one day the film may become an important art.' I do not know what is his definition of art, and I admit my own confusion on this elusive topic. But there need surely be no dispute between us in acknowledging the truth of Ruskin's broad assertion that it is the language of the imagination; a language in which the best film directors, actors, and technicians of Britain, America, France, and Russia are often exquisitely fluent. (Fifteen years ago the inclusion of Germany would also have been possible.) The apparent disdain with which your critic dismisses their inspiration and ability, and his condescension towards all that the cinema, in its short history, has achieved aesthetically needs no comment.

His oblique denial of the cinema's importance as an art seems as difficult to follow as to justify. The ubiquity of the film, whether good or bad, assures its affecting the ideas and emotions of a far greater number of people than is at present influenced by any other form of art. To dismiss it, therefore, as unimportant admits a degree of oblivion or partiality which is painful to observe in one who speaks with the authority of a critic.

I remain, Sir, yours truly,
NICOLAS BENTLEY

[*The Magnificent Ambersons* was the second film made by Orson Welles but, unlike *Citizen Kane*, it divided critical opinion. Both are now generally regarded as masterpieces]

W. C. Fields as Micawber

From Mr James Agate   *28 December 1946*

[drama critic of *The Sunday Times* 1923 – 47; author of eight volumes of autobiography, *Ego*; to be remembered with Hazlitt, Lewes, Shaw, Walkley, Beerbohm and Tynan]

Sir,

Your obituarist says of W. C. Fields that he was 'an almost ideal Mr Micawber in the film of *David Copperfield*.' Sir, you will permit me to say that he was not, and demonstrably not, and could not be. Consider Micawber's first appearance in the novel. '"This," said the stranger, with a certain condescending roll in his voice, and a certain indescribable air of doing something genteel, which impressed me very much, "is Master Copperfield. I hope I see you well, sir?"' There was nothing remotely genteel about Fields's Micawber, who in the film made his first appearance by a highly ungenteel fall through the roof of his own house.

Consider again. '"Under the impression that your peregrinations in this metropolis have not as yet been extensive, and that you might have some difficulty in penetrating the arcana of the Modern Bablyon in the direction of the City Road – in short, that you might lose yourself – I shall be happy to call this evening, and install you in the knowledge of the nearest way.'" Fields's Micawber would not have used the word 'peregrination,' or known the meaning of 'arcana.'

Mr Micawber's manners which 'peculiarly qualify him for the Banking business'? Not even Mrs Micawber at her most doting could have said that of Fields. Micawber is a gentleman who keeps his fallen day about him, and if he is not played like this he is not played at all. Fields was a glorious buffoon. But being possessed of no more gentility than a pork pie he could do no other with Micawber than turn him into an obese Ally Sloper, with very much the same nose and hat. And that, I submit, is not Dickens's character.

I am, Sir, your obedient servant,

JAMES AGATE

[In his youth a great juggler admired by Edward VII, Fields had three funerals – non-sectarian, Catholic and Spiritualist – the first organized by the ventriloquist Edgar Bergen]

The Television Habit

From Mr T. S. Eliot, OM   *20 December 1950*

Sir,

In your issue of 17 December you announce that the BBC proposes to spend over £4m during the next three years on the development of television. I have just returned from a visit to the United States, where television (though not, I believe, more highly developed technically) has become an habitual form of entertainment in many more households than here. Among persons of my own acquaintance I found only anxiety and apprehension about the social effects of this pastime, and especially about its effect (mentally, morally, and physically) upon small children.

Before we endeavour to popularize it still further in this

country, might it not be as well if we investigated its
consequences for American society and took counsel with
informed American opinion about possible safeguards and
limitations? The fears expressed by my American friends were
not such as could be allayed by the provision of only superior
and harmless programmes: they were concerned with the
television habit, whatever the programme might be.

Your obedient servant,

T. S. ELIOT

Interviews on Television

[A correspondent had complained that television
interviewers were a law unto themselves and did not show
proper respect to statesmen]

From Mr Malcolm Muggeridge   *9 April 1966*

Sir,

Professor H. D. Lewis's attitude to television interviewing is
surely rather heavy handed.

At least so it seems to me, who have been engaged, admittedly
in a desultory sort of way, in this bizarre activity for some 12
years past, beginning with Billy Graham, taking in Salvador Dali
and the late Brendan Behan (both highly successful interviews,
which I attribute to the fact that the former's English was totally
incomprehensible, and the latter — God rest his soul — too
drunk to utter), and including a fair proportion of those set in
authority over us. Professor Lewis equates the television
interview with questions in Parliament and at public meetings;
a truer comparison, it seems to me, would be with newspaper
interviewing, whether in the frivolous gossip-column style, or
with a view to seriously probing political views and intentions.

Politicians, in my experience, began by taking far too lordly
an attitude towards being interviewed on television. I name no
names, but there were, I assure you, those who confidently
expected one (in my case always in vain, I am happy to say) to
go over in advance what one proposed to ask, and to provide
assurances that this or that topic would not be touched on. They
gave one the feeling that coming to the studio at all was a great
act of condescension on their part. Now the tendency is to go to
the other extreme, and have so feverish a sense of the
importance of television in building up their public image that

some politicians, I really believe, would walk barefoot from John o' Groat's to Shepherd's Bush if they were assured of a peak-viewing time appearance on arrival there.

Of course television is important to politicians, as the press has been and to a great extent still is; but not as important as all that. They should take it easy. No one is going to make them appear if they don't want to, and they are under no obligation to answer a question which seems to them impertinent or irrelevant. By refusing to answer it, and giving their reasons for so doing in as emphatic terms as possible, they may rest assured that all the viewers' sympathies will swing to them and away from the interviewer. Mr Hogg – and excellent performer with whom it's always a pleasure to appear – has demonstrated that this is so again and again.

In general, however, men-of-letters and other non-politicians, who are less desperately concerned about how they are going to appear on the screen than politicians are, find it easier to fend off the too obdurate interviewer. Mr Robert Graves, the other day, fended off some questions of mine very skilfully and amusingly, making me, as we say in the Centre, look a proper charlie. Mr Evelyn Waugh, likewise, easily and adroitly turned aside Mr John Freeman's expert assaults in their super Face to Face interview.

De Gaulle is one of the few politicians who has grasped the point that the balance of advantage is always with the man being interviewed if he cares to seize it. I saw him on French television being asked why he had delayed releasing the Ben Barka story till after the presidential election. Instead of getting hot under the collar, sending for the French equivalent of Sir Hugh Greene, transferring his favours to Radio Monte Carlo, or otherwise manifesting his displeasure, he just hung his old, battered head sheepishly, and muttered in a woeful, strangled voice: *'C'était mon inexpérience!'*

It really might be a good idea if in Downing Street they had a look at these Graves and Waugh interviews, and at the General's press conference, instead of fretting about well-informed and courteous interviewers like Robert Mackenzie.

Yours, &c.,
MALCOLM MUGGERIDGE

[Hogg (now once again Hailsham), Graves, Waugh, de Gaulle: add Lady Violet Bonham Carter, Sir Compton Mackenzie, Harold Macmillan and Sir Mortimer Wheeler, and it would seem that the best television performers are no longer young]

Television Breaks

From Mr E. H. Dare   *11 March 1959*

Sir,

When consideration is being given to a third television channel could not a way be found out of the 'advertising break' problem by devoting the new channel entirely to advertising? In that way the present commercial channel could be left free from programme breaks (natural or otherwise), thus satisfying those of us who object to these interruptions while those millions who are alleged to prefer 'the adverts' will also be made more happy in their viewing.

Yours faithfully,

E. H. DARE

Henry Irving and Coquelin

From Lady Oxford   *8 February 1938*

Sir,

I knew Henry Irving and his lovely leading lady well. I had a passionate admiration for both of them, and after my marriage my husband and I often joined them at supper.

Irving had the sort of face which I most admire, nor can I recall any face at all like it. He did not seem to be looking at you but through you when he was talking to you. He would have enforced attention even if he had not been famous. There were many criticisms which could be made about his acting – a halting gait, a curious intonation; nevertheless, in some of the parts he played he was unrivalled and was thrilling to all theatregoers. He was the greatest impresario who has ever been connected with the English stage. In spite of his fame and his genius, and even some natural affectation, he was a lovable and authentic person and fundamentally humble.

When I first met him I was a friend of Coquelin, who visited London every season with his company from the Comédie Francaise. During these short visits he gave me lessons for love in the art of acting. He had made a great hit in a Paris play called *Le Juif Colonais*, which Irving bought and produced at the Lyceum under the title of *The Bells*. After seeing Coquelin perform the tortured part of Mathias – the innkeeper who had thrown one of his lodgers from his sleigh to be devoured by wolves – I went to see Irving. Two more different interpretations of the same part cannot be imagined. Coquelin enjoyed an even greater fame than Irving, and was the most accomplished actor of his day. But he had the sort of face which you could never associate with melodrama. It was as round as a Swiss roll, and had the agricultural smile of a peasant; the cleverest make-up could never have made him look sinister. Well aware of this, he played the part in a rollicking manner. However much his conscience pricked him, he appeared to be always at his ease when surrounded by his boon companions at the bar of his famous inn. He laughed louder and drank deeper when he fancied he heard sleigh-bells in the snow, which, whether they were there or not, were haunting his guilty imagination.

Irving took a different line. He never attempted to calm his conscience. When sitting in the inn with the same boon companions, however much he discoursed and declaimed he shuddered at the sound of sleigh-bells and raised his glass in both hands to distract his listeners from observing the anguish of his face.

When I praised this performance to Coquelin I could see that he was a little jealous and thought that I was exaggerating. (With all his charm and genius he had a certain vanity.) He asked me to take him to see *The Bells* and return afterwards to have supper with him. Sitting alone together, I asked him what he thought of the play, to which he replied that he had been thrilled by Irving's acting and doubtless he was a man of genius.

But, he added, the difference between our two interpretations is that the stupidest detective would have clapped Mathias (Irving) into prison, whereas I would never have been caught.

The last time I talked to Irving was when he came to see me at the end of a London season (I do not remember the date). I said that I was sorry to say goodbye to him, but I might by luck see him at the Palace garden party. He said that no actor was ever invited to a royal party unless he had a title. I told him that there would be no difficulty about this, as all our Royal Family were patronizers of the stage. I am proud to think that it was through my husband's influence that Irving was knighted.

Yours, &c.,

MARGOT OXFORD

[Margot Tennant married H. H. Asquith (later Earl of Oxford and Asquith) in 1894 when he was Home Secretary. Irving was knighted the following year]

The St James's Theatre

[which had seen the first performances of Pinero's *The Second Mrs Tanqueray*, Wilde's *Lady Windermere's Fan* and *The Importance of Being Earnest*, Lonsdale's *The Last of Mrs Cheney*, and Rattigan's *Separate Tables*. More recently the Renaud-Barrault company from Paris and Olivier's production of the two Cleopatra plays had filled the St James's]

From Mr Alan Dent   *28 June 1957*

Sir,

'Zealacious commerciality!' murmured Wells's Mr Polly when the ironmonger opposite took no notice of his 'Good morning!' – being far too busy arranging his shop. The St James's Theatre is to be pulled down and a block of offices reared in its place. At the confirmation of this threat, I can only repeat – 'Zealacious commerciality!' But the deplorable decision merits far more than a whimsical jest. It is an occasion for dismay and outcry.

As a Londoner by adoption (and in view of my present address), I may be permitted to end this roar of indignation on a personal note and as a practising dramatic critic. For 18 years I lived in Covent Garden, which I liked because I was close to most of the theatres. For the past three years I have lived in St James's which I like because it is close to St James's Theatre. On the day the demolition-man removes the first stone of this theatre, I shall sell the lease of my present flat at whatsoever personal loss. This will not, of course, matter to anyone but myself. But the loss of this old, endeared theatre will matter tremendously to the whole community – or at least to that section of it which persists in thinking that grace and glory and tradition are things worth striving to maintain.

Not until the demolition actually begins shall I really believe that this world has grown so bad, or that this town has grown so mad.

Yours faithfully,

ALAN DENT

[The world grown bad and the town so mad, Mr Dent moved]

The Purpose of a National Theatre

From Mr Laurence Irving   *28 April 1961*

[designer; biographer and grandson of Sir Henry Irving]

Sir,

The establishment of a National Theatre, if it is at all desirable, calls for clear thinking, particularly by those upon whom the Government must rely for professional advice.

The theatre is the domain of the actor; all other artists are ancillary to his performance. Though at this time his authority and prerogative have been usurped by others, it must be the purpose of a National Theatre to restore him a stage whereon he can maintain and demonstrate the highest standards of his art, assured of continuity of possession and freed from the speculative hazards of the so-called commercial theatre.

How can this be done? Let a noble theatre be built, with all its services under one roof, fitted for the production of plays on any scale and for the comfortable participation of the audience. Let a young actor-producer be appointed to direct it – one who will commit himself entirely to the living theatre. Let him enlist a company of similarly dedicated players – young enough to mature and to grow to full stature in the new dispensation. Let the salaries of these players be sufficiently generous for them to be able to ignore the distraction of films and television. Let the board of management give the director a mandate to re-create a style of acting and presentation capable of interpreting to perfection the whole range of drama from *Oedipus* to *The Caretaker*. Let it be made clear to him that for five or 10 years he must work to this end, disregarding favourable or adverse criticism and popular success or failure. Let no leading players be asked to give more than three performances of a major role in one week. Let all members of the National Theatre, artists and staff, be assured of pensions commensurate with their service.

Is all this the expression of Utopian folly? For certain the English theatre (including its critics) is in some disarray. Young players visiting European countries, which they have been led to believe are less enlightened than their own, return amazed by their glimpse of exemplary theatres in which all those who serve in them from director to call-boy strive only to aid and reinforce the actor in his task of creating illusion on the stage. Among these young people are many with high professional ideals who are resigning themselves to an acceptance of second-rate

268

standards and to the surrender of their artistic integrity. Never was there so much promise in the English theatre; never was the outlook for theatrical artists so unpromising.

Sir Ralph Richardson wrote recently that a National Theatre is not comparable to a National Gallery in that the exhibits are alive and kicking. Yet it can be compared with a national or municipal orchestra. In both cases, under the hand of an ardent director an association of artists with individual skills can reach a measure of perfection interpreting classic and modern repertory conscious of their corporate being and assured continuity of purpose.

Those who disagree may well ask what I mean by style. Perhaps it is totality of presentation in a well-conducted, well-equipped and disciplined theatre. The Royal Shakespeare Theatre and the Old Vic have whetted our appetites for a National Theatre; neither, owing to its chartered obligations, can qualify as a substitute.

The experiment will be costly and, at first trial, may fail. So it is with rockets.

Yours, &c.,
LAURENCE IRVING

[The Lyttelton Theatre opened with *Hamlet* (Albert Finney; director Peter Hall) on 16 March 1976. The Olivier and Cottesloe Theatres − the other buildings in Sir Denys Lasdun's complex − opened, respectively, on 4 October 1976 and 4 March 1977]

Olivier's Othello

From Professor J. Dover Wilson, CH   *17 October 1964*

Sir,

All the world is flocking in relays to the National Theatre to see our greatest actor performing a part which he had hitherto not attempted, the title role of Shakespeare's greatest tragedy; and having just returned from this exciting spectacle I think that perhaps some of your readers may care for a word from one who has been editing Shakespeare's plays for over 40 years, especially if you number one or two of my contemporaries still alive among them.

Ay there's the rub! For in 1964 I am 50 years out of date; I am still a believer in the essential dignity of man which is the basic assumption of dramatic tragedy as Bradley taught us, and for him Othello was the greatest of tragic heroes. Such was the reading of his character in all performances of the play that I had yet seen, including that of the noble African Paul Robeson with Peggy Ashcroft as Desdemona.

How proud then must be Dr Leavis when he finds himself the inspirer of this Othello quite new to the theatre! That it was a Leavis Othello was made clear to all spectators when they brought the Book of the Play with the programme as they entered, for there was the quotation from his famous essay in *Scrutiny* as they opened it; and as they watched Sir Laurence's performance it became clearer still.

Unhappily I could not follow the expressions on his face with my imperfect sight except every now and then, but I saw enough to glean a strong impression that the whole conception of the character he was attempting to give us was a Leavis one, which incidentally hasd also been made in an essay by T. S. Eliot, first published in 1919. Its upshot is that the 'nobility' upon which Bradley insisted (as did Shakespeare) gives place to a 'habit of approving self-dramatization' which is often a 'disguise for the man's obtuse and brutal egotism'; and at the theatre this became especially evident in the second half of the play in which I could discover no dignity in the character at all while the end was to me, not terrible, but horrible beyond words.

Every age rediscovers its own Shakespeare and I suppose that, after two great wars and the Nazi eruption from the nether region which seemed to drag our poor human nature through the loathsome filth of the concentration camps, to say nothing of the disintegrating influence of Freud, it is difficult to think nobly of Man. Yet it was surely not necessary for a Bradley to teach us, what Aristotle had long since taught us, that the essence of Greek tragedy, as of all great tragedy, is to think of the hero as *heroic*, through scene after scene that harrows us with terror and pity until in the end we are purged by the catastrophe which leaves us reconciled, even exalted.

Must we give up Shakespeare's heroes? Must we refuse to admit that the basis of his tragedy was his belief in the integrity of Man? If so, *nunc dimittis* – or I might say so if I were not certain that the whirligig of time would bring in his revenges, that Shakespearian criticism would presently emerge from its 'dark house' and learn again to 'think nobly of the soul'.

Yours, &c.,

J. DOVER WILSON

[*Othello*, 'Shakespeare's greatest tragedy': in *The Essential Shakespeare*,1932, Dover Wilson awarded the palm to *King Lear*. Had thirty years changed the critic's mind, or was it an unconscious tribute to the power of Olivier's performance?]

Much Ado About Nothing

[Franco Zeffirelli's production of Shakespeare's play for the National Theatre – with Maggie Smith as Beatrice, Robert Stephens Benedick, Albert Finney Don Pedro, Ian McKellan Claudio, Derek Jacobi Don John and Frank Finlay Dogberry – had caused *The Times* drama critic to remark that 'one of the most Italianate figures is Dogberry – a wrong-headed reading if ever there was one']

From Sir Laurence Olivier   *18 February 1965*

[Life peer 1970; Order of Merit 1981; Director of the National Theatre 1962 – 73]

Sir,
First of all, let me say, that the idea that the sound of the production should be Italianate, as well as the look, the feeling, and the atmosphere of it, was one that I most strongly encouraged and I promised the director that I would take full responsibility for it if it was brought into question.

What your critic has to say brings into the open a question which has been vexing me, and I am sure many of us in the theatre business, for some years. How should the peasant class speak in a Shakespeare play? What also vexes us is how these people should sound in English adaptations in foreign plays of all periods. These two questions are not unrelated, and I feel we can take them together to some extent.

We do not know, we cannot guess, how Shakespeare would like his plays to be interpreted in this day and age, any more than we know how Cervantes would like Sancho Panza to speak in an English version. We can only hazard that both would like the interpretation to be made so that the work can be appreciated by the greatest number of people, including intellects both high and low.

In general practice, and in the general way of vaguely localized Shakesperian presentation, our peasant can get away with regional, Mummerset, or a vaguely 'off' accent, or has done so up to now. Nobody has required Bottom the Weaver to have Athenian characteristics, and the Fourth Citizen in *Coriolanus* has not been reproached for coming straight from Salford, but I can't believe that Shakespeare intended an English atmosphere to pervade all his plays, much as I feel some people would wish it to be so.

There are times when his specified choice of place and character-naming brings this very much into question and invites exploration and expedition into further fields. I think that most would agree that *Romeo and Juliet* invites an Italian atmosphere, *Macbeth* a Scottish one, and *Antony and Cleopatra* largely an Egyptian one. The porter in *Macbeth* has been presented with a native accent with impunity on countless occasions.

For some mysterious reason the Cockney accent is very seldom welcome in Shakespeare except in the Eastcheap scenes in the histories.

On the very 'First Night of Twelfth Night' (January 6, 1601, according to Leslie Hotson), the most daring jape lay in the fact that a distinguished member of the audience was a Duke Orsino, Italian Ambassador to the English Court, and popularly supposed to have a béguin for the Queen. Did the first actor playing Orsino speak with an Italian accent by any chance? I'm only asking.

Now every producer has the right to express a point of view on any play, in fact that is one of the main things required of him and if the point of view taken is one that requires strong local characteristics, then this promotes a problem that has yet to be solved somehow or other.

In his production of *Much Ado About Nothing*, Mr Zeffirelli has been inspired by the tradition created by the Teatro San Carlino in Naples. This tradition has ceased to exist in Naples for some years but still survives in Sicily. This influence, being applied to this production, must bring with it a strong atmosphere, redolence and impression of Sicilian character and characteristics in the behaviour of the people concerned, and consistency requires that it sounds as well as it seems.

What would the captious find preferable in these circumstances? Cockney? Mummerset? English regional? I think not.

Proper logic is not by any means always to be applied to the stage which owes far more to the instinctive, the intuitive, the inexpressible, even to clown's logic. (Grock's way of getting down from a high piano stool.)

True logic will dictate to us that if a play is translated into the English language it must therefore be translated into English custom and characteristic, but do we really believe it is more fulfilling to Shakespeare to have Don Pedro behave like a gentleman from the Marlborough Club, than to suggest the kind of blood and ésprit that made Shakespeare choose his name and station.

Is Dogberry worse and less real as a low down carabiniero or a Warwickshire buffoon? The question I say is a vexed one and it cannot be answered by the bigoted or the severe logician. The answer can only lie in the mysterious impulse of stage logic.

Yours faithfully,
LAURENCE OLIVIER

[There is another answer – see Bernard Shaw's *Our Theatres in the Nineties*, vol. III, p. 325. 'Of all Sir Henry Irving's manifold treasons against Shakespeare, the most audacious was his virtually cutting Dogberry out of *Much Ado*.']

Cleopatra as the Dark Lady

From Dame Agatha Christie   *3 February 1973*

Sir,

I have read with great interest the article written by Dr A. L. Rowse and published by you on 29 January, on his discovery of the identity of Shakespeare's Dark Lady of the sonnets. She has always had a peculiar fascination for me, particularly in connexion with Shakespeare's *Antony and Cleopatra*.

I have no pretension to be in any way a historian – but I am one of those who claim to belong to the group for whom Shakespeare wrote. I have gone to plays from an early age and am a great believer that that is the way one should approach Shakespeare. He wrote to entertain and he wrote for playgoers.

I took my daughter and some friends to Stratford when she was twelve years old and later my grandson at about the same age and also some nephews. One young schoolboy gave an immediate criticism after seeing *Macbeth* – 'I never would have believed that was Shakespeare. It was wonderful, all about gangsters, so exciting and so real.' Shakespeare was clearly associated in the boy's mind with a school-room lesson of extreme boredom, but the real thing thrilled him. He also murmured after seeing *Julius Caesar* – 'What a wonderful speech. That Mark Antony was a clever man.'

To me Cleopatra has always been a most interesting problem. Is *Antony and Cleopatra* a great love story? I do not think so. Shakespeare in his Sonnets shows clearly two opposing emotions. One, an overwhelming sexual bondage to a woman who clearly enjoyed torturing him. The other was an equally passionate hatred. She was to him a personification of evil. His description of her physical attributes – such as 'hair like black wire' – was all he could do at that time (1593 – 4) to express his rancour.

I think, perhaps, that as writers do he pondered and planned a play to be written some day in the future; a study of an evil woman who would be a gorgeous courtesan and who would bring about the ruin of a great soldier who loved her.

Is not that the real story of *Antony and Cleopatra*? Did Cleopatra kill herself by means of an asp for love of Antony? Did she not, after Antony's defeat at the battle of Actium, almost at once make approaches to the conqueror Octavian so as to enslave him with her charms and so retain her power and her kingdom? She was possibly by then tired of Antony, anxious to become instead the mistress of the most powerful leader of the time. But Octavian, the Augustus of the future, rebuffed her. And she – what would be her future? To be taken in chains to Rome? That humiliation for the great Cleopatra – never! Never would she submit; better call for Charmian to bring the fatal asp.

Oh! how I have longed to see a production of *Antony and Cleopatra* where a great actress shall play the part of Cleopatra as an evil destroyer who brings about the ruin of Antony, the great warrior. She has finished with Antony.

Dr Rowse has show in his article that Emilia Bassano, the Dark Lady, described by one of her lovers as an incuba – an evil spirit – became the mistress of the elderly Lord Chamberlain, the first Lord Hunsdon who had control of the Burbage Players. Presumably she abandoned the gifted playwright for a rich and power-wielding admirer. Unlike Octavian he did not rebuff her. In his mind Shakespeare kept that memory until the day that he wrote, with enjoyment and a pleasurable feeling of revenge, the first words of *Antony and Cleopatra*.

Shakespeare was probably not a good actor, though one feels that is what he originally wanted to be. All his works show a passion for the stage and for comparisons with actors.

How odd is it that a first disappointment in his ambition

forced him to a second choice – the writing of plays – and so gave to England a great poet and a great genius. Let us admit that his Dark Lady, his incuba, played her part in his career. Who but she taught him suffering and all the different aspects of jealousy, including the 'green-eyed monster'?

Yours faithfully,

AGATHA CHRISTIE

[Had Verdi turned his attention to *Antony and Cleopatra*, and awaited Maria Callas . . .]

Theatre's Fashion for Despair

From Mr J. D. Brown   *5 February 1972*

Sir,

Having read your correspondent's review of the play (if that is the right word) *Insulting the Audience* at the 'Almost Free Theatre' I am forced to ponder on the likely future direction of the theatre. As I understand it, this pay (evidently written for masochists) consists of four actors (again, if that is the right word) who shout miscellaneous insults at the audience until they have run through their script. This is, by all accounts, the sum total of the performance.

Various critics seem to have taken the playwright, Mr Peter Handke, to task for writing a play which 'goes too far'; which transcends the bounds of what is normally regarded as theatre. I would suggest from reading these reviews of the play that this is a false argument. It seems to me that the fault of such a play is that it does not go far enough.

For a truly revolutionary theatre, the audience should hurl insults at the actors using scripts provided as they enter the auditorium. The actors should then show their contempt of the whole proceeding by performing some task which totally ignores the audience, such as eating a meal or playing bridge. The audience would leave when they became bored or felt they had had their money's worth.

As an extension of this, every now and again, the actors could break off from their activity and join the audience to shout insults at the empty stage. This would produce the unsettling effect which is a hallmark of all true masterpieces.

Perhaps a more perfect system would consist of having the audience and actors mingle together throughout the performance. They would then hurl insults at one another, taken at random from the script provided. Two refinements would of course, be important; the actors would not identify themselves so that nobody would know whether he was insulting an actor or a member of the audience and the shouters could make up their own insults if they did not like the scripts provided.

This leads to a still more perfect concept. That is, handing out scripts to random members of the population at some central point, such as Oxford Circus underground station (charging a nominal fee of course) and leaving people to insult their fellow travellers all the way home.

In contrast to the various critics concerned, I do not feel the slightest despondency for the future of the theatre. Indeed, I am full of optimism for it. I would even go so far as to say that should any theatrical management wish to take me up on any of the creative suggestions given over, I would be only too happy to provide them with full scripts.

Yours faithfully,

J. D. BROWN

The Agonies a Comedian Bears

From Mr Tommy Steele   *8 February 1969*

Sir,

Having just read the wonderful article in your paper (Saturday Review, 1 February), I feel that perhaps a little more could be said concerning the profession, the environment, the very existence of a comedian.

The big difference between a dramatic actor and a comedian is basically one of 'sound'. They both thrive in creating emotions in their audience, but it is the lot of the comedian also to create a sound — laughter. It is not enough for him to feel the moment he is amusing, he must *hear* the audience feel it. This can, and quite often does, cause deep anxiety to the man whose task it is to make an audience forget their anxieties.

Throughout the theatrical profession you will find it is the funny man who is the worrier, the crier, the creator of difficulties. He dreads the day his timing goes; he fears his audience; he thrives on laughs and dies with silence.

The comedian is never off stage. He has to prove 25 hours a day that he still has control over his listeners. He always has new material to test. He has his act which he protects like a tigress guards her young. He lives in constant fear that his 'gems' will be stolen, and they often are.

It is said that when the end of a comedian is at hand, he 'dies from the eyes'. Sit in an audience long enough and you have to see it at least once in your life. He stares transfixed. You will feel his animosity with every line. He loved you once, but now you frighten him. He knows you will never laugh for him again.

Such a comedian is not unlike Manolete. He faces the same dangers, he is tortured into risking all to please his audience and, alas, as in the case of the great Tony Hancock, he comes to the same end for the same reason.

Yours,
TOMMY STEELE

[The article which so moved Mr Steele had been written by Michael Wale, scriptwriter to Tony Hancock towards the end of the comedian's life]

Kick in the Lear

From Mr Basil Boothroyd   *28 November 1985*

Sir,

It is difficult for us old Shakespeare-goers. Are we cultural Blimps or justified deplorers of the new Shakespeare-makers?

The notice (November 25) by Mr Irving Wardle, a critic I follow with respect, sharpens our dilemma with his warm approval of the Kick Theatre *Lear* and its "amazing sequence of fresh and potent dramatic images".

These include a belly dance by the frock-coated king, who also conducts the thunder effects up a step-ladder with a riding crop and (though I read this elsewhere) wheels his clown on in a trolley.

Dare we any longer go to see Shakespeare? Worse, dare we introduce him to our younger relations? All very well to fire them in advance with promised wonders. But dubious fulfilment in Lady Macbeth on a monocycle, Bosworth Field fought with rolled umbrellas, "O, what a rogue and peasant slave" delivered from a balloon.

Not that I want to put ideas into anybody's head. Were that necessary.

Yours sincerely,
BASIL BOOTHROYD

Tongue-Tripping

From Mr Ned Sherrin   *4 March 1985*

Sir,

The best genuine malapropisms regularly committed these days come from one of the most talented and beautiful actresses to appear with the National Theatre in recent years.

Authenticated instances include her comment on a best friend who, 'went to live in Israel and worked on a kebab'; her dismay at the treatment of, 'the ostriches'. 'What ostriches?' 'The ostriches in Iran'; her dislike of, 'ejaculated lorries'; her admiration for the actress 'Joan Playwright' and her work at the 'RAC' and, perhaps most surreally, her recovery from a back-flip when she arrived at an upright posture saying, 'I'm Tallulah Bunkbed! Whoops! Sorry, I mean Tallulah Handbag!'

While training for her career she sought advice on how to be a better actress. She was advised to read Stanislavsky. She asked how the name was spelt. 'S.T.A.N. . . .' She looked hurt. 'I know how to spell his first name,' she said.

Yours faithfully,
NED SHERRIN

Sharing the Cup

From Mrs Dora Haley   *14 April 1973*

Sir,

It seems that the rules of hygiene are paradoxical – to say the least. Nowadays, a shop assistant who licks her fingers in order to facilitate the picking up of a paper bag in which to put cakes, or similar items of food, risks dismissal. Yet, during Eucharist Services in church, the chalice is passed from mouth to mouth along a row of a large number of communicants, usually without even a wipe (not that this would make much difference, as generally the same small piece of cloth is used. I saw this in a cathedral recently.)

Is there some magic, some mystical element? Because the chalice is a sacred vessel, is it considered to be immune to germs? One only asks where is the sense or reason in preaching hygiene when such anomalies prevail?

No wonder that the common cold develops into a widespread influenza epidemic – not to mention other diseases. I know that many folk will disagree with my viewpoint on this subject, but during a recent sermon on Radio 4 it was stated that we must not be afraid to speak out against something which we consider to be wrong, and I think that this is definitely wrong. I heard of a woman who contracted a lip infection.

However, it must be mentioned that in the majority of Nonconformist churches tiny individual communion glasses are now being used. Why not in Anglican churches, and cathedrals, too? Surely, prevention is better than cure?

Your sincere reader,

DORA HALEY

From Mrs M. Fletcher   *18 April 1973*

Sir,

I write at once to endorse most heartily every word of Mrs Haley's letter today (14 April). This is a subject dear to my heart, as in 40 years of regular church attendance there has not

279

been a single occasion when I have approached the altar rails with anything but a heart full of the ordeal that lies ahead of me. If coughs and sneezes abound among the congregation then my anxiety to be first in the queue far outweighs any other emotion, and totally obscures for me the true meaning, purpose and beauty of the Sacrament.

If in a restaurant one is handed a cup with traces of lipstick upon it one does not hesitate indignantly to return it and demand a clean one. Why then should I, in church, be expected to place my lips upon not one but many fresh and fruity impressions with never a qualm? I know for a fact that many old people, living alone and dependent upon good health to look after themselves, eschew the service of Holy Communion for dread of infection picked up from the chalice, greatly though this goes against the grain for them − it is a very real fear. My daughter once took a Roman Catholic friend to Sung Eucharist in York Minster at the height of the tourist season. When he saw the four-deep queue of communicants and the chalice passing from mouth to mouth with never so much as a token wipe he confessed that he was so revolted that he felt he could never attend an Anglican service of Communion again.

I have sincerely tried, over the years, to overcome my revulsion and distaste and have failed utterly. To me there is only one change necessary in our church service in this day of so many and such seemingly unnecessary changes, and that is the archaic practice of having to take wine from a communal chalice.

Yours sincerely,
MONICA FLETCHER

From the Reverend Maurice C. Garton　　　*18 April 1973*

Sir,

I fully agree that from a practical point of view Mrs Haley has a strong case, but the fact is that millions of people of all races, all over the world, use the common chalice regularly, and have done for centuries; and yet there is no strong evidence that there has been an epidemic as a result. The Church has many enemies, and if there was conclusive proof that disease has been spread by this means, the enemies would have published it abroad. Moreover at the end of the service the priest usually consumes what is left, and therefore would be most liable to be infected, but the life insurance companies give the clergy a 'good life'. The one instance Mrs Haley adduces is irrelevant, as there may have been other causes of infection. You cannot argue from a particular to a general.

I agree that the use of a purificator is useless from a hygienic point of view. I use it in case some other matter gets on to the chalice. It has been argued that as wine is alcoholic the alcohol will kill any germ, and therefore the Free Churchmen who use non-alcoholic wine are wise to use the individual cup. I leave this point to the scientists as I am not competent to give an opinion. What seems to me important is that the priest repeats the words of Our Lord 'This is my Blood', and by this he understands 'Blood' to mean 'Life', and if we receive Christ's Life then that will not result in physical death. In a materialistic world it is well to remember that spiritual values are more important than material ones, and the Communion Service is a constant reminder that Christ's values overturn material ones.

Yours, etc.,

MAURICE C. GARTON

From the Reverend T. J. Marshall   *18 April 1973*

Sir,

With reference to the complaint of Mrs Dora Haley, all that is required is for the General Synod of the Church of England to pass a Measure rescinding the Act of Parliament of 1574 (1 Edw VI c 1) which introduced Communion in two kinds into the Church of England.

If Holy Communion were given in one kind only, not only would it be more hygienic, but it would restore the practice of our national church for a thousand years and bring the Church of England into line with the greater part of Christendom and so promote the cause of Christian unity.

Yours faithfully,

T. J. MARSHALL

From Mrs Patricia Collins   *18 April 1973*

Sir,

As an Anglican and a bacteriologist I share Mrs Haley's doubts about the common Communion cup.

However, would not the Church of England Rubric preclude the use of individual cups?

Why not Intinction?

Yours faithfully,

PATRICIA COLLINS

From Bishop Thomas S. Garrett   *17 April 1973*

Sir,

Our commendable, if sometimes excessive, concern with hygiene needs to be counter-balanced by the reflection that every time one comes in contact with infection and gets away with it one builds up one's resistance.

Most worshippers accustomed to share one cup in Holy Communion would be loth to give up its symbolism, particularly when that of the one loaf advocated by many would-be reformers of worship has largely failed to oust the individual wafer. But why not experiment with the use of a spoon in administering the cup, as is the custom in some Eastern churches, and as is recommended (though by no means universally practised) in the Church of South India? The wine is poured from the spoon into the mouth of the communicant without touching the lips. It needs some practice by both clergy and their congregations: but one they are used to it they might well agree that it is the best way. The inkwell-sized individual Communion glasses to which Mrs Haley refers involve an enormous amount of washing up in large congregations.

Yours faithfully,
T. S. GARRETT
Bishop in Tirunelveli, Church of South India

From Mrs Pamela Vandyke Price   *17 April 1973*

Sir,

Mrs Dora Haley is right to be concerned about hygiene. Would that – as she supposes – the finger-licking shop assistant did risk dismissal! Also those who handle food and money at the same time, who wear long hair while serving in food shops – and would that the customers who bring in animals and who smoke in these shops were asked to leave.

But Mrs Haley's fears about hygiene at Holy Communion can be allayed. It is wine, fermented liquor, which is used in the Anglican Eucharist. Wine is one of the very oldest disinfectants in the world, which is why wounds were washed with it. Others in authority will be able to answer Mrs Haley as to the exact role and significance of the wine at Communion, but any layman reading the New Testament should be in no doubt that Our Lord took a cup of wine at the Last Supper and that this cup was shared among those present.

In the world of wine, it is routine for glasses to be shared and sometimes a number of people will taste along a line of wines,

282

each using the same single glass. I have never known anyone contract any infection by doing this, although naturally anyone with a cold or any kind of mouth infection would not taste in this way. It is to be supposed that anyone with a communicant's sense of responsibility would take thought and either decline to take the chalice or, if merely in doubt, arrange to take it last. But in any case and in a wholly material sense, the wine itself is a safeguard.

Yours truly,
PAMELA VANDYKE PRICE

From Commander E. Astley-Jones
(RN, Retired)   *17 April 1973*

Sir,

Mrs Haley's letter prompts me to suggest that celebrants could follow the practice of Bishop James, who, when he administered this sacrament at his church in Basil Street in London in the 1930s, dipped the wafer into the wine and then put it into the mouth of the communicant.

Yours faithfully,
E. ASTLEY-JONES

From the Reverend Sydney Linton   *17 April 1973*

Sir,

Mrs Dora Haley appears to over-estimate the risk of germs in the use of the common cup at Holy Communion. The clergy, whose duty is to consume what remains after all have communicated, far from being more infected than the laity, have an above-average expectation of life.

Yours faithfully,
SYDNEY LINTON

From Dr A. F. Foster-Carter   *19 April 1973*

Sir,

I am afraid it is impossible to deny that sharing the cup at Holy Communion is an unhygienic procedure. For instance, smears of lipstick can be very unpleasant and many priests fail to wipe the rim of the chalice. Even this practice does little to lessen the risk of infection, which is undoubtedly a theoretical possibility and I doubt whether any bacteriologist would share Mrs Vandyke Price's faith in the very low antiseptic properties of wine.

At the Brompton Hospital, during the years when it was the

'Hospital for Consumption' and the danger of infection with tuberculosis was greatly feared, Holy Communion was always administered by intinction (dipping the wafer in the wine, as described by Commander Astley-Jones; the words of administration being modified to include both elements). The wider use of this simple practice deserves serious consideration by the Church authorities. It is much easier than employing a spoon and there is no danger of spillage because the wine is absorbed into the wafer. Also it has the advantage of speed and this can be a blessing in these days of large parish Communion services.

Yours faithfully,
A. F. FOSTER-CARTER

From Mr H. D. F. Taylor   *17 April 1973*

Sir,
   The true believer at the Eucharist is not concerned with hygiene but trusts in God.

Faithfully yours,
H. D. F. TAYLOR

[Then came Aids]

In Time of Peace – 2

Saluting the Auschwitz Dead

From Group Captain Leonard Cheshire, VC   24 April 1967

[the official British observer at the dropping of the Atomic Bomb on Nagasaki, 1945; later founded the Cheshire Foundation Homes for the Sick; Order of Merit, 1981]

Sir,

To many in this country the absence of an official British representative at the unveiling of the memorial dedicated to the four million people of 23 nationalities exterminated at Auschwitz – and so movingly described in your issue of 17 April – is an occasion of the utmost regret.

Japan came, Italy came, India came, practically the entire Western Alliance came; alone Britain did not. Our dead who lie there were saluted by the Union Jack and by a handful of private pilgrims, not by our Government,

Whether political considerations, not apparently applicable to the rest of Europe, necessitated this decision, or whether in the official mind the occasion was not of sufficient significance there is no means of telling. Either way we have failed to measure up to the occasion and have lost in stature, not least because we have withheld an honour due to the dead.

It is sometimes thought, I know, that ceremonies like this are occasions for beating the drum and reviving old hatreds. Such is very far from the truth. One finds among the survivors, a hundred thousand of whom were present that day, not only a remarkable absence of bitterness but a solidarity and affection which transcends every frontier of race and political allegiance, and from which we have good reason to draw inspiration and hope. Out of evil God knows how to draw forth good.

I am, Sir, yours, &c.,

LEONARD CHESHIRE

285

Jewry's Debt to Bernadotte

[Count Bernadotte's progress report on his mission as mediator of the United Nations in Palestine reached the Palais de Chaillot on the very day of his assassination. Its first conclusion was that the Jewish State in Palestine is a 'living, solidly entrenched, and vigorous reality.' He also recommended the protection of all Arab rights in Jewish territory]

From Mr R. A. Hewins   *21 September 1948*

Sir,

In common with most Englishmen I have had a number of Jewish friends.

I have visited Auschwitz, the liquidation camp which will ever stand as one of the supreme infamies in world history. I have wandered aghast over the flat wastes of what was once the Warsaw ghetto. Near Danzig I have handled soap manufactured by Germans from Jewish corpses. I have seen and interviewed trainloads of the Jewish wrecks whom Count Folke Bernadotte as vice-chairman of the Swedish Red Cross rescued by his own exertions at the end of the war. I have seen the pioneer work done by Jews in Palestine. I know and respect a number of their leaders. I hope, therefore, that nobody will accuse me of being anti-Semitic. Yet in this hour of Jewish shame it is hard to remain objective and to fight the virus of anti-Semitism, which vitiates the world, turns all life sour, and converts the subject into an imitation of a Nazi, the very species we fought for six years to tame.

My friends in the Mandatory Government, with whom I had been a few days earlier in the King David Hotel, Jerusalem, were blown up in the midst of their thankless duties by Jews. Two British sergeants have been hung like dogs by Jews, although these simple soldiers were non-political and doing irksome duties far from home. The harmless brother of a Palestine police officer has been murdered by a Jewish infernal machine in his English home. The Jews have villified the British, their best friends, who fought Hitler for one year alone and made the very idea of the National Home feasible. The Jews have turned much of the great American republic, on whom we lean for our very bread and butter, against us. The Jews have embroiled us with our teeming Arab friends, who substantially paved the way for the destruction of the Hohenzollern confederation against us in the first world war. They threaten openly to engulf our trustiest

Arab friend, King Abdulla in Transjordania, which alone in the Middle East never for a second wavered against us in the late war and is still a friendly pivot of the Empire. This, and more, is a lot for the most tolerant Englishman to bear. It is almost enough to turn a saint anti-Semitic.

Now the Jews have murdered Folke Bernadotte. No more infamous (nor more unjustified) crime was, in my opinion, committed throughout the war. The Germans could argue that the shooting of innocent hostages and the razing of defenceless towns and villages was "war," and that these measures were "necessary politically." No such vestige of excuse can be offered for this, the supreme Jewish atrocity of modern times.

Count Bernadotte, whom I was proud to call my friend for eight years, was indisputably non-political and moved by exclusively humanitarian ideals. Nephew of a king, he had no name to make, no titles to win. Husband of a millionairess, he was above the sordid considerations of gain. He was deeply religious, and schooled himself for years in the organization of the Swedish boy scouts. When he had won his spurs he threw himself wholeheartedly into the perfection of the Swedish Red Cross organization.

When the late war broke out he was ready. The International Red Cross entrusted him with the first exchange of allied and enemy invalid prisoners. Such was his integrity and indisputable impartiality that the allies and Germans alike gave him free passage on his work of mercy. At the end of the war, on his own initiative and by his own opportunism, he rescued thousands of Jews from liquidation in German concentration camps: in doing so he confronted none less than Heinrich Himmler and got his way. Altogether Bernadotte rescued 40,000 lives, irrespective of race or creed. The new Civilian Convention, which was passed by the Seventeenth Red Cross Conference in Stockholm last month, was his inspiration and largely his work. Because of his proved idealism, efficiency, and impartiality Uno chose him as their Palestine mediator – Uno without which the provisional State of Israel could hardly exist to-day. And the Jews have struck him down – as they have struck down their other friends, the British.

It makes one almost despair of the human race. But in this woe-begotten hour one must look for some compensation and hope, rather than give way to rage and grief. That has been the British way during the thankless discharge of our mandate. That was Bernadotte's fearless way, too. Surely this shocking moment is the one for Jewry to set its house in order by deeds instead of words. The various Jewish factions must surely realize

287

that they cannot for ever go on "passing the buck." One can believe verbal Jewish protestations of horror, sympathy, regret, and disownment for a time, but surely the hour has struck when the Jews' most ardent well-wishers must shed their ingenuousness, measure the sympathy for Jewish suffering, and cease making allowances for the ignorant excesses of American Zionists — yet without taking the easy, self-destructive course of anti-Semitism.

Is it not time for world, American, and Palestinian Jewry to get together to root out the murderers and their organization, even if some international force is necessary? If civilized Jewry does not take drastic action now, when the iron is hot, I fear universal horror at Bernadotte's assassination must crystallize into a new and lasting wave of anti-Semitism. Not only for their own peace of mind but their own safety it seems that Jews should seize this opportunity.

The Stern gang, to whom the crime is attributed, is, I believe, not more than 1,500 strong, and it should not be beyond the power of Israel to deal with it. The prerequisite of Israel's recognition as a sovereign State and its admission to Uno is that the Jewish provisional Government should prove itself capable of preserving law, order, and discipline among its potential subjects. If Uno demands anything less, its authority as a civilizing force is dead.

I have the honour to be, Sir, yours, &c.,

R. A. HEWINS

Causes of Violence

From Mr N. F. Simpson   *14 August 1973*

Sir,

During the course of some researches into the causes of violence in our modern society, I have had my attention drawn to what would appear to be yet another instance of the sort of mindless thuggery with which in recent times we have become, alas, all too familiar.

In this case, a young man, pleasant, likeable and totally inoffensive, known to those around him simply as Abel, is attacked in a field by a psychopathic elder brother by the name of Cain, and receives injuries from which he subsequently dies.

One is loath indeed to draw overhasty conclusions from insufficient data, but one cannot but be forcibly reminded of scenes in *A Clockwork Orange*, where I believe similar muggings result, likewise, in the deaths of the victims concerned.

It is, of course, a matter for speculation whether it was this or some other film or television programme that in fact triggered off this abominable crime, but, bearing in mind that it had the effect of reducing the total world population at that time by no less than 25 per cent at a single stroke, it seems to me that the makers of films and television programmes, together with the writers of the books on which films and television programmes seem so often to be based, have a good deal to answer for.

Even though, as my assistant now somewhat belatedly tells me, the crime was committed some time before a good many of them were made, the principle remains the same, and the lesson is crystal clear to those not too wilfully blind to see it.

Yours in anger,
N. F. SIMPSON

Violent Youth

[There had been riots in Bristol]

From Mr David Holbrook   *April 1980*

Sir,

Over the last decade some of us have been warning about the effects on consciousness of a massive assault on human values. Through the powerful influences of film, television, "pop" and other media people have been subjected to the idolization of violence and aggression, as solutions to the problem of life. I recall a letter in *The Times* about the possible influence on youth of a certain film in which the anti-hero represents an idolization of violence, and an article of my own in which I warned of imitation in this realm.

Our intellectuals have indulged in their own cults of hate, from full-page advertisements in *The Times* calling for soft drugs to be legalized, to favourable reviews of stage shows in which the most fundamental of our values have been subjected to insult and inversion. The roots of my own objections are in the thought of the effect some of the powerful media might be having, on the kind of disturbed child I have taught in the past. Yet to my dismay, intellectuals on the whole have denied that what happens to consciousness can have any deleterious effect in society – while they must be "free" to indulge in any debasement.

Now, a new feature appears in our life — youthful riot. The whole of London's Underground system is brought to a halt by an outburst of destructive rage. In a provincial city there is rioting and destruction — an area, significantly, noted for its "red light" activities and its drug traffic. People are stunned by these new developments. But they are what we forecast, those of us who are aware of the deeper effects of the new cultural barbarism. Our nihilistic culture has created a new mental sickness, not least among the young, and especially the socially deprived young. Life has no meaning except immediate sensual satisfaction, and the only possible stance is one based on hate: this has been the sinister message. (It is interesting to note that in Germany the "porno-topia" euphoria has now given way to deep cynicism and apathy.)

Yet during this period our intellectuals have not only refused to accept that what happens to consciousness is important (not least because they wanted to indulge in mental rage themselves): they have also opposed and suppressed debate, treating those who raised a warning voice like pariahs. Now we are reaping the whirlwind of the pseudo-revolution of the seventies, and the victims, as usual, are the poor and weak: and those who have to keep order. The political implications are extremely grave.

Yours, &c.,

DAVID HOLBROOK

[The Child Poverty Action Group announced that the average family will spend £100 on presents for each child aged between 8 – 14 at Christmas. Television advertising for the latest toys puts added pressure on parents. 'Low income families will have to spend an entire week's social security benefit to buy a £60 talking teddy.' — *The Times*, 18 December 1986]

Implications of Inter-city Rioting

From Mrs Vivien Noakes   *8 July 1981*

Sir,

Before Freud responsibility for all shortcomings fell, often unjustly, upon the miscreant. We now know that such shortcomings often grow from maltreatment of the individual, either directly by another person or through society overall. However, this once necessary shift has now reached absurd lengths, so that no one dare say that a person is responsible for his own deeds without seeming to be unfeeling and reactionary.

In the case of the recent street riots we have heard that unemployment, racial prejudice, the police, outside provocation and that omnipresent factor of post-Freudian society, frustration, are all to blame. Such forces undoubtedly have an important part to play and must be carefully examined. In the end, however, it is surely the individual who stones and loots and burns who is responsible for making the decision to stone and loot and burn.

And yet, ironically, perhaps society is to blame, for as long as these people continue to receive our tacit complicity in what they are doing, until they hear unequivocally that what they are doing is wrong, however provoked they may feel themselves to be, there will be no end to incidents such as those we have been witnessing.

Yours faithfully,
VIVIEN NOAKES

From Dr Alexander Cooke   *8 July 1981*

Sir,
When 250 policemen are injured in a riot, why are there no protests from the Council for Civil Liberties?

Yours faithfully,
ALEXANDER COOKE

Streakers and Quakers

From Mr Ben Vincent   *13 March 1974*

Sir,
May I, a Quaker Elder and 'publick Friend' protest against the attitude of the authorities to 'streaking'? In the seventeenth century young Friends, male and female, were often moved to parade naked 'as a sign' (I'm not sure of what, except high spirits). They were hounded by the Justices but I should have expected modern governments to be less interfering.

Solomon Eccles, alias Eagle, destroying his musical instruments, not only went nude throught the City but bore on his long locks a burning brazier and cried 'Woe unto the bloody city,' James Nayler rode into Bristol while Friends cast their clothes before him shouting 'Hosanna' for which he suffered a punishment so atrocious that even the grim parliamentarians were ashamed fo themselves afterwards.

Such punishments proved of no avail. The Society proliferated. But it began to shrink when the eighteenth-century descendants of these young enthusiasts, now no longer ferociously penalized, became so staid that their shovel hats and bonnets attracted more derision than their grandparents' nudity. Early the following century they became a bourgeois coterie of bankers, brewers and cocoa-growers.

If you leave the streakers alone the same fate will befall them. Meanwhile I think we should be grateful to a set who, at great inconvenience to themselves, provide us without charge such innocent entertainment. I'm a bit fed up with *The Times* for denying us pictures of them.

Yours faithfully,
BEN VINCENT

[A good week for streaking: in Calgary, Alberta, despite a temperature of $-4°F$, and in St Louis, Missouri, where two students entered the front door and left by the back of the Penrose district police station]

Horse Sense

From the Reverend, I. H. G. Graham-Orlebar   26 April 1980

Sir,

Some years ago, I had a horse called Ministry so that if the Bishop called when I was out riding, he could truthfully be told: 'The Rector is out exercising his ministry.' I now have a new horse to be named. Could your readers make any suggestions along similar lines?

Yours faithfully,
I. H. G. GRAHAM-ORLEBAR

From Mrs J. G. Cliff Hodges   *1 May 1980*

Sir,

'I'm afraid the Rector is unable to see you – he's just fallen from Grace.'

Yours faithfully,
LINNEA CLIFF HODGES

From Mr Francis Hopkins   *1 May 1980*

Sir,

Considering the supposedly low level of stipends may not the Rector have gone to collect 'Social Security'?

Yours faithfully,
FRANCIS HOPKINS

From Canon George Austin   *5 May 1980*

Sir,

May I suggest that the Reverend Ian Graham-Orlebar calls his horse Praxis? Thus when the Bishp telephones he may be told that the Rector 'is developing Praxis in an on-going interface situation'. Such a use of current liberal ecclesiastical jargon will surely, by its very incomprehensibility, convince the diocesan hierarchy that here indeed is one parochial clergyman attempting to meet with contemporary society in relevant and meaningful confrontation.

Yours,
GEORGE AUSTIN

From Mrs P. C. Stephens   *9 May 1980*

Sir,

When the Rector of Barton-le-Cley is out on Parish Business (or away on Retreat), are Tact and Great Discretion exercised by his staff?

Yours faithfully,
PATSY STEPHENS

Sir,
   The horse is to be named Sabbatical at the suggestion of
Canon Eric James of St Alban's Abbey, who thinks I need one,
having been in the same parish ten years on the trot.
Yours faithfully,
I. H. G. GRAHAM-ORLEBAR

From Mr R. J. Paine   *9 May 1980*

Sir,
   If the gentleman gave his correct name and address and his
Bishop reads *The Times*, whatever he calls his horse the game is
up.
Yours faithfully,
R. J. PAINE

Feeling the Pinch

From Mr Frank Muir   *27 April 1985*

Sir,
   I left a famous bookshop in Piccadilly clutching a plastic bag
of paperbacks and proceeded along the pavement in a westerly
direction. I paused opposite the door of a famous grocer's shop,
waiting for the traffic lights to change, when a man and a
woman came out of the grocer's and made for me.
   They were small, apparently from South-east Asia, and were
clearly rich; the lady was swathed in furs and glittered here and
there. She rushed up to me, smiled delightfully, and said "you
have the most beautiful trousers I have ever seen".
   Now this was not unwelcome news; the trousers I was wearing
happened to be brand-new, with a highly colourful pattern in
what used to be called "bookmaker's check" and I was a bit
worried about them. So when the lady indicated with a gesture
that she would like to see the trousers on the move I obligingly
prinked up and down the pavement, smiling remotely like a
model and swinging my plasting bag.
   The lady said 'Beautiful! Beautiful!" Then she put her right
hand on my left buttock, caressed it for a moment, then gave it
a very strong pinch. As my eyebrows went up she said "In my
country we always give a pinch when we give praise."

I was in no danger, of course; in broad daylight the pinch would hardly have been followed by the hypodermic syringe and a spell of white slaving overseas. But I would be immeasurably relieved, for several reasons, to hear that in some parts of the world it really *is* the custom – much as we traditionally give a coin when we present somebody with a knife or a pair of scissors – to accompany the bestowal of praise with a pinch.

Yours faithfully,

FRANK MUIR

From Dr Jacqueline Simpson   *4 May 1985*

[Honorary Editor of *Folklore*]

Sir,

May I hasten to reassure Frank Muir? His alarming experience in Piccadilly simply illustrates the misunderstandings that arise when people who do not traditionally believe in the Evil Eye encounter those who do.

The belief is common in India, the Near East and many parts of Europe; its core is the notion that if anyone or anything is praised, this will arouse the envy of some malevolent onlooker with magical powers, who will "cast the Eye" upon it.

If nothing had been done to counteract the praise, Mr Muir's fine trousers would undoubtedly soon have met with some dire accident – some soup, perhaps, or too hot an iron. Maybe even the anatomy within would have withered under the glance of the unknown Eye.

Counter-charms are many and various. The lady might have thrown salt at him, spat at him, made indelicate gestures, or urged him to festoon himself with blue beads, coral horns, bits of sheepskin, or a fox's tail.

And yes, she could pinch him, and she did. His ensuing squeal of anguished astonishment converted him into a figure of distress which no Eye, however Evil, could envy. A great peril was thus averted.

Yours sincerely,

JACQUELINE SIMPSON

From Mr J. R. Burg   *6 May 1985*

Sir,

The custom of pinching to express admiration and liking was reported by the 14th-century Chinese traveller Chen Tsan as a ceremony practised at the court of the ruler of a large island in the Indian Ocean, probably Sumatra.

Chen's *Voyages* have not survived, but what are generally accepted to be extracts were early translated into Persian and late from Persian into Italian by "Christoforo il Armeniano" whose version, entitled *Peregrinaggio per terra e per mare*, was issued at Venice by Michele Tramezzino in 1551.

According to this source there were different kinds of pinches, using either two or three fingers, to express different degrees of appreciation, and when the pinching ceremony took place all present bowed and smiled.

It would be interesting to learn from Mr Muir how many fingers were used by the lady who pinched him in Piccadilly and whether, while he was receiving her unexpected compliment her gentleman companion bowed and smiled.

I am, Sir, yours etc,

J. R. BURG

From Mr P.J. Barlow   *7 May 1985*

Sir,

Mr Muir should think himself lucky. Where his charming assailant came from I have no idea. But had he been an Arab (or even a Spanish) gentleman of the old school he would, of course, have been honour bound to whip his trousers off on the spot and offer them to the lady.

Yours etc,

P. J. BARLOW

The Lady

From the Reverend Canon J. G. Grimwade 28 December 1983

Sir,

I find it surprising that you give only four lines to the statement in today's *Times* (December 21) that if there were a chance to be anyone else, Mrs Thatcher would choose to be Mother Teresa.

If this is how the Prime Minister feels it implies an immense change in the Government's health and social policies in the coming year.

Yours faithfully,

JOHN GRIMWADE

Americana

Violation of Stoke Poges

From Mr E. H. Parry   *29 July 1907*

Sir,

  Can you find room for a complaint from one of the custodians of a well-known churchyard? On Wednesday, the 24th inst., among the many Americans who visited Stoke Poges Church was a party of three, two ladies and one boy of about 18. The last-named succeeded, in spite of the protests of an elderly lady who acted as cartaker of the church, in carrying off a notice to visitors, which hangs up in the churchyard, having first tried unsuccessfully to smuggle out a similar notice from the church. He said he wanted it as a souvenir, and, though hotly pursued by the caretaker, the party succeeded in reaching their motor and went off triumphantly with their booty. Even 'the chill penury' which prevents our having a policeman to guard our treasures cannot 'repress our noble rage' at this dastardly act of petty larceny, which will perhaps not be repeated if you could kindly record it in your columns.

Yours faithfully,

E. H. PARRY

President Roosevelt

[On 9 August 1941 *USS Augusta* and *HMS Prince of Wales* were anchored in Argentia Harbour, Newfoundland. The Prime Minister of Britain clambered abroad the American heavy cruiser to be greeted by the President: 'At last we've gotten together.' Next day Mr Roosevelt paid a return visit to *Prince of Wales*. H. V. Morton later described the occasion in *Atlantic Meeting*]

Sir,

In August, 1941, a tall man suffering from the after-effects of infantile paralysis and leaning upon the arm of his son, walked from the waist to the quarter-deck of H.M.S. Prince of Wales, then anchored in Newfoundland waters. This was no mean walk and President Roosevelt said at the time that it was the longest walk he had taken for years. But he was resolved to reach the quarter-deck on foot and he insisted upon leaving his wheeled chair at the gangway.

As he moved, the cinema operators dropped their hands and the shutter ceased to whirr; for it was a rule in the United States that the late President was not photographed in the act of walking. Those who were there will never forget the painful sight of that splendid athletic body struggling to move, each forward inch a victory; and, as I saw him, I knew that I was watching a man propelled, not my muscles and sinews, but by the power of his mind. Sympathy was overwhelmed by admiration as we saw him, and we realized also that the lines of calmness, strength and purity which we saw upon his face had been engraved in a lonely but triumphant battle of suffering. There can be no doubt that this great and noble man would have approved, with one of his almost saint-like smiles, of the suggestion, put forward in your columns and elsewhere, that his memorial in this country should be an endowment for the study and cure of the disease which stuck down his body but failed to conquer his spirit.

Yours faithfully,

H. V. MORTON

[Four months later *HMS Prince of Wales* was sunk off Malaya. *USS Auguta* survived to carry General Omar Bradley to Europe in June 1944]

221b, Maryland

[The death of President Roosevelt on 12 April 1945 had stunned the world. Some political opponents at home celebrated; on Radio Tokyo an announcer read the bulletin and presented special music: 'in honour of the passing of a great man'].

From Mr Adrian Conan Doyle   *20 April 1945*

[son of Sir Arthur Conan Doyle]

Sir,
   In common with all the truly great, President Roosevelt was
a man of many facets. It is not generally known in this country,
for instance, that he was a keen member of the American
organization called 'The Baker Street Irregulars'. In a letter that
lies before me, the President writes: –
   'I cannot restrain the impulse to tell you that since I have had
to give up cruising on the Potomac I sometimes go off on
Sundays to an undisclosed retreat. In that spot the group of little
cabins which shelter the Secret Service men is known as Baker
Street. I am glad to play any part in keeping green the memory
of Sherlock Holmes. *Honoris causa*!
                                        Yours faithfully,
                                        ADRIAN CONAN DOYLE

[The President's retreat – called 'Shangri-La' after the city
in James Hilton's *Lost Horizon* – was in the Catoctin
Mountains about 60 miles north of Washington. The
Roosevelt cottage had two baths: one of them his, the other
shared by three bedrooms. The guests' bathroom door did
not close securely]

'To See Oursels'

From Mr James P. Dean   *19 September 1953*

[writing from New York]

Sir,
   At last, you English are achieving the impossible – you are
making us lose our national sense of humour. For years, insults
and sneers have been wafted across the ocean at us and we even
imported lecturers who told us in clipped, forceful speech that
we were braggarts, uneducated, money-mad, homicidal, crude.
Then a lot of us began to travel in England. We searched
almost in vain for the Oxford and Cambridge accent we had
admired in the movies – it appeared once in a while, but the

rest of the time it was smothered under the broad Lancashire and Yorkshire speech and the amazing, almost foreign, accent of the Cockney. We met people who told us we 'didn't sound American' – that being a wondrous compliment.

We met a man who kept £10,000 in his safe and counted it for us, not once but three times. We read about whole families being poisoned and attended the trial of a murderer who made Jack the Ripper sound mild. A woman expectorated out of the window of a crowded bus, and we thought longingly of the $50 fine that she would have received in America. We had tepid baths in cracked bathtubs, almost swallowed pits [stones] that loitered in plum puddings, choked over watery brussels sprouts, and watched butchers chasing flies from meat left exposed to the elements. We attended vaudeville shows which for sheer vulgarity could not be matched in any country – and the chief comedian invariably did an American characterization which was unfunny and untrue. We spent one unforgettable day at Blackpool and decided that our counterpart, Coney Island, is a model town of chivalry and refinement.

We rowed on the Thames with an ex-colonel who blamed us for both wars, and played darts with a mole-catcher who told us the citizens of Chicago were mowed down by machine-guns every day. We were asked by a delightful, bedridden lady if we knew some people named Smith in New York, and if there were any hospitals in Philadelphia.

We visited a large estate and the hostess asked us, while the maid was serving tea, if we had as much difficulty in America with our servants as she did with hers . . . and we immediately thought of our Swedish gen who called us by our first names and received $35 a week for telling us what to do and when to do it. We watched a four-year-old boy pick up a discarded cigarette and smoke it. We questioned children of 14 or 15 who had left school and were working and thought of the law that keeps our children in school until they are 18 years of age. And we searched in vain for one woman or one man who was serving on a charitable committee and thought of the long hours and days and years we had spent collecting money and clothes for unfortunate people of other countries.

We came home and forgot all this. The remembrance of the smiling policemen, the fascinating Tower, the succulent beef (we forgot the flies) – the statue of our George Washington – the people who were genuinely interested in America – the beautiful children – was stronger than the disagreeable experiences. But now – the cartoons and the speeches and the newspaper articles from England that are flooding this

300

country – are bringing them all back. And we are forgetting that a strong Britain and a strong Europe are necessary for our survival. We are beginning to wonder if the large slice deducted from our salaries is worth the survival of a lot of alphabetical absurdities.

We might suggest a remedy – just ignore us. Forget the 'Bundles for Britain' and the 'Flood Relief' and the help that has helped you to regain some sort of economic steadiness – we have forgotten your marvellous bravery during the last war and the delight we shared with you when your Queen was crowned. If you ignore us, we may be able to regain the friendship which is so necessary – when you are tempted to tell us our shortcomings, remember you have a few of your own. Above all, ignore us – and we can regain our sense of humour – we know people who turn the dial on TV when an English movie comes on!

Sincerely yours,
STELLA DEAN

Ad-Lib

[Adlai Stevenson, probably the most civilized man to contest the US Presidency (he lost to Eisenhower in 1952 and 1956), had died in London on July 14, 1965]

From Mr Cyril Clemens　　　　　　　　　　*4 August 1965*

[Editor, *Mark Twain Journal*; writing from Missouri]

Sir,

Your readers may be interested in what the late Adlai E. Stevenson wrote me shortly before his sudden passing:—

'My grandfather who was Vice President of the United States from 1893 to 1897, and had the same name as myself, was often asked how his name was pronounced. Many called him "Ad-*lay*", and many "Ad-*lie*". He was a good friend of Mark Twain, and at a banquet Mark Twain said he had resolved once and for all the controversy about the pronunciation. Whereupon he recited the following, he had just composed on the back of a menu:—

"Lexicographers roar
  And philologists bray.
And the best they can do
Is to call him Ad-*lay*.
But at Longshoremen's picnics
  When accents are high.
And fair Harvard's not present
They call him Ad-*lie*." '

CYRIL CLEMENS

Racing Handicaps

From Ms Bo Goldman   *14 November 1986*

[writing from California]

Sir,
  'These other horses couldn't beat (Dancing Brave) with a hammer in Europe,' said Pat Eddery after his mount finished a gasping fourth in Santa Anita's Breeders' Cup.
  But an hour earlier, France's Last Tycoon didn't need a hammer, only four hooves to trounce his competition over the same race course, despite the tight turns, the bumping in the stretch, the clods of flying grass, the terrible airplane flight, the California heat, the exhausting European racing campaign, and all the other excuses trainer Guy Harwood trotted out in defence of 'Europe's greatest since Mill Reef and Nijinsky'.
  How can you be English if you don't know how to lose gracefully?

Sincerely,
BO GOLDMAN

[Ms Goldman is referred to Bernard Shaw's *Saint Joan*, Scene IV: 'No Englishman is ever fairly beaten']

The Famous

Sandhurst Punishments

[After the latest instance of incendiarism at RMC Sandhurst, the Commander-in-Chief, Lord Roberts, decided in effect that all cadets in 'C' Company should be considered guilty unless able to prove their innocence. Some agreed with this procedure]

From Mr Winston Churchill, MP   *9 July 1902*

[Conservative Member for Oldham; Companion of Honour 1922; Order of Merit 1946; Nobel Prize for Literature 1953]

Sir,

The Headmaster of Sherborne writes you a truly remarkable letter. He says that a large part of the prosperity of the British Army depends upon the learning of lessons of general punishment. 'The innocent, doubtless, suffer with the guilty; but then they always do. The world has been so arranged.' Has it indeed? No doubt he has taken care that the little world over which he presides is arranged on that admirable plan, but it is necessary to tell him that elsewhere the punishment of innocent people is regarded as a crime or as a calamity to be prevented by unstinted exertion.

So long as the delinquencies of a schoolmaster are within the ordinary law the House of Commons has no right to intervene; but when a Commander-in-Chief and a Secretary of State are encouraged to imitate him, it is time to take notice.

Does Mr Westcott flog his boys in their corporate capacity?

Your obedient servant,
WINSTON S. CHURCHILL

[The Commander-in-Chief later promised that each individual case would be investigated again]

A Glimpse of J. S. Mill

From Mr Thomas Hardy   *21 May 1906*

[Order of Merit 1910]

Sir,

This being the 100th anniversary of J. Stuart Mill's birth, and as writers like Carlyle, Leslie Stephen, and others have held that anything, however imperfect, which affords an idea of a human personage in his actual form and flesh, is of value in respect of him, the few following words on how one of the profoundest thinkers of the last century appeared 40 years ago to the man in the street may be worth recording as a footnote to Mr Morley's admirable estimate of Mill's life and philosophy in your impression of Friday.

It was a day in 1865, about 3 in the afternoon, during Mill's candidature for Westminster. The hustings had been erected in Covent-garden, near the front of St Paul's Church; and when I – a young man living in London – drew near to the spot, Mill was speaking. The appearance of the author of the treatise 'On Liberty' (which we students of that date knew almost by heart) was so different from the look of persons who usually address crowds in the open air that it held the attention of people for whom such a gathering in itself had little interest. Yet it was, primarily, that of a man out of place. The religious sincerity of his speech was jarred on by his environment – a group on the hustings who, with few exceptions, did not care to understand him fully, and a crowd below who could not. He stood bareheaded, and his vast pale brow, so thin-skinned as to show the blue veins, sloped back like a stretching upland, and conveyed to the observer a curious sense of perilous exposure. The picture of him as personified earnestness surrounded for the most part by careless curiosity derived an added piquancy – if it can be called such – from the fact that the cameo clearness of his face chanced to be in relief against the blue shadow of a church which, on its transcendental side, his doctrines antagonized. But it would not be right to say that the throng was absolutely unimpressed by his words; it felt that they were weighty, though it did not quite know why.

                    Your obedient servant,

                                        THOMAS HARDY

[Mill, one of whose supporters was Bertrand Russell's father, began his campaign only nine days before the poll on 12 July 1865. Asked if he had written a passage stating that the English working classes were 'generally liars', he replied 'I did.' Grosvenor (Whig) and Mill (Radical) were elected, the defeated Liberal-Conservative being W. H. Smith, later Gilbert's 'Ruler of the Queen's Navee']

Cromwell's Head

['I to Westminster-hall where I . . . saw the heads of Cromwell, Bradshaw, and Ireton set up upon the further end of the hall.' – Samuel Pepys' *Diary*, 5 February 1661]

From Mr C. R. Haines   *11 April 1911*

Sir,
Now that the identity of Cromwell's embalmed head is generally acknowledged, is it not high time that some steps should be taken to put an end to the national scandal of keeping this ghastly relic as a curio? Cromwell was one of the greatest men the English race has ever produced. Only two of our long list of Kings deserve to be named in the same breath with him. He became King because he was the best and ablest man in the country, a thing that has happened but once besides in our history. In war he was one of the very few generals who were never beaten. He was a true patriot, and made England great and feared among the nations of Europe. He was a doer and not a talker, and, to the great benefit of the nation, he shut up for a time the House of Commons.
Surely it is possible for the Government or some public body to recover this head of Cromwell by purchase or otherwise and restore it to its grave in the Abbey. He deserves to rest in an honoured grave far more, to say the least, than Charles II. Where is the Nonconformist conscience that allows this desecration of the remains of the greatest (in the realm of action) of all Nonconformists?
I am sure the Rev. H. R. Wilkinson, the present owner, would be horrified if the skull of an eminent parishioner whom he had buried were exhumed and kept as a curio in a box. When a perfectly innocent and justifiable proposal was made to open the grave of Shakespeare and inspect its contents for historical purposes, a deafening outcry was raised, but what would have been thought if his skull were in private hands?

305

May I appeal to you, Sir, to use your great influence in this matter?

> I am, Sir, etc.,
> C. R. HAINES

[The Reverend, later Canon, Wilkinson, vicar of Stoke-by-Nayland, Colchester, had inherited Cromwell's head. He later bequeathed it to Sidney Sussex College, Cambridge, where Cromwell had been a Fellow Commoner, 1616–17]

Letter from Rome

[*The Times* had criticised the Duce]

From Signor Mussolini   *26 June 1925*

Sir,

I am very sensible of the fact that your most important paper attentively follows my political and polemical manifestations. Allow me, however, to rectify some statements contained in your last editorial.

It does not correspond with facts that the last Bills voted by the Italian Chamber are against the most elementary liberties, whereof you will be convinced by carefully considering the article of the aforesaid laws. It is not true that patriots are discontended. On the contrary, the truth is that the opposition is carried on by a small dispossessed group, while the enormous majority of the Italian people works and lives quietly, as foreigners sojourning in my country may daily ascertain. Please note also that Fascism counts 3,00,000 adherents, whereof 2,000,000 are Syndicalist workmen and peasants, these representing the politically organized majority of the nation. Even the Italian Opposition now recognizes the great historical importance of the Fascist experiment, which has to be firmly continued in order not to fail in its task of morally and materially elevating the Italian people, and also in the interest of European civilization. Please accept my thanks and regards.

> I am, &c.,
> MUSSOLINI

[There is no record of Hitler or Stalin writing to *The Times*]

Chamberlain's maiden speech

[*The Times* had been serializing extracts from J. L. Garvin's *Life of Joseph Chamberlain*]

From Professor A. E. Housman   *25 November 1932*

[Latinist and poet who, like Kipling and Shaw, declined the Order of Merit]

Sir,

On page 14 of your issue of today it is said that Joseph Chamberlain wore an eye-glass when he made his first speech in the House of Commons. He wore a pair of spectacles with black and rather thick rims. Disraeli is described as 'frail and cadaverous.' His complexion was a pale olive, but did not look cadaverous from the Strangers' Gallery; and of frailty there was not a sign. Sitting as he did with one knee crossed over the other, he showed a very good pair of legs; he walked in and out of the House with a long, easy stride; and after answering a speech of Hartington's, a few days earlier or later, about the Suez Canal shares, he threw himself back into his seat almost with violence.

Chamberlain's speech was very rapid, and at first too loud for the size of the Chamber. He showed no trace of nervousness except that once, after saying 'I protest, Mr Speaker,' he rather hurriedly changed the phrase to 'I humbly protest.'

Yours faithfully,

A. E. HOUSMAN

[Disraeli's reply to Hartington was made on 8 August 1876. Housman was then aged 17.

Also on 25 November 1932 *The Times* carried a report of an address – 90 minutes long – to the Fabian Society by Bernard Shaw: 'The whole history of Parliament is a vindication of Guy Fawkes']

Enforced Abdiction of the Cuckoo

On Monday, 26 October 1936, the front page of the New York *Daily Mirror* contained the photograph of a woman surmounted by four words:

KING WILL WED WALLY

Other American newspapers preferred the vernacular and alluded to the 'King's Moll'. Three days later, *The Times* printed at the foot of otherwise unremarkable home news page this item.

UNDEFENDED DIVORCE SUIT

'At the Ipswich Assizes yesterday Mrs Wallis Simpson, who gave her address as Beech House, Felixstowe, with a London address at Cumberland Terrace, Regent's Park, NW, petitioned for the dissolution of her marriage with Mr Ernest Aldrich Simpson on the ground of his adultery at the Hotel de Paris, Bray-on-Thames, in July this year. MR JUSTICE HAWKE granted a decree *nisi* with costs.'

The name of the woman with whom Mr Simpson was alleged to have commited adultery was not disclosed in open Court. However the petition mentioned a certain "Buttercup Kennedy' which seemed to some as fictitious a name as the 'Leon Trotzky' once given to a magistrate by Bertie Wooster's friend Sippy Sipperley. Mr and Mrs Simpson's marriage had lasted eight years, happiness evaporating in the autumn of 1934 when Mr Simpson's manner changed, though whether this was the outcome of an Independence Day dinner which Mrs Simpson gave for the Prince of Wales the previous year (blackbean soup, grilled lobster, fried chicken Maryland, raspberry soufflé) was not clear.

In this same issue of 29 October, *The Times* informed readers that H. Macbeth-Raeburn, RA was engaged on a portrait of the Kind in Highland dress, that Mrs Baldwin — wife of the prime minister — had held an At Home in Downing Street where madrigals were sung in aid of the Safer Motherhood Appeal, and that Mr L. S. Amery, MP was urging the use of tear gas to quell rioting, though not of course in Britain. The Spanish civil war raged, Walter Hammond batted finely for the MCC tourists in Australia, and Sir Thomas Beecham was about to make the first orchestra of the Royal Academy of Music sound almost as brilliant as the London Philharmonic.

The conflagration, when it came, was of a dual nature. One fire was thought to have started in a staff lavatory, the other in a bishop's palace. The former publicized itself, the latter was for a while dampened by a unanimous decision of newspaper owners. *The Times* lent its correspondence columns to one, not to the other. Around six o'clock in the evening of Monday, 30 November 1936, the Crystal Palace at Sydenham, south London began to blaze. Next day, when addressing his diocesan conference, the Bishop of Bradford, Dr Blunt, accidentally entered a Royal minefield. Devoting most of his remarks to a criticism of Bishop Barnes of Birmingham for suggesting the Coronation ceremony should be changed, Bishop Blunt added 'It has for centuries been, and I hope still is, an essential part of the idea that the King needs the grace of God for his office'. In all probability Dr Blunt read *The Times*, had never heard of the New York *Daily Mirror*, and did not know that King Edward had – what both papers would now term – a girlfriend. Similarly, readers of *The Times* were unaware of what awaited them when they tuned to the BBC's 9 o'clock News on Monday, 30 November.

'We hope to take you over to the Crystal Palace, where our observer has been watching.' That observer was the young Richard Dimbleby who, with his sound engineer David Howarth, had rushed to Sydenham earlier in the evening. The broadcast was a triumph for Dimbleby and the BBC; unfortunately, it alerted all London to the spectacle of the century. A million or so south of the river converged on Sydenham, tens of thousands within access of Hampstead Heath invaded those grasslands. The outcome was inevitable: *The Times* received, and published, a letter rebuking the BBC for calling 'Fire!' When some other Crystal Palace suffered from careless flames, the Corporation would do well to restrain its enthusiasm. Listeners expected news from the BBC and not, as on this occasion via a charred Dimbleby, hot news. The true significance of Sydenham could be stated simply: what alternative accommodation could be found for the annual meeting of the National Cat Club?

Because the *Yorkshire Post* has seized upon Bishop Blunt's mention of God's grace to break the press silence on the King and Mrs Simpson, *The Times* entered the fray with a mild leading article – The Kind and a Crisis – which alluded to a marriage 'incompatible with the Throne'. Only by turning to another page could readers grasp the gravity of the situation. In the Potteries the production of mugs bearing the likeness of King Edward VIII had been halted. What would happen to eight million mugs were the Coronation to be cancelled?

Friday, 4 December restored sanity of a kind. Mr Edward Meyerstein suggested the Crystal Palace site might be occupied by a convalescent home to serve London's hospitals. Should this idea appeal to the King, Mr Meyerstein would at once subscribe £100,000 (about £17m today in property values). *The Times* Fourth Leader offered counter-intelligence: the Crystal Palace goldfish had survived their boiling and were in excellent condition, though black in colour.

The nation's morale rose on Saturday, 5 December when the art editor of *The Times* filled much space with a superb picture of snow in the Highlands, the news editor counterpointing neatly with a brief paragraph announcing Mrs Simpson's departure for France.

On Tuesday, 8 December *The Times* decided to tell the truth. The crisis had flooded Printing House Square with so many letters that acknowledgement was impossible. 'To publish would have been indecent.' On the other hand, certain sentences from the letters merited the supreme accolade of a fleeting though anonymous appearance in *The Times*.

The King of England, of the Dominions, of the Colonies, Emperor of India, as the third husband of a woman who has failed to hold two husbands? Would not each and every one of us question the wisdom of such a marriage if it were to be undertaken by our brother?

Meanwhile the Standing Commitee of the House of Commons prepared to resume consideration of A. P. Herbert's Marriage Bill.

A supporter of King Edward was discovered:

I for one will never acknowledge any other King while King Edward lives. I will recognise the women he chooses for his wife as his Queen Consort. Let him who is without sin, in any way, cast a stone at the King.

On this same day, 8 December, the Marriage Bill's Standing Committee began to consider collusive divorce.

On 10 December another sentence was plucked from the thousands littering Printing House Square.

If the King marries a *divorcée* without the sanction of the Church, of which he is the Defender, how can he retain his holy office of Kingship, having just infringed the regulations that he is supposed to enforce, or at least uphold?

The sponsor of the Marriage Bill, A. P. Herbert (Oxford University, Independent), said divorce was a release from misfortune and not a crime.

Friday, 11 December was overcast. *The Times* suspended publication of its Fourth Leader, the BBC broadcast solemn music and — unable to foresee the future when he would be the harbinger of all Royal tidings, joyful or distressing — confined Richard Dimbleby to Portland Place.

King Edward VIII abdicated, to be succeeded by his brother the Duke of York as King George VI. The Established Church triumphant, the Archbishops of Canterbury and York contacted all clergy and ordered changes in relevant prayers — 'Delete "Edward", substitute "George".'

On Monday, 14 December *The Times* resumed publication of its Fourth Leader, the BBC returned to normal with a diet of dance music and emasculated comedians. The Crystal Palace so much ash and twisted girders, Paddington Baths were made ready for the annual meeting of the National Cat Club.

General de Gaulle

From Mr Robert Cary, MP   *1 July 1940*

[Conservative Member for Eccles, later for the Withington Division of Manchester, Sir Robert Cary contested every general election between 1924 and 1970]

Sir,

May I be allowed to comment on the excellent letter of your Military Correspondent, Captain Cyril Falls?

I too have heard a little of the cautious talk about General de Gaulle. His age is a refreshing innovation in Allied leadership: the quality of his rank can easily be determined by the British Government — particularly if it were coupled to a gracious offer to be designated an honorary aide-de-camp to the supreme head of the British armed forces. General de Gaulle made a bold and superb gesture which was based upon a high strategic comprehension. The widening of the circle of the war away from the land-locked misery of the defensive to a wider perimeter where sea power could play its decisive part would give to France the energy and resource of successful counter-attack. An answer to the Panzer divisions could not be mounted on the soil of France, but their limitations — rooted in one dimension — defined their possibilities. In changing the nature of the war and given the naval and military weaknesses to Italy to bite upon, General de Gaulle discerned the seed of ultimate victory.

I cannot understand that anybody could be dilatory in recognizing General de Gaulle, unless dilatoriness is merely another symptom of those two diseases of the British method — caution and understatement. His recognition should have been automatic. Problems of rank, pay, allowances, and conditions of service for him and his followers were not insurmountable obstacles of negotiation between the British Government and the separated interests of the French Empire.

It would be difficult to find in military history characters more attractive than Hoche or Marceau, than Desaix or Richepanse. Any one of them, had he risen to supreme power, would have served France better than Napoleon. Perhaps it may be reserved to General de Gaulle to occupy the premier place in the military history of the French Republic.

Yours, &c.,

ROBERT CARY

Voice for de Gaulle

[On 24 July 1967 the General had roused Montreal with a cry of 'Vive le Québec libre!', so uniting *The Times*, the BBC, the Canadian Prime Minister Lester Pearson, *Le Monde* and *L'Humanité*]

From Dr A. L. Rowse   *12 August 1967*

Sir,

Since it is clear that no one is going to speak up for de Gaulle, perhaps an historian may – it would be a pretty poor show if there were no one in this country to understand his point of view. Isn't it desirable, even important, that it should be understood?

De Gaulle is the most historically minded of statesmen, along with Churchill, and he has an historian's memory. Neither the United States nor Britain, after liberating France, showed any interest in supporting or maintaining the French Empire. Why should he show any interest in maintaining what is left of the British Commonwealth?

Thrown back on France, what he has achieved for France is nothing short of miraculous – the tranformation of a defeated country into the most potent power in Western Europe, with a decisive voice in its construction and shaping. If only we had had a de Gaulle in the postwar period to take the right options! But there has been nobody up to the level of our needs since Churchill.

Any fool can spend, any party can whittle away a country's resources, weaken it by endlessly outbidding each other for the support of an electorate that cares for neither and can never

312

understand the country's long-term interests. I am sure politicians do not understand the contempt serious-minded people feel for both their parties and for what they have brought the country to. The sinister dialectic of political parties is ruining this country as it ruined France. De Gaulle put a stop to that.

I do not suppose that he wishes to disrupt Canada, merely to underline and draw international attention to the Frenchness of Franch Canada. In that he has certainly succeeded as usual, and accomplished precisely what he intended in going there, nothing more and nothing less. It will be interesting to watch the reverberating effects of the emphasis he has given into the 1970s.

Yours, &c.,

A. L. ROWSE

No Soup for the General

From Mr W. R. Sellar   *16 February 1968*

Sir,

Your Cookery Editor, with all the authority of *The Times* behind her, advises us to make cream of asparagus soup by opening a tin (10 February).

No wonder, Sir, that General de Gaulle considers that we are not yet ripe to enter Europe.

Yours faithfully,

W. R. SELLAR

Bertrand Russell

[The philosopher died on 2 February 1970, aged 97]

From Mrs T. S. Eliot   *10 February 1970*

Sir,

My husband, T. S. Eliot, loved to recount how late one evening he stopped a taxi. As he got in, the driver said: 'You're T. S. Eliot.' When asked how he knew, he replied: 'Ah, I've got an eye for a celebrity. Only the other evening I picked up Bertrand Russell, and I said to him: "Well, Lord Russell, what's it all about," and, do you know, he couldn't tell me.'

Yours faithfully,

VALERIE ELIOT

313

This England

'Oh, Mr Porter . . .'

From Mr Richard Harvey   *18 October 1968*

Sir,

This afternoon I caught the 15.05 train from the recently modernized Euston Station.

According to the new electronic departure indicator, its destination was Rugby; according to the ticket collector and a notice on the platform it was Coventry; according to the destination blind on the train it was Wolverhampton. I got off at Watford, to hear the station announcer declare it was Wolverhampton; and walked home to look it up in my copy of the timetable and discover it was Birmingham.

Perhaps now that their modernization scheme is complete British Rail's executives will have enough time to decide where their trains are going to?

Yours faithfully,

RICHARD HARVEY

BR Dialogue

From Mr Winston Fletcher   *4 October 1977*

Sir,

On the fecund subject of overmanning and productivity I thought that you would wish to have recorded for posterity the following conversation which occurred yesterday evening on a train from Paddington.

Guard to barperson: Tony's serving toast, on the other train.

Barperson: Toast? on his own? I'll have the union on him.

Guard (apparently taken aback by the vehemence of the barperson's reply): Well his customers seem to like it.

Barperson: Pleasing customers is all very well, but you can go too far. Making toast's a two-man job.

Only the reprobate toastmaker's name has been changed, in the probably forlorn hope that it may still be possible to protect him.

Yours faithfully,
WINSTON FLETCHER

The Trade Disputes Bill

['Acts of Parliament are not passed to make illegal specific acts that either you or I think are legal. They are passed to define what illegality is, i.e. a political strike . . .' – Ramsay MacDonald to Neville Chamberlain]

From Mr A. P. Herbert   *9 February 1931*

Sir,

The Prime Minister, in his last letter to Mr Neville Chamberlain, has burst, somewhat unexpectedly, into humour. Perhaps, therefore, I may trespass into politics.

Is there not a simple solution to this rather childish controversy? I suggest that the Trade Disputes Bill be withdrawn and a two-clause measure be substituted as follows:

REVOLUTION (ENABLING) BILL

(1) A revolution shall be lawful if it be conducted by the manual workers in two or more basic industries.

(2) It shall be lawful for the income-tax payers to combine together to refuse payment of income-tax, provided that the primary purpose of such refusal be to further a financial dispute and not to embarrass the Government.

This, unlike most modern legislation, would be not only lucid but just. I cannot hope that even this measure would goad the parliamentary Liberal Party to unanimity, but almost every other citizen would be satisfied.

I am, Sir, your obedient servant,
A. P. HERBERT

Man goes to the Moon

From Mr P. A. Williams   *26 November 1969*

[from deep in the heart of Sussex]

Sir,
On Thursday evening my wife and I watched the truly wonderful programme on BBC television showing the American astronauts on the moon. We thought how incredible that this programme was coming 'live' from the moon on BBC-1 when we cannot even receive in our house BBC-2.

We could not telephone the BBC to offer our congratulations because our telephone has been out of order for four days and the Post Office engineers cannot trace the fault. Last Friday we had to hand-milk our cows with the aid of torches and candlelight because the power supply had been cut off in a very small area in which our farm lies, and the South Eastern Electricity Board only apparently possessed one mobile generator which was urgently needed at a nearby chicken farm.

It seems that the Americans have a monopoly of technological progress.

Yours faithfully,
P. A. WILLIAMS

Say No More

From Mr M. L. Charlesworth   *11 October 1973*

Sir,
Amongst the memorable notices displayed by London Transport and recently reported by your readers, let this one find a place:

Gents and lift out of order
Please use the stairs.

Yours faithfully,
M. L. CHARLESWORTH

A Volga Boatman

From Mr Laurence Viney   *1 April 1949*

Sir,

Coming to London in the train this morning, a man sitting next to me was reading the *Daily Worker* while all the time softly whistling the Eton Boating Song.

I am, Sir, your obedient servant,
LAURENCE VINEY

Booking a Hotel Room

From Professor John Hutchinson   *2 August 1977*

[writing from the Graduate School of Management, University of California at Los Angeles]

Sir,

I was recently in London to hold discussions *inter alia* on the expansion of North American investment and trade in the United Kingdom, my homeland.

I had a meeting in Newcastle and went to a travel agency in the West End to buy my train ticket. I also asked the lady behind the counter (I think it was a female) if she could reserve me a room at the Royal Station Hotel in Newcastle.

'Well, not really,' she said.

'What do you mean, not really?'

'Well, you'd have to pay us for the room now. Then when you got to Newcastle you'd have to pay the hotel. Then you'd have to come back here and ask us for a refund. But you can't do it anyway, because you haven't got an account with us.'

Where, Sir, do we go from here?

Yours faithfully,
JOHN HUTCHINSON

World Service

From Mr John Le Carré   *1 July 1981*

Sir,

At a moment when, thanks to the failure of diplomacy, we are spending £33.7m a *day* (and rising) on defence, and wondering whether we are getting value, for Foreign Office is aiming to save £3m a *year* by cutting BBC foreign language broadcasts to three of the most important unaligned countries of the world: Burma, Somalia and Brazil. At a saving of £10,000, which is a fraction of the cost of keeping a very average ambassador in the style to which he is not accustomed, they are also disconnecting Malta.

By what conceivable right? Are we to believe it is not worth one tenth of our daily defence expenditure to be revered as the distributors of sober, accurate and impartial news to unaligned countries who are otherwise without it?

Does the Foreign Office itself believe that the pulp distributed by its information services and spokesmen commands a particle of the same respect, let alone the same audience? Have we forgotten that two years ago the Foreign Office ordered cuts in the Turkish broadcasts, only to come running back a year later, asking for them to be expanded?

The BBC's foreign language broadcasts achieve something which goes far beyond the capacity of any foreign office. They enter the homes of thousands of ordinary people. They are taken to their hearts. They inform and educate. They set standards of objectivity. They inspire gratitude and even, now and then, actual love, as any traveller to those regions can establish for himself.

Really, it is obscene to imagine that the Foreign Office, whose emissaries have scant contact, at best, with the ordinary people of the countries to which they are accredited, should presume to sit in judgement over our most effective, popular and trusted spokesman.

If Mrs Thatcher is looking to bring reason to bureaucracy, let her do it here, and sharply. Better to shed an embassy or two, and slim a few more, than sack our real ambassadors.

Yours faithfully,
JOHN LE CARRÉ

[John Le Carré was a member of HM Foreign Service 1960–64]

Postal Delays

From the Dean of Canterbury   *5 February 1970*

Sir,

A few days ago I received a communication addressed to T. A. Becket, Esq., care of The Dean of Canterbury. This surely must be a record in postal delays.

Yours truly,

IAN H. WHITE-THOMSON

From the Reverend I. J. M. Haire   *3 February 1978*

[Missionary to Halmahera, Indonesia]

Sir,

Yesterday (Monday, 23 January) I received, in this Northern Moluccan island in Eastern Indonesia, a parcel posted in Belfast on Saturday, 8 June 1974. It took exactly three years, seven months and 15 days on its journey. I wonder if this is a record, at least for the fast-moving seventies?

Yours faithfully,

JAMES HAIRE

From Mr John Turner   *4 October 1976*

Sir,

A letter was delivered this week to a busy doctor's surgery in a scarred and perforated envelope. In explanation a Post Office official had added the legend 'Found adhering to a snail.'

Comment would be superfluous.

Yours faithfully,

JOHN M. TURNER

[The letter addressed to T. A. Becket was apparently delayed for 800 years or so. (It may even have come from King Henry II suggesting a happy coalition of interests.) But as the Dean omitted to mention the envelope's postmark, an arbitrating Cuckoo has decided that both the Dean and Mr Haire may claim their records.

If, as seems likely, T. A. Becket's letter has been entrusted to a snail, we may assume the gasteropod's progress was the first recorded instance of a postal employee working to rule]

320

'Dear Reverend'

From the Reverend E. H. W. Crusha   *12 March 1976*

Sir,

May I enlist your support in restraining the use of 'Dear Reverend' and 'Dear Reverend So-and-so' in letters to clergyman? It appears to be increasing among people of standing and education who might be expected to be readers of *The Times*.

Yours faithfully,
EDWIN CRUSHA

From Mr Arthur Bond   *16 March 1976*

Sir,

As a boy in a solicitor's office I was taught that a clergyman one knew and liked was addressed as 'Dear Vicar' or 'Dear Rector'. If oen disliked him or did not know him well enough to form a view one said 'Reverend Sir' unless his help was needed, in which case one said 'Dear *and* Reverend Sir'. It seemed to work very well.

At home at the manse callers who asked 'Is the Reverend in?' were usually gentlemen who had already been to the Presbytery but decided that, on this one occasion, and strictly off the record, they would like a second opinion.

Yours faithfully,
ARTHUR BOND

From Mr Peter du Sautoy   *16 March 1976*

[Chairman, Faber and Faber Ltd]

Sir,

I learnt from T. S. Eliot, the politest of men, that letters to clergymen one does not know personally should begin 'Reverend Sir'.

Yours faithfully,
PETER DU SAUTOY

From The Revered R. W. D. Dewing   *18 March 1976*

Sir,

A certain firm which had my name on its mailing list as 'The Rev Dewing', sent me a 'personalized' circular letter which commenced 'Dear The Dewing' and continued in the same fashion: 'You see The Dewing . . .', and, 'The advantages to you The Dewing are . . .'

When I wrote and expressed by surprise and amusement at this strange form of address, I was told that the fault lay with the computer, which was unable to distinguish between clerical and other gentlemen. Programmed to omit initials, had I been entered on the mailing list as Mr R. W. D. Dewing, my letter would have commenced 'Dear Mr Dewing', but, concluding that Rev must be initials, it obeyed its instructions and produced 'The Dewing'.

I remain, yours faithfully,

R. W. D. DEWING

From the Reverend F. P. Coleman   *19 March 1976*

[Rector, St Andrew-by-the-Wardrobe, with St Ann]

Sir,
Reverence to whom reverence is due. The morning's post recently included a letter addressed to 'The Reverend St Andrew-by-the-Wardrobe'.

Yours truly,

F. P. COLEMAN

From Mr Peter Faulks   *20 March 1976*

Sir,
I remember being told by a cleryman that when in India a parishioner wrote to him as 'Reverend and Bombastic Sir.'

Yours faithfully,

PETER FAULKS

From Canon Allan Shaw   *23 March 1976*

Sir,
There are degrees of reverence. When I was a Dean and very reverend I once received a letter addressed to 'The Very Shaw'. I thought that took some beating.

However, it was bettered by the present Bishop of Lincoln. He once told me that he had received a letter directed to 'The Right Phipps'.

Yours obediently,

ALLAN SHAW

322

'Dear Rabbit'

From Rabbi David J. Goldberg   24 March 1976

Sir,

While Christian clergymen ponder their correct form of address, they might also spare a thought for the difficulty experienced by thir Jewish colleagues. On several occasions (and usually from the Inland Revenue) I have received letters which address me as 'Dear Rabbit'.

Yours sincerely,

DAVID J. GOLDBERG

A Major Problem

From Mr Adrian R. D. Norman   25 March 1976

Sir,

Your surprised and amused correspondent, the Revd R. W. D. Dewing, reminds us that though to err is human, to mess things up consistently requires a computer. On behalf of my colleagues and fellow acolytes at the shrines of the computer, may I beg his forgiveness for those sins of commission, our programmes, and invite through you, Sir, the help of your readers?

Those who have finished the crossword 20 minutes short of the terminus today might bend their minds to devising an algorithm for deducing accurately and infallibly the correct form of address from the name line of a properly addressed envelope containing up to 36 capital letters and punctuation marks. It may be that the problem is insoluble because, as with the crossword, logic alone cannot decide whether the clue conceals an anagram or a classical allusion. The computing professional will be greatly in the debt of the solver of this now classic problem and the usees (alias: victims of the computer's users) will have one less cause for complaint.

For those who take up the challenge, the test data base contains records with the following name line fields: Danie Van Der Merwe, The Master of Ballantrae, The Mistress of Girton, C. M. Gomez de Costa e Silva, Mrs Mark Phillips, Earl Mountbatten, Count Basie, Sir Archie McIan of that Ilk, Adm. Hon Sir R. A. R. Plunkett-E-E-Drax, J. Smith Esq, Sister Mary-Paul, A. d'Ungrois, the Revd Dewing.

Of course, any abbreviation needed to fit into 36 characters must be accepted. Confident of the continuing superiority of the product of unskilled labour, the human mind, over its most marvellous artifact,

I remain, yours faithfully,
ADRIAN R. D. NORMAN

Back Gradually to Reverends

From His Honour Judge Irvine   25 *March 1976*

Sir,

The clergy may have their tribulations in the modes of their computerized address, but the law is not without its trials in that respect. At least the Lord Bishop of Lincoln remained 'Right', but judging from the nature of the particular envelope's contents I fear as 'Honour Irvine' I may have changed my sex.

I have the honour to be, Sir,
your obedient servant,
J. E. M. IRVINE

From the Bishop of Repton   26 *March 1976*

Sir

His Honour Judge Irvine is not alone in having his sex changed by letter. The Gas Board have just stopped addressing me as Archbishop and simply begin 'Dear Grace'.

I have the honour to be, Sir,
your obedient servant,
† WARREN REPTON

From the Reverend D. F. C. Hawkins   27 *March 1976*

Sir,

A young member of my congregation in Nigeria once addressed me in a letter as 'My dear interminable Canon'. I try to believe he intended it kindly.

Yours obediently,
D. F. C. HAWKINS

From the Reverend S. H. Chase

Sir,

Surely few can rival my claim to temporary reverend fame.

When serving in Holland in 1944, as Chaplain to the 7th Bn The Duke of Wellington's Regt, a parcel of games and other comforts arrived from a well-wisher at home.

The parcel was addressed to 'The Rev The Duke of Wellington', and without a moment's hesitation was handed to me.

Yours faithfully,
STEPHEN CHASE

From Mr Christopher Child   *27 March 1976*

Sir,

It is not only the style of an opening address that can be reverent. As a young District Officer Cadet, I received an application for employment as a junior clerk in the District Office. After setting out his qualifications, the writer finished his letter by saying that 'nightly, I pray to the Almighty, to whom Your Worship closely resembles, that my application may be successful.'

I have the honour to be, Sir,
your obedient servant,
CHRISTOPHER CHILD

From the Reverend Adrian Benjamin   *29 March 1976*

Sir,

Further to the Revd R. W. D. Dewing's letter on his being persecuted by a computer, may I as a fellow clergyman suggest that this is by no means a lone martyrdom? Tired of replying to the National TV Licence Records Office's constant enquiries as to why we did not possess a TV Licence, with the statement that it was because we did not possess a TV, my wife and I gave way, bought one, and wrote and told them of our surrender. A month later there came yet another letter with the question reiterated.

I had snatched up my biro ready and angry to reply − when suddenly I noticed the address to which the letter had come. This time, All Saints' Vicarage having had a TV safely installed, the letter had come to 'The Present Occupier, All Saints' Church . . .'

Should I tell them that we have more interesting things to do there? That the Almighty manages without? Or simply give way and install one in the pulpit, so we can watch ours at home?

Yours faithfully,
ADRIAN V. BENJAMIN

How to Get a Letter in *The Times*

From Mr J. Armour-Milne   26 January 1970

Sir,

You're joking. You must be. 'Who will be writing to *The Times* tonight?' is printed on the face of an envelope containing a letter to me from *The Times*. The letter 'assures you that your remarks were read with interest'. But not sufficient interest to warrant publication. I wonder why when one considers the amount of drivel that is to be found in the Letters to the Editor.

Three times in my life I have written a letter to the Editor. Three times he has found my letter interesting, but not sufficiently so to warrant publication.

The first was on the subject of east Germany, on which I have had a book published. Probably I was not considered an expert on east Germany.

The second was a protest, and an invitation to others to do so, against the victimization of Lieutenant-Colonel Emil Zátopek, the Czechoslovak Olympic athlete. Presumably I was not considered an expert, although, in Prague itself, at the height of his career and for seven years, I advised Zátopek on his training. And wrote two books on sport in Czechoslovakia under the communists.

The third, recently, was a reply to Sir Peter Mursell, a member of the Royal Commission on Local Government, on the implications of the Maud Report. Again, I assume, I was not regarded as an authority on the subject, although the Guardian has given a pen picture of my work against Maud spread over four columns and I have been invited to debate Maud with Lord Redcliffe-Maud at University College, Oxford, of which he is Master.

What does one have to do in order to be recognized by the Editor of *The Times*? Bring about a counter-revolution in communist east Germany? Run faster than Zátopek? Become chairman of a new Royal Commission on Local Government in England?

Yours faithfully,
J. ARMOUR-MILNE

First and Foremost

From Miss Sylvia Margolis   *28 January 1970*

Sir,

The answer to Mr J. Armour-Milne's question is simple.

Last year I had two letters published in *The Times* and I've been dining out on them ever since. They involved me in an exchange of letters of ever-increasing lunacy with other correspondents. I can bear witness that the prime qualification you need to get letters published in *The Times* is eccentricity.

Yours faithfully,

SYLVIA MARGOLIS

Closed Shop?

From Mr W. P. Courtauld   *28 January 1970*

Sir,

Mr J. Armour-Milne asks what does one have to do in order to be recognized by the Editor.

The short answer would seem to be either a Member of Parliament or of the Athenaeum. Needless to say I am neither one myself.

Yours faithfully,

W. P. COURTAULD

[Correspondents writing from the House of Commons or the Athenaeum are outnumbered three to one in these pages by academics and clerics. This may of course indicate that the latter are underemployed]

Deterrent

From Mr P. H. H. Moore   *28 January 1970*

Sir,

Mr J. Armour-Milne refers to 'the amount of drivel that is to be found in the Letters to the Editor'.

Whether or not you, in fact, publish drivel is not for me to decide, but a sure method of raising the standard of letters that you receive would be not only to publish your usual selection of letters, but also to print, each day, a complete list of the names of those correspondents whose letters you have rejected.

The thought of possibly being included in your Rejects List, and then to have one's acquaintances saying, 'I see that you have had yet another letter refused by *The Times*', would be too much of a risk for most people.

Yours faithfully,

P. H. H. MOORE

Homage

From Mr J. S. Hocknell   *29 January 1970*

Sir,

In his letter Mr J. Armour-Milne asks 'What does one have to do to be recognized by the Editor of *The Times*?'

I hope nothing will move you to answer such a presumptuous question.

The criteria by which you recognize your correspondents are no more to be bandied about by ordinary people than those governing the nomination of bishops, Royal Commissioners, Presidents of MCC or even newspaper editors.

I had not intended to reveal that I have been making a study of what I like to imagine is your epistolatory policy. But Mr Armour-Milne has forced my hand.

Until it can be published (perhaps in your pages?), I ask him to ponder his fortune. To have received your invariably courteous but *private* acknowledgements of 'interest' is to have moved in the foothills of immortality. Only grosser spirits would seek public proof of your editorial regard.

Yours faithfully,

JOHN HOCKNELL

The Penalty

From Mr Thomas Frankland   *31 January 1970*

Sir,

Aspirant contributors to your correspondence column should beware. My last letter, on conserving British butterfies, a rather esoteric matter, produced 63 replies — from as far afield as Iran, Kenya and St Helena. It took me a fortnight to write suitable replies. I vowed never again to subject myself such possibilities; the vow is broken only to protect, dissuade and enlighten.

Yours faithfully,

THOMAS FRANKLAND

Animal, Vegetable or Mineral

From Mr Hockley Clarke   *31 January 1970*

[editor, *Birds and Country Magazine*]

Sir,

It may be of interest to state that I have been privileged to have had over 40 letters published in *The Times*, and to indicate some of the subjects to which they referred: birds, animals, tomato plants, bats, caterpillars, hotels the Christmas post, chemical sprays, railway closures, wintering in England, &c.

I am, Sir, yours faithfully,

HOCKLEY CLARKE

An Outcome

From Mrs Mary Powell   *31 January 1970*

Sir,

If my husband had not written to *The Times* on 16 January 1930, there might never have been a Crossword Puzzle to intrigue your readers.

Yours faithfully,

MARY E. POWELL

[The *Times* Crossword Puzzle dates from 1 February 1930]

Definition

From Gimpel Fils   *31 January 1970*

Sir,

René Gimpel (1881–1945) – French art dealer, collector and diarist – was a noted Anglophile.

His sons remember his definition of an English gentleman: 'A man with a passion for horses, playing with a ball, probably one broken bone in his body and in his pocket a letter to *The Times*.'

Yours faithfully,

GIMPEL FILS

Royal Nod

From Mrs Helen Reid   *4 February 1970*

Sir,

King George V, approached by a friend who hoped that a word from His Majesty in the right quarter would solve a difficulty, said 'My dear fellow, I can't help you! You'd better write to *The Times*.'

I have the honour to be, Sir,

Your obedient servant,

HELEN REID

Till the cows come home

From Mrs Jan Pahl   *5 August 1982*

Sir,

The English language is a subtle and flexible instrument, but it does have various lacunae; I am writing to invite your readers to repair one such gap.I am concerned that there seems to be no way of ending a letter with a phrase which conveys the idea of 'in friendship' or 'with warm and friendly feelings'.

There is 'love from', but that is perhaps a little naive; there is 'with kind regards' but that seems rather formal; 'best wishes' is too like a Christmas card, and 'yours ever' implies all sort of long-term commitments; *amicalement* comes closest to the phrase I mean − but I want something in English.

Yours sincerely,

JAN PAHL

From Mr Vivian Vale   *9 August 1982*

Sir,

A well-tried French acquaintance of ours invariably ends her English letters to us with 'Yours friendly', which we love. But perhaps Mrs Pahl might prefer to employ the simple American coda of 'Cordially'?

Yours faithfully,

VIVIAN VALE

From Dr J. R. Butler   *9 August 1982*

Sir,

I once taught an attentive student who ended her little notes to me with the valediction 'Yours eventually'. I assumed that this was intended to convey warm and friendly feelings.

Yours sincerely,

J. R. BUTLER

From Mrs Gavin Lyall   *10 August 1982*

Sir,

Jan Pahl wants a letter-ending to convey friendship, not love or formality. How about 'yours cordially', with which I have been ending letters for years (including one to her)?

The 'yours' form is capable of all sorts of individual variations: 'yours apologetically', 'yours disgustedly', 'yours in sackcloth and ashes', 'yours delightedly' and I have used them all. But perhaps 'yours' itself is absurd; so what about just Cordially'?

Until this is an accepted form, however, I remain,

Yours cheerfully,

KATHARINE WHITEHORN

From Mrs P. A. Jerram   *12 August 1982*

Sir,

Mrs Pahl finds a gap in English in ways of signing off her letters. There is no gap in the language; it is a question of looking a little further to find an expression unhappily fallen into desuetude. When I wish to convey 'warm and friendly feelings' to my correspondent, I sign myself

Yours affectionately,

PAMELA JERRAM

From Mrs Brigid Grafton Green   *13 August 1982*

Sir,

Is 'Yours affectionately' *too* affectionate for Mrs Pahl? It offers warmth of feeling without pushiness.

Incidentally, why never '*Dear* Sir' nowadays – even when one is feeling particularly friendly towards *The Times*?

Yours sincerely,

BRIGID GRAFTON GREEN

[Writing to *The Times*, 17 January 1930, Mr E. S. Campbell began 'Dear Sir' and ended 'Yours affectionately']

From Mr P. A. Davies   *13 August 1982*

Sir,

I have always thought of Evelyn Waugh's immortal phrase 'with love or what you will' as the ultimate end to my correspondence.

It has disarmed my sternest critic and redeemed my dullest prose.

Yours faithfully,
PHILIP A. DAVIES

From Mr George Gale   *13 August 1982*

Sir,

Amiably yours,
GEORGE GALE

[The Cuckoo-in-Chief is grateful to the *Daily Express* for the only non-letter to appear in the correspondence columns of *The Times*]

From Mr John Housden   *16 August 1982*

Sir,

Mrs Jan Pahl, whos seeks an English equivalent for *amicalement* with which to end her letters, may be interested to know that when I was a District Officer in Barotseland in the nineteen-fifties all official letters in English to the local African chief commenced with the salutation 'My Friend' and ended 'I am Your Friend'.

I never discovered the origin of this strange mode of address, which was in frequent use at the time but may be a little too regal for Mrs Pahl's purposes.

Yours sincerely,
JOHN HOUSDEN

From Professor I. M. Mills   *17 August 1982*

Sir,

My son, who is 22, began writing to me a year or so ago with the ending: 'Your friend, William'. This seems to be a simple and unaffected ending that conveys the desired feeling.

Yours friend,
IAN MILLS

From Mr Bernard Kaukas   *17 August 1982*

Sir (and Mrs Jan Pahl):

Yours till the cows come home.

Yours sincerely,
BERNARD KAUKAS

From Mr David Peace   *19 August 1982*

Sir,

I hope it may help Mrs Pahl to hear of the endings of two
letters I found especially engaging. A servant ended a letter to
George IV, 'Invariably Yours'. (Incidentally it began, 'My
dearest Sir . . .') And I will end this letter as did my 10-year-old
granddaughter,

Ever wishing good,

DAVID PEACE

From Mr Gervase Craven   *19 August 1982*

Sir,

Some years ago a young distant relative wrote to thank me for
a Christmas present. With an obvious wish to express some
sentiment of friendliness, without appearing too effusive, she
brought her letter to a close with the words 'most of my love'.

Yours faithfully,

GERVASE CRAVEN

From Mrs Phyllis Gascoin   *21 August 1982*

Sir,

Mrs Pahl is perfectly correct. There *is* a gap in the language.
The problem is one of long standing.

Did not Miss Austen, in the person of Miss Mary Crawford,
say to Fanny Price: 'You must give my compliments to him.
Yes, I think it must be compliments. Is there not a something
wanted, Miss Price, in our language – something between
compliments and love, to suit the sort of friendly acquaintance
we have had together? . . . But compliments may be sufficient
here.'

I present my compliments to your correspondents and to
yourself, and sign myself *simpliciter*.

PHYLLIS GASCOIN

From the Under-Sheriff of Greater London   *24 August 1982*

Sir,

I remember a lady anxious for a reply from my office to her
letter seeking to be excused from jury service as she was eight
months pregnant, ending appropriately,

'Yours expectantly',

ALASTAIR BLACK

From Vice-Admiral Sir Louis Le Bailly   *25 August 1982*

Sir,

During the period he was spring cleaning the Royal Navy,
Admiral Jackie Fisher didn't do too badly.
To Viscount Esher: 'Yours till a cinder'.
To J. A. Spender: 'Yours till the Angels smile on us'.
To F. E. G. Ponsonby: 'Yours till death'.
To George Lambert: 'Yours till Hell freezes'.
From 1908 onwards the last appeared most frequently.

Yours faithfully,
LOUIS LE BAILLY

From Dr R. W. K. Paterson   *31 August 1982*

Sir,

When the contents are appropriate, we can end our letters, as
our Victorian forefathers often did, by giving final encore to the
dominant theme or delicately reiterating the emotional gist: by,
for example, 'Yours in great distress of mind' or 'Yours in
heartfelt gratitude and relief'. In this way we can, so to speak,
round off our letters pointedly.

Yours in earnest hope of publication,
R. W. K. PATERSON

From Mr Stelio Hourmouzios   *14 August 1982*

Sir,

Mrs Pahl is treading on delicate ground. The moment you
depart from the accepted forms of salutation you inevitably
endow any new formulas with some specific value, whereas the
present time-honoured conventional forms, inane as they are, no
longer have any significance in themselves.

We could, of course, revert to the extravagant protestations
that our great-grandfathers liked to use when rounding off a
letter, but life is too short for that: and quite honestly I do not
see members of our contemporary society tamely subscribing
themselves as most obedient, humble servants.

Believe me to be, Sir,
Not your anything but simply
STELIO HOURMOUZIOS

INDEX OF SUBJECTS

abdication crisis, *Times* coverage of 306–11
address, forms of 230–1
    clerical 321–6
advertisements, as musical instruments 252
aeroplanes 134–5
    sensation of travel in 138–40
    and war 136
Albania 9–10
albatross 134–5
anti-cyclone, alternative word for 17–18
Antony and Cleopatra 273–5
Arabic, translation of *The Times* into 58
archaeology
    clay pipe 213–14
    gladius, how to draw 224
archery 177–8
army
    nicknames 152–7
    uniforms 161
artistic ability, assessment of 259

barristers, wigs for women 160–1
BBC 53, 90
    pronunciation 189–91, 198, 215–16
    Third Programme 191–2; interruption of
        music on 240, 245–6
    World Service 319
beards, and bicycle chains 59
Bernadotte, Count
    assassination of 286–8
'blackthorn winter' 229–30
Boer War 1–2, 4, 143
    concentration camps 113–15
Brandenburg concerto, correct tempo for
    241–2
British Rail
    express trains 99–100
    modernization 315
    radio nuisance on 246
    restaurants 193
    safety regarding hats 21–2
    sleepers 117, 131
    station masters 98
    toast 315–16
Buckingham Palace
    tourists and sentries 63
Byrne, Tom (VC) 61–2

Ca Passe 50
Canterbury, Archbishop of
    Cosmo Gordon Lang
    Runcie 27
chamber pots 116–18

Chamberlain, Joseph, maiden speech of 307
cheese 73–4
    Danish blue and chianti 74
    stilton 76–7
chewing gum
    police and 16
children
    death by overlaying 118–19
    violence against 128
    at war 119–120
Church of England
    Alternative Service Book 29
    Bible, The; Authorized Version 3; New
        English 3; New Testament 27
    communion chalice, communal, as
        source of infection 279–84
    Hymns for Today's Church 83
Churchill, Winston
    journalistic skills 53–4, 62
    portrait by Graham Sutherland 256–7
cocking a snook 231–2
comedian, art of being 276–7
computers, and forms of address 323–4
concert halls, acoustics of 247–8
concorde 141–2
Cornish, Charles John 1–2
cows, in St James's Park 16–17
cricket
    bodyline bowling 184–5
    Meredith at Melbourne 185
    Test Match of 1882 182–4
    Times misprints concerning 28
Cromwell, Oliver
    head 305–6
cuckoo
    in *Blithe Spirit* (Noel Coward) 49
    hearing the 5, 23–7
    last 1, 2–3, 5
    song of 10, 24

dancing, manners and 40–3
Daphnis et Chloe (Ravel) 239
death
    customs concerning 212–13
decimalization 220–1
dogs
    licences 148–9
    in London 44
    musical 250–2
    rail travel 43, 131
doodle-bug 151–2
dustmen, and dukes 218–19

earwigs 216–17
education
　allocation of dons' time 165–6
　philistines in 173–4
　selection principle 166–7
　of West Indians 167–8
EEC
　De Gaulle opposing British entry 313
Einstein
　Times reports of date of birth 84
England/English
　ability to lose 302
　impressions of American visitor 299–301
　pedigrees 226
　reasons for greatness 20–1
　royal hat rights 227
English language 187–201
　Americanisms 187
　collective nouns 221–3
　economic jargon 194
　foreign place names 67–8
　foreign words 188
　non-sexist 196–7
　phrases 93–6, 198–201
　plain 193–4, 230–1
　pronunciation 198
Enigma Variations
　performance by Toscanini 243
Eton
　unusual singer of boating song 318

farthing 212
Fascism
　defence of by Mussolini 306
Fields, W. C.
　as Micawber 261–2
film
　as art 260–1
　history of cinematograph 233–4
flies
　hibernation of 47–8
flight 134–42
　birds 134–5
　sensation of 138–40
food 69–77
　ideal 69–71
　ministry of 74
　shortages 73, 147
　squirrels 74–6
foot
　measurement of French 36
football (association)
　violence 128–9

Gaulle, General de 311–13
generation gap 55–6
Germany
　language 150, 151
　war with *see* World War II
glasses, musical 248–9

golf 178–9
　caddies 179–80
Gorbunov, Posadov 58–9
Gothic
　new age 162–3
grass mowings
　as food 71
hair
　cutting 57
　long 163–4
hedgecutting 39
hip baths 64
Holloway Prison 123–6
honours
　reputed sale of 202
hooligans 4–5
　Teddy boys 130–1
　transistor louts 246
　see also football (association), violence
horses
　naming 292–4
　and spectacles 127–8
hotels
　booking a room 318

immigration 132–3
imposters 33–4
indexes 210
Inland Revenue
　sale of brides 103–4
intellectuals 210–11
inventions
　cinematograph 233–4
　in war 143–5
Iran-Iraq war 119–20
Irving, Henry
　and Coquelin 265–6
St James's Park 16–17, 19
St James's Theatre
　closure of 267

Keeble, Sir Frederick
　definition of perfect meal 70
Kew Gardens
　repercussions of fire at 122–6
Kitchener, Lord 53–4

leeches 45–7
legal system
　sentencing 128, 231–2
Lenton, Miss Lilian 122–6
letter writing 235–6
　ending letters 331–5
letters to *The Times*
　influence of 58–9
　successful correspondents 326–30
Light Brigade, Charge of 62
Locke, Joyce 123

337

Mahler, Gustav
  first symphony 243–4
malapropisms 278
manners
  and men 168–70
  and women 171–3
marriage
  betrothed or financé 187–8
  cuckoos and 27
mathematics
  octal system 220–1
May Day
  customs 40
memories
  of nineteenth-century 44–5
Metternich
  journey 66–7
Mill, J. S. 304–5
Miró, Joan 257–8
misprints 28–31
motor cars 34, 39
mouse
  coal-heaving 217–18
  death of 84
  singing 217
Mozart, Wolfgang Amadeus
  and thrushes 247
MP
  experiences of a new 36–8
  and OMs 260

names 105–111
  abbreviations 110
  French 109–10
  horse's 292–4
  Russian revolutionary 109
  Spanish 108
  Sussex 110–11
National theatre
  purpose of 268–9
nightingale 53
notices
  London Transport 317
nowhere 207–8

old masters
  forgeries 253–6
Olympic Games 68, 175–6
opera
  dress at 13–15
  interrupted broadcast of 240
organ recitals 249–50
Olivier, Sir Laurence
  performance of Othello 269–70
owls
  luminous 209–10

Pakistan
  definition of 236–7

Parliament
  House of Commons rebuilt 87–90
  light 227
passports 21
Pauling, Dr 132–3
Pavlov,
  theories used in psychological warfare 85–7
philately 64
pigs 147–8
  names for 208
pinching 294–6
poltergeists 48–9
police
  and chewing gum 16
  injury in riots 291
postal services
  delays 320
  dispensibility of 195–6
  mail coaches 142
prison
  treatment of suspects 122–6
prostitution
  white slave trade 120–1
public schools
  manners 168–72

rainbows
  inverted 237–8
razor blades 148
Roget's Thesaurus 127
Roosevelt, President 297–9
Russell, Bertrand
  and T. S. Eliot 313
Russia
  phrases 95
  psychological warfare in 85–7
  revolution 50, 51–2
  revolutionary names 109
  Rolls Royce 228–9

sailing
  signals 94–5
sanctions
  economic, against South Africa 115–16
Sandhurst punishments 303
sausages, German 97
scaup 85
sentries
  mockery by tourists 63
sexism
  non-sexist language 83, 196–7
Shakespeare, William
  modern interpretation 277
  Zeffirelli production 271–3
shooting
  at aeroplanes 140–1
shopping
  shyness 122

338

sleeping
  out of doors 54–5
soldiers
  coloured 132
space travel 140–1
  contrast with British technology 317
spectacles
  historic evidence 127–8
squirrels, grey 74–6
Stevenson, Adlai 301–2
Stoke Poges churchyard larceny 297
streakers
  and quakers 292
summit conference 1960 85–7
swaging 63

Teddy Boys 130–1
Television
  commercial breaks 265
  effects of watching 262–3
  interviews 263–4
tennis scoring 180–2
Thatcher, Margaret 296
theatre
  suggested new directions 275–6
  see also National Theatre
Thule
  pronunciation of 90–1
ties
  staircase 207
  Wykehamist 159
Times, The
  fourth leaders 7–8
  misprints in 28–31
  price of 43
  see also letters to
Titanic, sinking of 92–3
toads
  and goldfish 234–5
tobacco
  alternatives to 203–5
Toscanini
  and Elgar 243
trade disputes bill 316
trespassing
  in aeroplanes 137–8
Trinity College, Cambridge
  jump 176–7

Trireme, Greek 65–6
Turkish delight 130
Tutankhamen, King 211

unions
  TGWU 218–19

Vermeer, Johannes
  stolen painting 258
vicars
  number of churches in the charge of
    232–3
Victoria, Queen 212–13
violence
  media and other causes of 288–91

wagtail, grey 19
waiters, ideal 71–2
walking, long distance 15–16
wasps, finding nests of 79–82
weddings, cost of 101–3
wife
  for sale 56, 101–4
  value of 104
Wilmington, Lord 33–4
women
  as medical students 51
Wooster, Bertie
  chin 203
World War II 26, 149, 145–6
  advice for gas attacks 150
  bureaucracy 146
  censorship 145–6
  commemoration of Auschwitz dead 285
  D-day 151
  food shortages 73
  fires and reconstruction 59–61
  House of Commons 87–90, 225
  Nazis, fate of leaders 223
work
  all must 49–50
  labourers' wages 126
Wren, Sir Christopher 59–61

Zog, King 9, 10, 162

INDEX OF CORRESPONDENTS

Abdullah, Imam S. M. 140
Acworth, C. B. 73
Adland, Miss Eleanor 205
Agate, James 261–2
Aggett, Mrs Hilary 154
Alexander, Mick 195
Alington, Dr C. A. 222–3
Allan, Miss Caroline 102
Allan, Terence 101
Allen, Sir Carlton 231–2
Allen, Major R. H. 148
Allison, T. J. 169
Antusch, Adolf 53
Armour-Milne, J. 326–7
Armstrong, Sir Thomas 228
Ashton-Hopper, A. 147
Astley-Jones, Commander E. 283
Austin, Canon George 293
Ayers, Ms Duffy

Back, Ivor 73–4
Bailly, Sir Louis Le 335
Barbirolli, Sir John 243–4
Barker, General Sir Evelyn 156–7
Barlow, P. J. 296
Barry, Gerald 199
Beecham, Sir Thomas 241–2
Beerbohm, Sir Max 231
Beesley, Lawrence 92–3
Benjamin, Rev. Adrian 325–6
Bentley, Nicolas 260–1
Bentley Beaumann, Wing Commander E. 156
Berenson, Bernard 253–5
Best, Mrs S. 167–8
Betts, Herbert F. 225
Birdwood, Sir George 47–8
Bishop, Major General Sir Alec 152
Black, Alastair 334
Blagden, Judge J. Basil 221
Blaxland, Gregory 153
Blissard, Rev. W. 126
Bockett-Pubh, Charles P. 84
Bode, Dr Carl 162–3
Bodkin, Dr Thomas 105
Boggis, Rev. R. J. E. 127–8
Boland, Miss Bridget 68
Bond, Arthur 321
Bono, Percy 140
Boothroyd, Basil 277
Bosanquet, B. J. T. 178–9
Bosanquet, Reginald 152
Brabrook, E. W. 16–17

Bradbury, Ernest 246
Branson, J. R. B. 6, 71
Bratby, John 259
Brereton, Dr Cloudesly 56
Brogan, Prof. D. W. 207, 214–15
Brough, Edwin 208
Brown, H. H. 222
Brown, J. D. 275–6
Brown, Mrs Margaret 107–8
Buckley, Mrs Jean 94
Bullock, Miss E. M. 200–1
Burg, J. R. 9–10, 295–6
Burr, Malcolm 216–27
Butler, Dr J. R. 331

Campbell, Lieutenant-Colonel W. M. 149
Cantuar, Osric 5
Carré, John Le 319
Carter, D. I. 232
Cary, Robert 311–12
Chamberlain, Neville 6, 19
Charlesworth, M. L. 317
Chase, Rev. Stephen 325
Cheatle, Sir G. Lenthal 62
Chelmsford, Bishop of (John Edwin Watts-Ditchfield) 211
Cheshire, Group Captain Leonard 285
Child, Christopher 325
Child, Mrs H. M. 147
Chisholm, M. M. 214
Christie, Dame Agatha 273–5
Churchill, Sir Winston 303
Churchyard, Major J. H. 162
Churton Collins, Professor J. 187
Clarke, Hockley 329
Clemens, Cyril 301–2
Cliff Hodges, Mrs J. G. 293
Clout, Imogen 171
Coleman, Rev. F. P. 322
Collins, Mrs Patricia 281
Conan Doyle, Adrian 299
Conan Doyle, Sir Arthur 2, 53–4, 143–5
Conteh, Abdulai O. 26–7
Cooke, Alexander 291
Coote, Bernard 198
Cope, John 110
Copinger-Hill, Rev H. 226
Cottam, A. V. 117
Courtauld, W. P. 327
Coylar, Henry A. De 137
Crammond, John G. 175–6
Craven, Gervase 334
Crawley, Leonard 184–5

Crusha, Rev E. H. W. 321
Cunningham, R. E. D. 205
Curtis, Brigadier J. H. P. 154–5
Curzon, Clifford 245–6
Cust, Lady Sybil 55–6

Dahrendorf, Professor Ralf 28–9
Danckwerts, Professor P. V. 170
Dare, E. H. 265
Darling, T. Y. 164
Davie-Distin, D. 132
Davies, Alfred 36–8
Davies, Philip A. 332–3
Davis, N. R. 59
Davison, Miss Ivy 200
Dean, Mrs James 299–301
Dencer, D. 46–7
Dent, Alan 267
Devey, H. B. 137
Dew, G. D. 252
Dewing, Rev. R. W. D. 321–2
Dickens, C. E. C. 207–8
Digby, Bassett 21
Donnelly, Patrick 103
Dover Wilson, Professor J. 269–70
Drysdale, Patrick 28

Eagar, W. M. McG. 212, 248–9
Edgecumbe, Sir Robert 187–8
Edmondson, Miss Helen 228–9
Eliot, T. S. 76–7, 262–3
Eliot, Valerie 313
Ellis, Aytoun 110–111
Elsey, Rev. H. W. R. 98
Elton, Professor G. R. 165–6, 173–4
Emmott, Lady Constance 44
Ernle-Erle Drax, Admiral Sir Reginald 182
Evans, Edward 200
Everett, Oliver 155

Faulks, Peter 322
Fendley, J. A. 218
Feuchtwanger, Mrs Primrose 153
Fielding, Leslie 198
Fisher, Lord 6, 49–50
Fisher Evans, John 228
Flanagan, Dr Kieran 29–30
Fletcher, Anthony 64
Fletcher, Mrs Monica 279–80
Fletcher, Winston 315–16
Fordham, E. W. 199
Forty, Mrs Douce 172
Foster-Carter, Dr A. F. 283–4
Fowler, Professor Frank M. 30
Frankland, Thomas 329
Freeland, Nicholas 172
Friese-Green, W. 233–4
Fulham, Bishop of (Staunton Batty) 150

Galbraith, Professor J. K. 141–2

Gale, George 333
Galsworthy, John 136, 215–16
Garrett, Bishop Thomas S. 282
Garton, Rev. Maurice C. 280–1
Gascoin, P. A. 173, 250
Gascoin, Mrs Phyllis 334
Gillett, James W. 82
Gimpel Fils 330
Godding, Mark 15–16
Goldberg, Rabbi David J. 323
Goldman, Ms Bo 302
Goodchild, John 31
Gordon, Sir Charles 168
Grafton Green, Mrs Brigid 332
Graham-Orlebar, Rev. I. H. G. 292–3, 294
Grattan-Doyle, Sir Nicholas 69–71
Graves, Robert 235–6
Greene, Graham 28
Gregory, Kenneth 260
Griffith, John G. 196–7
Grimwade, Rev. Canon J. G. 296
Grove, Dr Victor 150

Hachette et Cie 36
Hagberg Writhe, Sir Charles 58–9
Hagne, D. B. 213
Hailsham, Lord 206
Haines, C. R. 305–6
Haire, James 320
Haley, Mrs Dora 279
Hall, Andrew 79
Hardy, Thomas 304
Harmsworth, St John 326
Harris, Walter B. 57–8
Harrison, G. M. A. 90
Harvey, Richard 315
Haward, Edwin 98
Hawkins, Rev. D. F. C. 324
Hayter, Sir William 95
Healey, Dr T. 224
Heiney, Mr and Mrs 94–5
Henderson, P. G. 166
Hendricks, Cecil A. C. 191
Herbert, A. P. 6, 193–4, 316
Herbert, John 118, 172
Hereford, Bishop of 113–15
Hewins, R. A. 286–8
Highlock, Stephen 103–4
Hill, George E. 250
Hill, Mary M. 94
Hocknell, J. S. 328–9
Hodgson Burnett, W. 122
Holbrook, David 289–90
Holmes, Miss Alison 217
Holmes, Rev. Cecil 97
Hopkins, Francis 293
Horsley, Victor 122–5
Hourmouzios, Stelio 335
Housden, John 333
Housman, A. E. 307

Hoyle, Professor Fred 220–1
Hughes, Richard 195–6
Hughes, Spike 247
Hummel, Sidney A. 96
Hutchinson, Professor John 318

Illingworth, Dudley H. 217–18
Impey, L. A. 201
Irvine, Hon. Judge 324
Irving, Laurence 268–9

Jackson, N. L. 183–4
Jeffries, Sir Charles 84
Jenkins, A. R. D. 99–100
Jerram, Mrs P. A. 332
Johnson, Dr Claire 93
Johnstone, James 170
Jones, L. E. 161
Jordan, Philip 199

Kaukus, Bernard 333
Kinneir, Dr Guy 226

Ladenbury, Baroness Aster 97
Lascelles, Sir Alan 156
Lawson, D. F. 219
Leaver, John 106
Lee, Rev Reginald 232–3
Lethbridge, Miss Nemone 130–1
Lewis, Major C. J. L. 79, 80, 81
Lightwood, Max 131
Lindkvist, R. G. T. 257–8
Linton, Rev Sydney 283
Lofts, Mrs Norah 128
Lombard, Rev B. S. 51–2
Longrigg, John 74
Lydekker, R. 23

Macartney, C. A. 66–7
MacDermott, Rev K. H. 24
Macdonell, Lady Agnes 40
MacInnes, Colin 20–1
McIntyre, Dr W. D. 100
Mackenzie, Compton 201
McRobert, Sir George 98–9
Maitland Hawes, A. P. 181
Malcolm Carter, H. 19
Mallon, David 25
Mann, Edward J. 119–20
Manning, W. E. G. 102
Margolis, Miss Sylvia 327
Marshall, Rev T. J. 281
Martin, Gordon 29
Masefield, John 120–1
Masefield, Peter G. 221–2
Maxwell, Henry 63
Micholls, M. G. 237–8
Middleton, Lady E. 40–3
Miles, Sir Bernard 163–4
Miller, T. G. 191–2

Millington, G. 199
Mills, Professor Ian 333
Moncrieff, Charles Scott 50
Money Coutts, Miss Eleanora 139–40
Moore, John 211–12
Morgan, Charles 186
Morrison, Alastair C. 101
Morrison, John 65–6
Morton, H. V. 298
Morton, Tom 169
Moss, Rev Arthur 27
Motz, Dr H. 24–5
Moulin, Charles Marsell 122–5
Moynihan, Sir Bernard 179–80
Muggeridge, Malocolm 263–4
Muir, Frank 294–5
Mumford, William 71–2
Murdoch, Miss Iris 166–7
Murdoch, Mrs W. 151
Murray, E. 91
Mussolini, Benito 306
Mynors, H. C. B. 99

Nathan, David 30
Nash, Ogden 27
Newton, Rev F. H. J. 188
Noakes, Mrs Vivian 290–1
Norman, Adrian R. D. 323–4
Norrington, Sir Arthur 258

Odell, N. E. 151–2
Oetzmann and Co 33–4
Olivier, Sir Laurence 271–3
Olivier, Sir Sydney 48–9
Orchard, Dr Jennifer 173
Orde, Lady Eileen 200
Oulton, Mrs Derek 153
Oxford, Margaret, Lady 265–6

Pahl, Mrs Jan 331
Paine, R. J. 294
Palmer, G. H. 193
Palmer, William 83
Palmes, James 170
Parkin, Anthony 80
Parry, E. H. 297
Parsons, Mrs M. E. 234–5
Paterson, Dr R. W. K. 335
Peace, David 334
Pearsall Smith, Logan 17–18
Pendred, Loughlan 230–1
Philipson, A. G. 205
Phillips, M. T. 195
Pigott, Sir T. Digby 209–10
Ponsonby, Sir Frederick 159
Powell, Rev J. H. 208
Powell, Mrs Mary 330
Priest, Dr Pamela 26
Pring, Dr Charles H. 51
Purnell, C. J. 85

Ravel, Maurice 239
Reid, Graham L. 146
Reid, Mrs Helen 330
Repton, Bishop of 324
Richards, Rev D. G. 249
Risolo, Miss Silvia 21–2
Roberts, Rex 216
Robertson, Major H. N. 145–6
Robertson, Toby 117
Ronald, Sir Landon 243
Rosebery, Lord 202
Rothschild, Alfred de 43
Rowse, A. L. 312–13
Russell, Bertrand 132–3

Sackville-West, Vita 64
Sainsbury, Dr John 148–9
Salmon, F. R. 169
Samson, Mrs Rosemary 25
Sanders, G. T. St J. 155
Sargant, Dr William 85–7
Sargent, Sir Malcolm 244–5
Sautoy, Peter du 321
Savill, Dr Agnes 122–5
Scales, L. G. 157
Scholfield, B. 227
Sellar, W. R. 313
Shaw, Canon Allan 322
Shaw, Sir Bernard 6, 13–15, 189–91
Shaw, Sir Napier 229–30
Sherrin, Ned 278
Shipley, Sir Arthur Everett 45–6
Short, Philip 142
Simon, Timothy 80
Simons, Dr Peter J. 102–3
Simpson, Dr Jacqueline 295
Simpson, K. R. 154
Simpson, N. F. 288–9
Sitwell, Osbert 231
Skidelsky, Professor Robert 115–16
Smith, Canon A. C. A. 104
Smith, H. A. 149
Smith, John J. 196
Speaght, George 95
Spiegel, Fritz 29
Spring, Mrs Peter 169
Squire, Sir John 250–2
Steele, Tommy 276–7
Stephen, Sir Herbert 160–1
Stephens, Mrs P. C. 293
Stepney, Bishop of (Joost de Blank) 151
Stewart, Dr J. A. 204
Stewart, Paul 174
Stewart Roberts, Miss Margaret 218–19
Stokowski, Leopold 247–8
Strachan, J. G. 63
Strachan, M. F. 127
Strachey, Sir Charles 240
Sutherland, Millicent Duchess of 16
Symns, J. M. 204
Szamuely, Dr Nina 109

Tallents, Sir Stephen 75–6, 203–4
Taylor, A. J. P. 223
Taylor, H. D. F. 284
Taylor, Max 171
Temperley, Clive 177–8
Thompson, Professor Alan 117
Thompson, G. V. E. 140–1
Thompson, Sir Henry 34–6
Thomson, Rob 83
Tobin, Herbert C. 67–8
Tomlin, G. A. 205
Trevelyan, G. M. 176–7
Trewin, J. C. 213–14
Turner, John M. 320
Twickel, Baroness Ann 96

Vale, Vivian 331
Vandyke Price, Mrs Pamela 282–3
Varcoe, Jonathan 91
Verner, Colonel Willoughby 39
Vernon, Douglas 26
Vidler, Dr Alec 116–17
Vince, Mrs Sheila 96
Vincent, Ben 292
Viney, Laurence 318

Waldegrave, William 194
Warren, f. 57
Waterfield, A. J. 225
Watson, F. J. B. 200
Waugh, Evelyn 210
Wavell, Field Marshall Lord 61–2
West, Dame Rebecca 212–13
Whalley, Lieutenant Colonel P. R. 226
White, Arnold 138–9
Whitehorn, Katharine 332
Whitehouse, J. Howard 87–90
White-Thomson, Ian H. 320
Whittet, G. S. 256–7
Wilde, T. G. 90–1
Williams, Norman 80, 81–2
Williams-Ellis, Clough 59–61
Williams, Gerald 131
Williams, P. A. 317
Williamson, Henry 215–16
Willson, Dr Henry 118–19
Williamson, John 228
Wilson, Donald 156, 215
Wilson, Mrs Hal 171
Wilson-Barker, Commander 134–5
Wodehouse, P. G. 203
Wood, Canon W. 44–5
Woodman, A. J. 127
Wright, A. R. D. 100
Wyatt, Canon R. G. F. 204
Wykes, James 224
Wyllie, J. M. 236–7
Wynne Thomas, Dr H. 54–5

Young, B. W. M. 198
Young, James 91